A Penguin Books Canada/
McClelland and Stewart Book

THE DIONNE YEARS

Pierre Berton was born in 1920 and raised in the Yukon. He spent his early newspaper career in Vancouver, where at 21 he was the youngest city editor on any Canadian daily. He moved to Toronto in 1947 and at the age of 31 was named managing editor of *Maclean's* magazine. He was an associate editor and columnist at *The Toronto Star* from 1958 to 1962 and has written and hosted several national television programs. He is the author of thirty-nine books, as well as a Canadian history series for young readers, and has received three Governor General's Awards for works of non-fiction including *Klondike*. He is a Companion of the Order of Canada and a member of the Canadian News Hall of Fame. Mr. Berton lives in Kleinburg, Ontario.

The Dionne

"It [the Depression] bred a
generation determined to
give its children the good
things it had lacked and
spare them the harsh
disciplines it had known."

—*Hugh MacLennan*

"There was so much more
money than love in our
existence. It took a long time
to realize the effect it had on
all of us. ..."

—*The quintuplets*

A Thirties
Melodrama

Years

By Pierre Berton

A PENGUIN BOOKS CANADA/
McCLELLAND AND STEWART BOOK

PENGUIN BOOKS
Published by the Penguin Group
Penguin Books Canada Ltd, 10 Alcorn Avenue, Toronto, Ontario, Canada M4V 3B2
Penguin Books Ltd, 27 Wrights Lane, London W8 5TZ, England
Penguin Books USA Inc., 375 Hudson Street, New York, New York 10014, U.S.A.
Penguin Books Australia Ltd, Ringwood, Victoria, Australia
Penguin Books (NZ) Ltd, 182-190 Wairau Road, Auckland 10, New Zealand

Penguin Books Ltd, Registered Offices: Harmondsworth, Middlesex, England

First published in Canada by McClelland and Stewart Limited, 1977

Published in paperback by Penguin Books/McClelland and Stewart, 1991

10 9 8 7 6 5 4 3

Sources

Pictures: pages 41, 42, 43: *Toronto Star* photos by Fred Davis from Helen Dafoe; page 44, top: *Toronto Star* photo by Fred Davis from Joseph Sedgwick; bottom: *Toronto Star* photo by Fred Davis from Yvonne Leroux Davis; pages 45, 46, 47: *Toronto Star* photos by Fred Davis from Helen Dafoe; page 48, top left: *Toronto Star* photo from Yvonne Leroux Davis; top right, *Toronto Star* photo from Helen Dafoe; bottom, left and right: University of Toronto; pages 133, 134, 135, 136, *Toronto Star* photos by Fred Davis from Helen Dafoe; page 137: *Toronto Star* photo by Fred Davis from Yvonne Leroux Davis; page 138, top: *Toronto Star* photo by Fred Davis from Joseph Sedgwick; bottom: *Toronto Star* photo by Fred Davis from Helen Dafoe; page 140, top: United Press International; bottom: North Bay *Nugget.*

Cartoons: "Just Kids" : King Features Syndicate Inc., 1936; "Sentimental Old Reprobate" and "Toonerville Folks" reprinted with permission of the *Toronto Star.*

Excerpts from *We Were Five* by James Brough (New York: Simon and Schuster, 1965) by permission of the publisher.

Illustration on pages 8, 9 and map on page 13 by Jack McMaster.

Manufactured in Canada

Canadian Cataloguing in Publication Data

Berton, Pierre, 1920-
  The Dionne years

Includes bibliographical references and index.
ISBN 0-14-013952-4

1. Dionne quintuplets. I. Title.

CT9998.D5B4. 1991 971.062'3 C91-094183-1

Acknowledgements

This book could not have been written without the hard digging and persistence of my research assistant, Barbara Sears, who found the eyewitnesses to the story and dug out the documents that provide the underpinning. To her I owe an inestimable debt of gratitude.

Some fifty people were interviewed for this book, and I should like to thank them for taking time to see me or my assistant, often at personal inconvenience, and for sharing their memories of the Dionne years. They are Germain Allard, Olizine Arcand, Archie Arcieri, Margaret Legros Audy, Ross Beesley, Mrs. William Blatz, Marie Clouthier Chabot, Jack Chisholm, Silvain Corbeil, Frank Creasy, Senator David Croll, Mr. and Mrs. Bill Dafoe, Mrs. Helen Dafoe, Mrs. Carroll Davies, Yvonne Leroux Davis, Mrs. Wilf Dickey, Audrey Dionne, Mr. and Mrs. Léon Dionne, Ruth Pearce Donald, Alec Du Fresne, Lyle Evans, Mort Fellman, Margaret Fletcher, Isabell Girard, Stan Guignard, Dr. G. P. Hamblin, Florian Houle, Mrs. Leo Kervin, Luis Kutner, Louise de Kiriline Lawrence, Arthur Maloney, Rt. Hon. Paul Martin, Dr. J. S. McCleary, Mollie O'Shaughnessy McMillan, Marie MacNaughton, Dorothy Millichamp, Mrs. Ken Morrison, Dorothy Pinkham, Joseph Sedgwick, George Sinclair, Gordon Sinclair, Dr. Bette Stephenson, Cécile Michaud Stephenson, Roy Tash, the late Lord Thomson of Fleet, Kenneth Valin, Mr. and Mrs. Leo Voyer, and Dr. Harold Williams.

Special thanks go to Norma Dainard and Alan Walker for their cheerful assistance at the Metropolitan Toronto Central Library, to Gordon Dodds of the Ontario Archives, to Mort Fellman of the North Bay *Nugget,* to Len McDonald and Isla Rochette of the township office of North Himsworth, to Brad Claridge of the township office at Corbeil, to Mrs. P. M. Lindsay of the Surrogate Court of Nipissing, and to Jacques Grimard and Father Barsalou of the French-Canadian Research Centre, University of Ottawa.

I am greatly indebted to Helen Dafoe and her daughter Frances Dafoe for allowing me to examine the papers and scrapbooks of Dr. Allan Roy Dafoe and Dr. William Dafoe and for contributing several photographs for this book. Yvonne Leroux Davis, who made her diary available, also contributed many of her husband's photographs. Mollie O'Shaughnessy McMillan was kind enough to lend me a manuscript describing the quintuplets' activities in the nursery during her time there. Mrs. Margaret Thompson contributed three large scrapbooks compiled by her colleague, the late Dr. Norma Ford Walker. George Sinclair allowed me access to various letters and papers he had kept since his days as Dr. Dafoe's secretary. Joseph Sedgwick allowed me to tear apart his prized photograph album in order to make use of other pictures of the quintuplets.

Several people read the manuscript in earlier drafts and I should like to thank them for their many useful comments and suggestions. They are Barbara Sears, Janice Tyrwhitt, Charles Templeton, Elsa Franklin, Janet Craig, and Janet Berton. My secretary, Ennis Armstrong, saved me months of work by transcribing tapes and typing and annotating research notes and various manuscript drafts, often at the expense of her own weekends.

It is obvious from the above that a book of this complexity is never the work of one man; he remains, however, properly responsible for infelicities of style, imbecilities of construction, flawed judgements, and egregious error. But he refuses to answer for typographical misprints. The computerization of the printing process has made proof correction a matter of pure chance. In the final analysis the author, like everybody else these days, commits his work to the hands, not of an editor, but of a machine.

Kleinburg,
April, 1977.

Contents

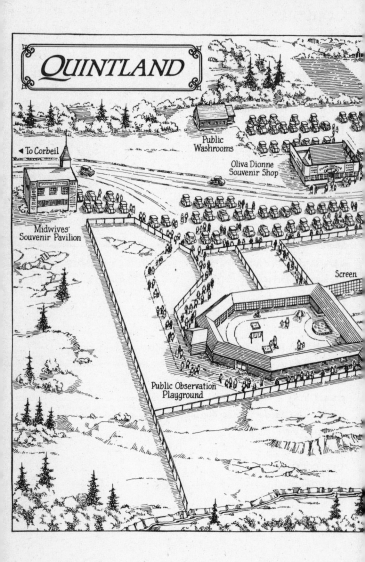

QUINTLAND

◄ To Corbeil

Public
Washrooms

Oliva Dionne
Souvenir Shop

Midwives'
Souvenir Pavilion

Screen

Public Observation
Playground

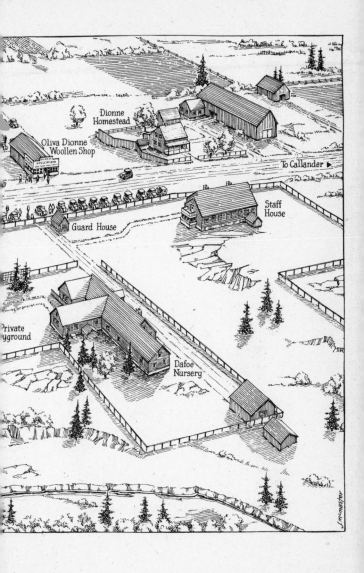

Dionne Homestead

Oliva Dionne Woollen Shop

To Callander ▶

Staff House

Guard House

Private Playground

Dafoe Nursery

J.mcmaster

ONE:
The road to Quintland

On May 28, 1934, between the hours of three and six in the morning, there were born to a farm-wife in the backwoods of Northern Ontario five identical girl babies. The event can properly be called a miracle. The chances of a woman giving birth to fraternal quintuplets were fifty-four million to one. The chance of such a child growing to adulthood was incalculable; there was no past record of any quintuplet living more than a few days. But the odds on the birth of identical quintuplets – all developed from a single egg, as these were – could not be reckoned; there had been only two cases in all medical history. Nor, in spite of fertility drugs, have there been any since. One cannot compute such odds because the choice is random. Identical quintuplets are a sport in human genesis.

Because the Dionne quintuplets survived and were on display for the first nine years of their lives, they became the world's best-known babies – better known than the princesses, Elizabeth and Margaret Rose, better known, even, than Shirley Temple. Millions, seeing their photographs almost daily on the front pages, in the rotogravure sections, on magazine covers, in countless advertisements, and in newsreels and feature films, were able to watch them grow, pound by pound and inch by inch, just like their own children.

Born in the blackest days of the Great Depression, they were as much a part of their time as Major Bowes, Frank Capra, Benny Goodman, or Father Coughlin, and just as influential. It is not possible to trace the social history of the Thirties without reference to the Dionne quintuplets. The reverse is also true. It is certain that, had they been born into an earlier decade, they would have expired swiftly – one-day wonders to be headlined briefly

11

and quickly forgotten. It is equally certain that had the miracle occurred a generation later, the spotlight would have been softer and the melodrama muted.

For a province struggling against economic strangulation they were as valuable a resource as gold, nickel, pulpwood, or hydro power. They saved an entire region from bankruptcy. They launched Northern Ontario's flourishing tourist industry. At their peak they represented a five-hundred-million-dollar asset.

Their proven attraction was so great that several cities offered them homes and three world's fairs wanted to exhibit them. The Ontario and federal governments passed unprecedented laws to protect them – as much with an eye to their economic potential as to their personal welfare.

Controversy swirled about them for all of their childhood years. They exacerbated the growing schism between Francophones and Anglophones in Ontario and Quebec. The prolonged struggle over their guardianship was fought on racial and religious grounds. When they refused to speak English on an international broadcast, they caused a backlash of anti-French and anti-Catholic resentment.

They influenced attitudes – towards child rearing, inoculation, and adoption. They boosted the sales of condensed milk, toothpaste, disinfectant, and dozens of other products. And they also changed for better or for worse the lives of many – from the doctor and the midwives who presided at their birth to those young couples who, determined never to bring children into a world torn by war and depression, changed their minds at the sight of five pudgy little girls romping merrily in their playground.

Between 1934 and 1943, close to three million persons made the long journey to the section of Lake Nipissing between North Bay and Callander that the travel brochures called "Quintland." The road led north from Toronto along the narrow lane of Yonge, the world's longest street, for two hundred and fifty miles, winding its way past straggles of tourist cabins, some hardly bigger than sentry boxes or outdoor privies; past service stations disguised as Cotswold cottages or storybook palaces with pink towers selling Marathon Anti-Knock Blue; past the jigsaw shapes of miniature golf courses, already falling into disuse; past snack bars made to look like ice cream cones, offering Eskimo Pies and ice-cold bottles of Whistle for a nickel; through the tight business sections of small red-brick towns, each with its Queen's or Empire hotel, and along the margins of smiling little lakes; and then, suddenly, just beyond Orillia, into the shattered rock of the Precambrian Shield, sombre with white pine and paper birch.

Long stretches of forest and gneiss, swamp and schist followed

and sometimes a farm struggling out of the wilderness, the barns unpainted, a tumble of stones gathered along the fencelines – harsh country, enticing for painters, grim for farmers, especially with pork retailing at less than fifteen cents a pound. But for the people of Quintland there was a new kind of profit: for these visitors belonged to the upper stratum of society – those who could afford a car and so had money to spend. They were a minority. In the mid-Thirties, fewer than 40 per cent of all Canadian families owned any kind of automobile. Four-lane highways were not needed. For the last eighty miles, the road to Quintland was not even paved.

The road led directly through Callander, the Cinderella city, better known in those days than Jack Benny's Waukegan. Here was the service station operated by Léon Dionne, the quintuplets' uncle, with its five pumps, each named for one of the babies. And here, up the street from the Log Cabin Lunch ("We don't know where Mom is but we have Pop on ice"), was the oblong brick house with the brass plate on the door bearing the name of the world's best-known doctor, A. R. Dafoe.

13

The turn-off road was heavy with automobiles. On peak days they formed themselves into a metallic snake, two and a half miles long, winding from Callander to the Dafoe Hospital. In one sixteen-hour period, in July, 1936, an observer clocked 1,956 cars on the turn-off – a rate of two cars a minute. They rumbled along through rough, inhospitable country, an unkempt mélange of dense brush and craggy outcrops interspersed with ragged hay fields. Except for a small sign, TO THE DIONNE QUINTUPLETS, there was no hint of anything unusual. But then, as the roadway rose to the crest of a low hill, each newcomer encountered a swirl of dust and was treated to a spectacle he could never forget.

Directly ahead a small community had been carved out of forest, swamp, and rock. Each summer morning and afternoon, seven days a week, it vibrated with people. The road spread out into a macadamized plaza, choked with parked cars and ringed with buildings and signs. At the far end, where the road curved, stood an ungainly frame structure on which were emblazoned the words MADAM LEGROS AND MADAM LEBEL MIDWIVES OF THE QUINTUPLETS BID YOU WELCOME! In the foreground, to the right, was the birthplace of the Quints, an unpainted farmhouse and a cluster of barns. Beyond it lay Oliva Dionne's two souvenir stands, with his name in gigantic letters and the words SOUVENIRS – REFRESHMENTS – OPERATED BY PARENTS OF THE WORLD'S MOST FAMOUS BABIES. Behind these were a parking lot for a thousand cars and a large log rest room.

On the left side of the plaza were more buildings: the nursery in the foreground, a neat, squat structure with a red roof and stained log walls, flanked by a staff house and a guardhouse. Beyond it lay the horseshoe-shaped playground building and observation gallery. The entire complex was surrounded by a seven-foot fence of meshed wire, like that of some minor correctional institution. Uniformed policemen stood guard at the gates.

There were people everywhere, pouring out of cars and buses, and spending money – buying souvenir postcards, pamphlets about the birth, binoculars at inflated prices, British woollens and china, candy, pop, hot dogs, and, for a quarter, Oliva Dionne's own autograph.

They came as early as six in the morning. By the time the first observation period began at 9:30, the queue could stretch back for half a mile or more. As the people moved forward they passed a long trough labelled STONES FROM THE QUINTUPLETS' PLAYGROUND. These were the famous "fertility stones," gathered each morning from the shores of Lake Nipissing in the trucks of the Ontario highways department and widely believed to be a boon to barren women. Everybody took one; like the view of the Quints, they were free.

The visitors were allowed to enter the gallery in groups of one hundred, peeling off in two directions, some moving counterclockwise and some in the opposite direction. No one was allowed to bring a camera. Only one man could take pictures: Fred Davis, late of the *Toronto Star* and now the representative of an American picture syndicate. Oliva Dionne himself could not photograph his own children.

The playground was surrounded on three sides by a U-shaped roofed passageway with windows facing inward and fitted with a silvery screen of wire mesh so closely woven that a pin could not be thrust through the opening. From this dark tunnel the five toddlers could be seen, playing on swings and tricycles or splashing in their shallow pool, apparently oblivious of the unseen thousands shuffling silently past them.

Few could resist a gasp on first seeing the Quints. By 1936, when the new playground was first opened, the two-year-olds were glowing with health, cheeks pink, enormous eyes framed by long lashes, hair in soft curls. The contrast between that spectacle and the memory of the early photographs, which had shown them as tiny inhuman creatures – "like skinned rabbits," as one report put it – was one reason why the sight of them was almost magical. To add to the fantasy, each was a carbon copy of the others. Which one was Cécile? Which Yvonne? Which Marie? Was that one Annette – or was it Emilie? In the gloom of the gallery people whispered those questions, but it was not possible to tell them apart.

The magic is still remembered. Those who saw the quintuplets at their cutest can never forget the spectacle. Forty years later, when other events have faded from memory, the enchantment of that moment remains. For many, such as Margaret Bennett of Windsor, who was eight years old when she saw the quintuplets in 1936, it was the thrill of their lives.

My memories of that trip are very strong – despite childhood visits to Banff, Yellowstone, and Quebec City during those same years – so it must have been a real milestone. The fact that both my parents were teachers in Windsor probably predisposed us all to an interest in children, yet I think we were, like all the other thousands of tourists, drawn by the fact that we were seeing a curiosity, a "wonder of the world," something we would never see again or hear of in our lifetime. It was really VERY exciting. That first sight of the five lovely baby girls playing innocently in an enclosed playground absolutely overwhelmed me. They were so adorable; it was like seeing a miracle.

When I returned to school that fall I boasted to teachers and class-mates alike that I had seen the Quints that summer, and they were terribly impressed. In other summers, coming back from long family camping trips to the Rockies or down East, there was no point in tell-ing anyone except the teachers where I had been because most of the kids didn't know enough geography to be impressed. So you can see, it was a real highlight in everyone's life to see the Quints.

The miracle was that the quintuplets were "normal." The press said so; the government said so; the official guardianship said so; Dr. Dafoe said so: normal and healthy in every way. Here was a paradox. If they were normal, why did they need to live in a hospi-tal, cared for by nurses in white? Why, at this point, could they not be returned to their parents?

Only the parents and a handful of their supporters asked that question. Few who saw the Quints that year had a critical word to say about their upbringing. The prevailing cant was that the little girls were receiving the best possible care, that they were the lucki-est children in the world, and, being a rare and exquisite species, they must be protected – protected from clouds of germs that could kill or cripple them; protected from curious crowds who could suffocate or crush them; protected from kidnappers, who would certainly steal them; protected from exploiters who would exhibit them as freaks; protected from the future, dark and uncer-tain; and, above all, protected from their own parents.

Even if the government of Mitchell Hepburn had wished to re-turn the children to the farmhouse across the road, the public outcry would have made the move politically impossible. But the government had no such intention. By 1936 the quintuplet indus-try was in full swing, and Quintland had equalled Niagara Falls as the biggest tourist attraction in Canada, rivalled in the United States by only Radio City, Gettysburg, and Mount Vernon.

In a year that produced some of the blackest headlines of the century, the Quints made the biggest news of all. By the end of 1936, *Time* magazine was able to report that they had become "the world's greatest news-picture story," subscribed to by 672 U.S. dailies with an aggregate circulation of more than thirteen million. One reason was that the Quints were *good* news, some-times the only good news on the front pages of the Depression years. Although 1936 was a wonderful year for newspaper writers and editors, it was not so wonderful for newspaper readers. Hitler marched into the Rhineland; Mussolini conquered Ethiopia; Gen-eral Franco touched off the Spanish civil war; Chiang Kai-shek declared war on Japan. It was also the year of the Rome-Berlin axis, the abdication crisis, the electrocution of Bruno Richard Hauptmann, the Moose River mine disaster, and the humbling defeat of Joe Louis by Max Schmeling of Germany. In contrast to all these horrors – not to mention the more routine fires, shipwrecks, wife beatings, gangland slayings, executions, suicides, sit-down strikes, hunger marches, and lovers' triangles that dominated the front pages of the period – the cheerful photographs and feature stories that streamed out of Callander were as welcome as rose water in a charnel house.

So were the films. By the time *The Country Doctor* was released by Twentieth Century-Fox, the quintuplets were, in the words of the *Literary Digest*, "acknowledged by the industry to be the greatest audience-drawing combine in the history of motion pictures." All the movies the quintuplets made were greeted by public and reviewers alike with wild enthusiasm. "The only movies we are able to sit back and enjoy in absolutely uncritical bliss are Chaplin comedies, Silly Symphonies and any picture at all about the quintuplets," wrote B. R. Crisler, the *New York Times* movie critic, in the spring of 1937.

They were, so Leo Dolan of the Canadian government tourist bureau told the North Bay Board of Trade in the spring of 1936, "the greatest tourist attraction on the face of the globe!" His listeners did not question that hyperbole, for all stood to gain from the accident of the quintuplets' birth. In 1939, when the children were five, American visitors answering Ottawa's tourist questionnaires still listed the quintuplets as the greatest drawing-card in Canada. Even in 1940, when wartime restrictions had cut deeply into domestic travel and the children themselves had lost some of their baby cuteness, a quarter of a million people were drawn to the U-shaped passageway and the sunlit playground. By that time more people had seen them in the flesh than had viewed any other Canadian, living or dead.

Millions around the world knew of Canada only because of the quintuplets. Callander was the one Canadian community with an international reputation. In 1935, Gordon Sinclair, the *Toronto Star*'s footloose reporter, interviewed in Indore a Brahman whose only interest was in Oliva Dionne, the quintuplets' father. He had a thick sheaf of clippings about the birth and wanted to know what the father of the famous five ate, so that he might copy it and enjoy a similar fertility. In 1936, Matthew Halton, travelling through France on assignment for the same paper, reported that he was peppered with questions about the quintuplets. A Toronto ophthalmologist, Dr. R. J. P. McCulloch, who spent six weeks in India in 1938, reported that in all that time he could find only one reference to Canada in the Indian press: a report that the five girls were confined with colds. And in Nigeria, the Reverend Harry Garbutt, an Anglican minister, was able to halt the sacrifice of twin children among the Sobo tribe by pasting photographs of the quintuplets on the walls of all his churches. The native mothers, who believed that at least one twin of a pair was filled with evil, were impressed by the fact that Canada had constructed a special hospital for its multiple birth, with obviously beneficial results.

TOONERVILLE FOLKS

That was perhaps the most extreme example of the babies' widespread influence. In North America in 1936, the Quints dominated Christmas toy sales; Shirley Temple dolls took second place to their Dionne counterparts. A photograph that same year showing them receiving diphtheria shots resulted in the heaviest attendance in history at Toronto clinics. When they helped launch an Adopt-A-Child campaign, eight hundred Ontario orphans found homes in three weeks – another record. *Time* reported that one of the reasons for the construction of the Ivy Lea bridge between New York State and Ontario was to make the Quints more accessible to American tourists. Conventions were planned around them: twenty-five hundred members of the Supreme Order of the White Shrine of Jerusalem came to Toronto in 1938 because the city "held out the inducement of the Quints."

The staying power of the quintuplets as a continuing story was phenomenal. They remained on the front pages for the first nine years of their lives and intermittently thereafter. There was scarcely a major magazine from *Parents* to *Click* that did not feature them at least once on its cover. At the end of the Great Depression they continued to be listed among the most popular of international celebrities, along with Mickey Mouse and Charlie Chaplin. They had, in fact, only one major rival for world acclaim, and that was the diminutive and deceptively shy recluse, Allan Roy Dafoe, the country doctor who had helped bring them into the world, a man universally venerated as a medical miracle worker. A hero in the eyes of everybody from Franklin D. Roosevelt to Rudy Vallee, he was without an enemy in the world; unless, of course, you counted the two sad-eyed people who lived in the farmhouse across the road: the parents of the world's most famous babies, Elzire and Oliva Dionne.

TWO:
Beyond the shores of Nipissing

Few countries were hit harder by the Depression than the Dominion of Canada. Few peoples suffered more severely than its citizens. No Western industrial nation entered the decade of the Thirties with fewer social services. No other had an economy so rigid. The fixed costs of three railways, built largely at public expense in the rosy glow of western expansion, had become a crushing burden on the taxpayer. The lifeline of an export trade based on staple raw materials was choked off by the economic nationalism of former customers. Between 1929 and 1933 the total national income dropped by almost 50 per cent.

Statistically, 1934 was a slightly better year than 1933, but few had reason to be aware of it. More than a quarter of all wage earners – and perhaps as many as a third – were out of work. The exact figures are not easily reckoned because tens of thousands of young men went unrecorded. They had never held a job; they had no idea what it was like to hold one; few could get relief. They moved aimlessly from town to town, dodging the railway police, sleeping under bridges, and accepting scant handouts in the local jails or soup kitchens before being hustled away by the authorities or by the pull of their own wanderlust.

In North Bay in May, 1934, the month the quintuplets were born, six thousand free meals were served to transients in the local jail. In the cold months as many as three hundred men crowded into the jail each night for warmth. The town of fifteen thousand could ill afford the charity. Almost 20 per cent of North Bay's population was on relief that year (the overall Canadian percentage was fifteen), a statistic that helps explain an editorial that appeared in the *North Bay Nugget* on May 28, in the same issue of the paper that carried the banner line: QUINTUPLETS BORN TO FARM

WIFE. The paper commented on the fact that enumerators for the coming provincial election "have remarked on the large number of voters who have expressed communist sympathies. Several of them have declared that a communist candidate would have little difficulty in carrying sections of the riding outside the urban centres."

Callander's plight was far worse than North Bay's. Seventy per cent of the town's population of nine hundred was on relief. Even at twenty-five cents, few men could afford a haircut, and the town barber, Eugene Dufresne, willingly took three jars of tomatoes as his fee. "No money and all on relief," Dr. Allan Roy Dafoe wrote to his brother Will (in Toronto) in January. "I don't know what some of the people will do when relief ceases. They are so used to getting it."

Relief payments were far below the survival level. In 1934, a family of five in Callander received $32.36 a month, of which $18.12 was for food, $7.00 was for shelter, and $7.24 was for clothing. That yielded an annual income of just over half of the seven hundred dollars the Department of Labour had established as the poverty level and only about one-third of what it defined as the minimum subsistence level for the same sized family. During its years in office, the government of R. B. Bennett spent less on relief than it did on meeting the annual deficits of the Canadian National Railways.

Relief recipients received vouchers, rather than cash; that branded them as indigents, dependent on public charity. To get on the relief rolls they were forced to submit to an investigation of their homes and their larders and to prove that they had no other income. Because the township of North Himsworth was virtually broke and could scarcely afford even the 10 per cent it contributed toward relief funds, borderline cases in the Callander area went without.

It was the same throughout Northern Ontario. In North Bay, a young unemployed couple, newly married, was denied any succour, the relief officer remarking that people who married in such circumstances could expect no sympathy or aid from the government. This attitude, which seems callous in the welfare state of the 1970s, was common in 1934. It left its mark on Lord Thomson of Fleet who, as plain Roy Thomson, was the North Bay councillor in charge of distributing relief in 1934. At the time, the future newspaper magnate owned a single tweed suit, patched by his wife, and was teetering on the edge of insolvency – kiting cheques between North Bay and Timmins to meet the payrolls of his two radio stations. But he had already announced that he intended to be a millionaire, and he had little use for those who took government handouts.

Yes, I was on the council, and we used to have to deal with relief recipients, and I think that experience gave me, well, prejudice. It prejudiced me against relief. I don't believe in relief at all, you see; I'm probably the most right-wing person you've ever met. I believe that you should look after yourself, and I think everybody could do it if they wanted to. Of course there were some unfortunates with medical trouble; maybe parents dying, children dying, or something. I had sympathy. Those kind of people would get relief. But I think we've ruined the calibre of our people with handouts. It wasn't so tough then, you know. My thought is this: before anybody should get any help from the government they should suffer a little. Now I don't mean by that, lay down and die. But adding everything up, it's probably better to try like hell to get a job and fail than just to walk in and take a handout; I did it, you know.

But in 1934 it was not always possible to follow the advice of the future press lord. A man or woman with a job was sometimes as badly off as the million and a half Canadians on relief: the average wage in a lumber mill in the Callander area was only twelve dollars for a sixty-hour week. By 1934, four of the five mills had burned down (along with the railway station), and the fifth had closed its doors. The woollen mill, the tannery, the paddle-wheel steamer that had been the outward symbols of the community's prosperity at the turn of the century were long gone. In the year of the quintuplets' birth, Callander was merely an abandoned lumber town of box-frame buildings, a flag stop on the main railway line between Toronto and the mining country of the North, hemmed in on three sides by wild, cut-over timberland and on the fourth by the slate waters of Lake Nipissing. A single frame hotel, its rooms rarely occupied and falling into disuse, catered to a trickle of travellers. A general store, a gasoline station, and a post office made up most of the business section. With taxes thousands of dollars in arrears, the community in that bleak spring of 1934 had reached its low point.

The farmers of North Himsworth and of the neighbouring township of East Ferris were not quite so destitute. They had a roof over their heads and grew their own food. It is ironic that Oliva Dionne, who was shortly to be portrayed in the international press as a wretched, poverty-stricken peasant, was in better financial shape than most of his neighbours in the towns of Callander and Corbeil. He owned 195 acres of land of which 70 were cleared; he grew his own vegetables and raised his own beef, pork, and poultry; he held title to his home, a one-and-a-half-storey farmhouse built originally of logs but now covered with siding and big enough to hold all of his five children; and he was one of the few people in the district to own a car. He had never been on relief and was proud of it.

Although his name would be linked inseparably with Callander, he belonged to the Roman Catholic parish of Corbeil in the township of East Ferris; his home lay about halfway between the two communities. The characters of the two villages differed as coal from kindling, and it is necessary for an understanding of what followed to comprehend that difference. Callander, with its equal mix of Anglo-Saxons and French Canadians, lying in the orbit of North Bay, was the more sophisticated. It had a doctor, a post office, and some of the accepted manifestations of civilization: hydro-electric power, telephone service, running water. Corbeil had none of these. Its people lit their homes with kerosene lamps and could not listen to the radio or ring each other up. The town had no medical services. It was not on any travelled highway. The railway station was closed; the agent had been withdrawn. The solidly French-Canadian population of five hundred lived very much as their ancestors had lived three centuries before on their farms in Normandy.

For the people of Corbeil science had little meaning. They preferred to believe in divine miracles. In May, 1934, a few days before the greatest miracle of all, they were observing *le rogation*, an interval of prayer for the fruitfulness of the soil and for rain for the crops. They were rarely sick – a vigorous people who sprang from sturdy stock with "the greatest vitality in the world . . . unspoiled by blood diseases for generations," to quote Allan Roy Dafoe. Doctors were called only in dire moments. At the approach of a birth a midwife was sent for – somebody like Madame Benoit Labelle, who had delivered some three hundred babies. Although the average size of the Canadian family dropped rapidly during the Depression, the rural *Canadiens* continued to rejoice in large numbers of children. To have a substantial family was considered a woman's greatest honour; the neighbouring parish of Bonfield boasted a Canadian record – one hundred and fifty of its families had more than ten offspring each.

The Catholic church was the hub around which the life of Corbeil revolved. In the light of what was to happen, it is important to understand that the priest's advice was rarely questioned or rejected. The code and conduct of his flock derived from him. The families of Corbeil literally prayed together and stayed together. Sons worked in the fields, inherited their father's land, and in turn supported their aging parents. Girls, who learned to sew and cook almost as soon as they learned to walk, married schoolmates or next-door neighbours. In a sense, children were property, to be protected and controlled like domestic animals and sometimes to be profited from. Marriages were made, not in Heaven, but by an arrangement between families, with the girl's dowry an important factor in the transaction. Morals were rigid. Boys and girls did not hold hands until they were engaged and then rarely.

The children of Corbeil were brought up on the virtues of obedience – to the parish priest and to their parents. The mothers ruled the kitchens; the fathers' words were law; the family was the real political unit. The people of Corbeil were a private people, a little shy if not downright suspicious of the outside world. Large families, such as the Dionnes', tended to turn in upon themselves, drawing their resources from within. The concept of the "nuclear family" would have repelled a man like Dionne. His immediate family group – the one he saw almost daily – included his father, at least one aunt and uncle, a spinster sister, a brother and sister-in-law, and his wife's aunt and uncle as well as his own children.

The old people of Corbeil – people such as Mr. and Mrs. Leo Voyer, who have run the general store for almost half a century – do not remember the Depression as a period of unremitting gloom. No one had any money, but most had enough food to eat: they grew it themselves; cabbages, turnips, carrots, and onions filled the root cellars each winter. The staple meat was salt pork with four inches of fat on it. They made most of their own clothes, carding, spinning, and knitting the wool, made their own soap from beef fat and lye, made their own wine from beets and cherries, made their own moonshine from barley and oats, made their own sleighs, skates, skis, and hockey sticks (the pucks, frozen blobs of manure) and, in doing so, made their own fun.

Oh, we had good times! Really good times. We had parties, we had dances, we always had somebody to play the violin. We had a big two-ton truck, and if we were going some place, we'd take all the gang and go just any place at all. We always had enough to make a dance. Couldn't cost anything because we had no money. Oh, there was dancing! And when you'd go to a party, at that time, you'd go in the house and you'd stay until about five o'clock in the morning. There were really more nice times, at that time, than you've got now. There'd be maybe ten, fifteen people. The house wasn't any bigger for more. And nobody going around in cars in those times, taking a bottle for a drink. At that time nobody was taking a drink – only moonshine.

This was the society to which Oliva Dionne and his young wife, Elzire, belonged. Except for a brief honeymoon trip to Masham Mills in the Ottawa Valley, they had never strayed more than a few miles from the farmhouse which Oliva's father, Olivier, had built at the turn of the century and in which all of Oliva's children, five living, one dead, had been born. Like his son, Olivier Dionne was a proud man who boasted that he had never owed a nickel in his life.

In 1934, Oliva Dionne was thirty-one years old, a wiry farmer with unkempt hair like Stan Laurel's. He had had nine years of schooling, four at Corbeil and then five at Callander, where he was sent to learn English. Like everybody else he walked to school – five miles every day. At sixteen he left his studies to help out on the farm; there was never a thought or a question that he would do anything else. His father ruled the house. If Oliva or any of his five sisters and brothers stepped out of line, they were smacked. It was the same at school.

Except for meals and sleep, his childhood was spent almost entirely out of doors. In the fall he hunted with his father. In the summer he fished in Nipissing, a lake then teeming with pike and pickerel. At school lunch breaks, the children rushed to the lakeshore and swam until the bell called them back. At haying time the children toiled in the fields from four in the morning until nine at night.

By 1925, the year in which he was married, Oliva Dionne was considered the best catch in the country. He had money in the bank, the only car in the community except for the one owned by the priest, and a hay press, which he rented out by the day. The girl who caught his eye, Elzire Legros, was only sixteen when they were married. They met, appropriately, at church. She was plump, pretty, and competent, perfectly able to help her husband cut hay within a week of bearing a child. The farm was their life; their most prized wedding present, from his father, was a new cow.

In the mid-Thirties a shrill press coarsened the image of Elzire Dionne almost beyond recognition. The public attitude toward her varied from pity at her being "forced" to bear children to censure of her ingratitude toward a government that wanted to care for them. It was widely assumed that with her lack of education (she had left school after Grade Three) and her peasant background, she could not possibly be a good mother to such a large family. On the contrary, she was, by the standards of her own community and even by the general standards of her time, a very good mother indeed.

It escaped almost everybody's notice that Elzire Dionne really liked having babies and that she loved children with a passion. For most of her childhood she had been a surrogate parent. Her mother had died when she was seven; before the age of twelve she assumed full control of the Legros household, cleaning the house, cooking meals, even cutting hair. It was not a normal childhood; in a family of seven children she was the only girl, and until her confirmation she always wore blue overalls. Her main recreation was playing baseball with her six brothers or the fiddle at dances. None of this fulfilled her maternal instincts. She collected soap wrappers, which could be sent away for a variety of premiums. Her brothers wanted baseball equipment; but she wanted dolls, and she got them. It is said that she had at least ten dolls and that after she was married she missed them so much that she brought them secretly to her new home. Before long, the dolls were replaced by babies. Her first child was born when she was seventeen. Five more pregnancies followed in rapid succession. By 1934, at twenty-five, she was mother to five living children and pregnant again – a two-hundred-pound woman, still with the face of a child.

Her life revolved around family and church. The Dionnes were not gregarious; they had little time for visiting or entertaining except with members of their family. Oliva Dionne had never celebrated his own birthday. His wife was not at ease with strangers. Though she could understand English, she was too shy to speak it. The high point of her week was Sunday Mass at the Corbeil church, which she attended regularly. Intensely religious, she believed implicitly that everything that happened to her and to her family was the direct result of the intervention of the Deity. Children were born, lived, or died as a result of God's will; no earthly power could interfere. This unquestioning acceptance of a divine order gave her a remarkable serenity. The early photographs of Elzire Dionne do not do her justice; almost everyone who met her commented on the unlined face, the childlike beauty.

Childbearing was to her a process as natural as eating. It was why women were placed on earth. She was determined that her daughters would also be good mothers. They must learn to cook, to sew, to clean the house, and to prepare food at any hour. The kitchen was their natural habitat; in the Dionne home it flowed into the parlour without a barrier. Few entered that home without being offered something to eat.

When the Depression came, the Dionnes were forced to struggle harder. Oliva Dionne found that he could no longer sell the produce of his farm or the furs of the animals he trapped each winter. Their savings kept them off relief but dwindled to almost nothing.

Elzire made over one of her husband's suits for Ernest, her eldest, and tore apart her wedding trousseau to fashion coats and dresses for Rose and Thérèse so that they would be presentable at church.

By 1934 there was very little money coming in, the house was mortgaged for three thousand dollars, and Elzire Dionne was experiencing disturbing complications in her pregnancy. The baby was not due until the end of July, but by May she was abnormally heavy and suffering from swollen legs.

Oliva Dionne had managed to wangle a job hauling gravel with his wagon and team at four dollars a day. He decided he could afford to consult a doctor. The only practitioner within a fifteen-mile radius was Dr. Allan Roy Dafoe of Callander. He had delivered three of the Dionne children and had just missed delivering a fourth, which was born before he arrived. For the other two, Mrs. Dionne had relied on the champion midwife of the district, Mme Labelle.

The doctor was not a man to waste time or mince words. He told Dionne that he must put his wife to bed at once and keep her there. She must not be allowed to do housework or farm chores; he would need a hired girl to look after the children. From Dionne's description he diagnosed Elzire's ailment as dropsy. Clearly, her condition was serious. He warned Dionne that if his advice was not taken, his wife might die.

The next morning, the doctor drove out to the farm to find Mrs. Dionne dragging herself about the kitchen, trying to keep house. She was in terrible pain, her legs swollen to twice their normal size. Dafoe was furious. He ordered her to bed and delivered a tongue lashing to her husband. Get yourself a hired girl, he told him, or get yourself a new wife; take your choice.

Here was a clash of cultures. One can understand the exasperation of the doctor, faced with two peasants who could not seem to fathom a clear and present medical danger. Dafoe's attitude was that of a stern father trying to knock sense into dull and uncomprehending children. Yet one must also sympathize with Dionne, who had been forced to mortgage his property to stay off relief. Where was he to find the means to hire anybody? As for his wife, she was doing her duty to her husband and her children as she saw it, in spite of considerable pain; her fate lay in God's hands, not the doctor's. Between Elzire Dionne and Allan Roy Dafoe there was no scintilla of understanding, nor would there ever be. If she could not grasp her peril, he could not comprehend her fatalism. He was a medical man, not a social worker. In twenty-five years in the district he had never bestirred himself to learn a word of French. But then, he had never tried to be popular with his patients in either of the two cultures; quite the opposite. Professionally he was impeccable, a tireless practitioner who came when he was called whatever the hour or the distance and who never gave a thought to his fee. Socially he was a cipher. Within a month, the international press would apotheosize him as the quintessential country doctor; but he was scarcely that. There was nothing typical about Allan Roy Dafoe.

Physically, he was unprepossessing. Everything about him was tiny except his head. He was only five feet five. His hands were so small he had to buy his gloves at the children's counter, yet his head size was so large he had trouble getting fitted for a hat. He stammered. His clothes did not fit. Financially, he was not much better off than his neighbours. He never sent a bill and often rejected fees in kind, such as firewood, because he knew his patients could not spare it. Almost all his income came from relief work. The government paid doctors ten dollars for delivering a baby and allowed fifty cents for each office call and two dollars for each house call. There was, however, a ceiling of a hundred dollars a month on such payments, and that, together with a small stipend as Medical Officer of Health for the municipality, made up the bulk of his income.

In small northern villages the turnover of GPs is continual. But at the time of the miracle birth, Dafoe had spent half his life – more than twenty-five years – in the Callander area, ministering to poverty-stricken farmers whose language he could not or would not speak and with whom he had not a shred of common interest. He had scarcely any close friends, lived a hermit-like existence, and, since he was on call at all times, rarely enjoyed a full night's sleep. In all those years he had taken only one two-week holiday.

Why? The Dafoes did not lack opportunity. His father was a successful doctor in Madoc, a small town in eastern Ontario. His younger brother, Will, was one of the best obstetricians in Toronto, an ambitious, well-to-do, and socially prominent specialist with an enviable medical and athletic record. Yet here was Roy, Will's senior by eleven years, hiding out in an obscure French-Canadian community in the inhospitable Precambrian desert of Northern Ontario.

"Hiding out" is the proper phrase. The persistent stammer is the giveaway. Psychologically, a stammer is considered the visible sign of inner childhood tensions. It was from these that Dafoe was fleeing. He had come to Callander at the age of twenty-five, fresh out of medical school, bent on escape – escape from the henpecking of four sisters, from the uncompromising ambition of his parents, and from a nagging sense of his own inadequacy.

Decades later in 1937, when his name was better known than that of Osler or Banting, Dafoe, in the course of a speech to the Conference on Research on the Dionne Quintuplets, unconsciously drew back a corner of the curtain on his own childhood: "This self-expression stuff – I don't know. Maybe it's all right. When my brother and I were little boys my father didn't let us have any self-expression. We were told what to do."

Dafoe's father was a stern, parsimonious, inflexible man, more than normally conscious of his professional position in a community of farmers. In the Dafoe household his will was law. This bred in the son a stubborn and perverse streak, as one painful incident from his childhood makes clear. The boy hated porridge so much that his father offered to pay him a penny each morning to choke it down. When summer came, young Roy had managed to save thirty-two cents. But his shoes needed half-soling, and when he announced that they had been repaired at a cost of thirty cents, his father simply told him: "That works out very nicely. You can take thirty of your pennies and pay for your own shoes." The boy did so, but that afternoon he flung them down in front of his father, crying: "H-here's your old shoes! You can k-keep them and your p-p-porridge, too!"

Dafoe's high-strung mother, too, had a strong personality and he was also, to quote his biographer, "waist deep in sisters." Until the age of eleven, he was the only boy in the household. Though they were all younger than he, the four of them did their utmost to run his life. The eldest, Norma, caught up to him in school and consistently topped him in class. He barely managed to scrape through his second high school year, a performance that did not sit well with his ambitious father.

By this time the stammer had become a severe handicap, preventing the boy from making close friends. He had, however, found a refuge, a six-foot hideaway at the back of the barn, burrowed in the hay. In this womb-like cavern he escaped to a vicarious existence. He read indiscriminately: everything from Nick Carter penny dreadfuls to the English classics. Neighbours said there weren't half a dozen grown men in town who had read as many books as the Dafoe boy at twelve.

His career at the University of Toronto was undistinguished. In his first year in Arts he failed every subject and had to repeat. He almost flunked out of medical school when he failed to answer a question in the final oral examination. The case was reconsidered and he got his degree. His father assumed that Roy would join him in practice in Madoc. Nothing was further from the son's mind. He took his internship at Bracebridge in the Muskoka lake district and then fled three hundred miles north into mining country, moving from town to town and mine to mine until, drifting south again to Lake Nipissing, he found what he was seeking. The practice of Dr. Emmett Scarlett at Callander was for sale for one hundred dollars. Dafoe bought it immediately.

In Madoc he had been under the thumb of his parents and his sisters. At university he had stood near the bottom of the class, an unathletic youth with few social graces. But in Callander he had few intellectual equals. He was *le docteur*, the healer, the miracle man. He could order people about and did. For the first time, the boy with the inferiority complex felt himself superior to his neighbours. His father and his sisters wrote, urging him to move to more prosperous surroundings. But he had no intention of ever moving again.

He developed a gruffness of manner that would one day charm and disarm the toughest members of the press corps. Part of this served as a mask for his shyness; part was the stock-in-trade of the rural practitioner. Like any doctor, Dafoe learned to hide his feelings. More than most, perhaps, he understood how important it was to transmit to his patients a sense of confidence. In his photographs, Dafoe is always poker-faced. Even when flanked by the famous five, he flashes no teeth for the camera. In New York for the first time, surrounded by reporters, he refused to be dazzled by the skyscrapers of Wall Street or the lights of Broadway. This non-reaction, startling to Manhattanites, made him front-page copy.

As a doctor and as a man he was liked and respected. His very bluntness was an advantage among the plainspoken people of Callander, Corbeil, and Bonfield. He had another asset, more valuable in those communities than surgical brilliance – a remarkable store of common sense. He prescribed few medicines; his patients could not afford them. His faith rested instead on the natural remedies of fresh air, sunlight, uncontaminated water, and a balanced diet. Once he encountered a sobbing mother trying to force a salt solution down the throat of a child stricken with pneumonia. "He's dying," she cried. "Can't you do something?"

"If you're sure he's dying, I'll try," the doctor stammered. He wrapped the baby in a blanket and put him out in the bright February sunshine and the fresh air. The baby recovered.

He quickly learned to improvise. One of his first patients was an eighteen-year-old boy who had mangled his hand in a threshing machine. Dafoe's instinct was to amputate, but he knew that a farmboy was helpless without his hands. He decided to take a long chance and save some of the fingers. Only then did he discover that he had no catgut to sew up the wound. Dafoe solved the problem by sending to the barn for a few hairs from a horse's tail; with this makeshift thread, carefully sterilized, he patched up the broken hand.

On another occasion, a man fighting a forest fire slipped and fell into the blaze, burning himself fearfully. It was Dafoe's first case of burns, but he remembered that his father had treated them with tea. He brewed a potful and wrapped the victim in soft bandages soaked with the strong tea. It was rough and ready treatment, but the tannic acid did the job.

The bulk of his practice consisted of delivering babies, usually in the small hours of the morning. May was the baby month, and the doctor used to joke that he could not count on much sleep in late spring. Ironically, he had managed somehow to get through his entire medical training without ever witnessing the birth of a child. As a young intern in Bracebridge, called upon to preside at a delivery, he stood helplessly by while a midwife took over. But by the time the quintuplets were born, Dafoe had delivered more than five hundred infants whose mothers ranged in age from thirteen to fifty-three. He delivered one woman in Astorville of twenty-three babies; all but two lived to adulthood. His pregnant patients seemed able to survive the worst shocks. One desperate woman shot herself through the throat at close range when six months pregnant with an unwanted child. The bullet ploughed upward through her skull, passing through part of the brain. Dafoe patched her up and three months later delivered her of a healthy boy.

In 1934, Dafoe was a near recluse, looking far older than his fifty-one years – a diabetic who had to give himself regular injections of insulin. He had never fully recovered from the blow of his wife's death in 1926. They had been married for only twelve years, and when she succumbed to a brain tumour, which followed an attack of meningitis, he was as usual out on call. Dafoe had another explanation for her death. "She wore herself out helping me, serving the people here," he told a Boston journalist. She was a public health nurse, and the two had worked together for days without sleep during the influenza epidemic of 1918; Dafoe always believed that that was the start of her failing health.

He lived a solitary existence in the two-storey brick house with the white picket fence that he bought in 1914, the year of his marriage. His only son, Bill, was away at boarding school and saw his father only during holidays. The two were not intimate; it was hard for anyone to be intimate with a man who shied away from betraying emotion. At the time of his wife's funeral, the doctor had refused to go to the cemetery for fear of showing his feelings in public. His letters to his teen-aged son were brief and stilted. In 1938, when Dafoe was famous and had ghost-writers, these letters were written for him by the secretary who also prepared his syndicated column. Dafoe barely bothered to read them before he signed them.

He lived for his work, his books, and his shortwave radio. Once he had owned a small pipe organ on which he played for hours – Bach and Handel, hymns and improvisations in a minor key – but after his wife's death this fell into disuse; some said he never touched the keys again. But he bought at least three books a week; his library was enormous, containing at least fifteen hundred volumes. The boy who had devoured Darwin's *Origin of Species* and Buffalo Bill dime novels at the age of twelve remained an eclectic bookworm. He gobbled up detective stories, but he also read the classics, contemporary novels (*Anthony Adverse* was the best seller that spring), and adventure and science-fiction pulps from *Argosy* to *Amazing Stories*. Piles of them cluttered his attic, dating back as far as 1914.

When he was not reading he was fiddling with his radio. Shortwave dial twisting had become a national craze, bigger even than miniature golf and producing the same kind of name-dropping that jet-setters were to indulge in half a century later ("I got Rio last night; can you beat it?" "Yep, *I* got Moscow!"). Night after night Dafoe sat huddled over his set, listening to distorted voices or snatches of nightclub music wavering across the Atlantic from the capitals of Europe. Yet, in spite of his library and his listening-post, he remained curiously unsophisticated. It is a measure of his withdrawal from the world that he had seen only one movie in his lifetime, *Sunshine Susie*, the 1931 British musical starring the German actress Renate Müller. He did not see another feature film until Twentieth Century-Fox made *The Country Doctor*, in which Jean Hersholt played a thinly disguised Dafoe.

"I don't know you from Adam, Mr. Hersholt," Dafoe remarked when he first met the actor, "but, please – that means nothing. I know no one in pictures."

"Surely," said Hersholt, "you have heard of Greta Garbo."

"Who's she?" asked Dafoe.

Here one's credulity is stretched to the breaking-point. It is impossible to believe that the omnivorous reader had never heard of the best-publicized screen actress of her time. It is easier to believe that Dafoe by 1936 had slipped comfortably into the role that the press had created for him – that of the simple, unworldly country GP, devoted to his patients, unblemished by the pox of sophistication. One cannot fault Dafoe for this; like many another public figure he learned to make a virtue of his shortcomings.

He was looked after by a housekeeper, a Mrs. Little, who invariably ate in the kitchen, away from the doctor, even when there
was no one else in the house. His one close friend was Kenneth
Morrison, the town's leading citizen, whose father had named Callander after his own birthplace in Scotland. Morrison, who had
been a member of the North Himsworth municipal council since
1921 and who became its reeve, also ran the general store. Occasionally, too, Dafoe would visit with one or other of the Roman
Catholic priests in the area, who were his intellectual equals as
Morrison was his social equal. His only other companion after his
wife's death was Madame Louise de Kiriline, the nurse at the Red
Cross outpost in Bonfield. For six years, from 1928 until 1934,
doctor and nurse worked side by side as virtual equals, establishing a rapport rare for Dafoe and a mutual respect that was dissi-
pated only after the tensions engendered by the quintuplets' first
year.

Louise de Kiriline was and is a remarkable woman with a
remarkable past. Tall, erect, and handsome, with dark close-
cropped hair and a strong, almost masculine face with deep-set
eyes and high cheekbones, she was a no-nonsense professional.
Her credo was Dafoe's: fresh air, sunlight, cold water, sensible
food, rest, and open bowels. She was perfectly able to remove an
appendix in the doctor's absence and to work round the clock.
During a smallpox epidemic in 1930, with more than one hundred
active cases, the two had toiled without sleep to vaccinate every
child in the area over the age of six.

De Kiriline sprang from aristocratic Scandinavian stock. Her
background was both adventurous and tragic, for she had married
a White Russian in a Danish prison camp during the Great War,
only to lose him to a Bolshevik firing squad when the two tried to
return to his homeland after the revolution. She herself had survived a bout in a Leningrad prison and had worked on the Volga
during the famine of 1921 before leaving Europe forever to try to
make a new life as an outpost nurse in Northern Ontario. In 1928,
because of her fluent French, she was posted to the new Red Cross
depot in Bonfield. Here she learned how to baptize babies and to
administer the last rites in the absence of a priest and, equally important, how to drive a dogsled over roads that, in the drifting
snow, neither horse nor automobile could negotiate.

*Dr. Dafoe? Well, Dr. Dafoe was quite a peculiar person. He was
not like everybody else. I remember he took me out the very first day I
met him and showed me all around – all the houses and all the places.
He knew all those families from top to bottom. He knew their health*

and everything about them. He was extraordinary! As a medical man I would say his greatest skill was diagnosis. He really did know exactly what was the matter. That was not so much from reading books as from his own experience with all those families – seeing them, you know, from generation to generation. His asepsis was not very good. It was always very hard for me to get him to wash his hands. That kind of thing didn't matter so very much because, you see, we never had any infections or anything like that.

You know the people lived very, very poorly at that time during the Depression, but he never refused to come and he never talked much about money. He was really very fond of this place, and he was very fond of the people. With Dr. Dafoe I was treated as I was in Sweden, where nurses and doctors are equal. We worked together just hand in glove. It was extraordinary. Of course, we were all over the place, but I just had to phone him, and he knew he could trust me and that I knew exactly what to do. We had such interesting things happen! I remember especially one time, away in the back country, a woman was going to have a baby and Dr. Dafoe knew the exact state of her condition . . . knew it couldn't live and we would have to take it out in pieces. I had all the instruments well arranged and sterilized when suddenly in comes the little old grandmother, and with her little hand she sprays me with holy water. I was listening to the baby's heartbeats to make sure it was still alive inside the mother because you see the priest had taught me how to baptize a dying child; and that was the time I baptized a child inside the mother. And I remember how helpful Dr. Dafoe was at the time, how easy he was.

He kept mainly to himself, but he was very open with me. We discussed all kinds of things. He was very interested in history. We discussed conservation. We discussed medical matters and so on. So spiritually, it was very interesting, because there were very few people he could talk to. Sometimes we listened to concerts together. He would tell me that such-and-such was going to be on the radio and would I come up and listen to it with him? And he monitored my social life so that I wouldn't go into places where he felt I shouldn't be. Of course, I was young in those days. But he'd say, No, no, you shouldn't go there – they'll all be drunk there.

Yes, I think he was lonely. I'll tell you a little secret: he proposed to me once! Dr. Dafoe! From behind the door. Of course, I didn't have any thought of that at all. But he was really touching and I felt so sorry for him because he was so very lonesome. And he was a nice man then. Of course, he changed . . .

THREE:
May 28, 1934

Few other births in history have been described in more detail, at greater length, and with more accuracy than that of the Dionne quintuplets. All of the witnesses to the event – both parents, the two midwives and, of course, the doctor – volunteered their versions of the miracle within a few days of its occurrence. In the decade that followed, the tale was repeated in books, magazine articles, medical addresses, learned journals, souvenir pamphlets, documentaries, and newspaper features. Hundreds of thousands of words have been used to tell exactly what went on in the Dionne farmhouse on that soft morning in May when the babble of frogs shrilled through the night and the perfume of lilacs lay heavy in the air. The five babies were still struggling for life when the lilacs expired, trampled to death by the curious.

One might expect that the narrative would have palled, so often was it repeated, but this was not the case. The two midwives were persuaded to put their names to a version; this pamphlet, hawked at twenty-five cents from their own booth, sold more than one hundred thousand copies. The parents told their story to a New York sob sister who made it the basis for *two* books, published ten years apart, as well as innumerable newspaper and magazine articles. The doctor dined out on it for almost a decade. Again and again he was urged to retell it for newspaper reporters, for his biographer, for radio audiences, from the lecture platform, and for the inspiration of his colleagues at medical conventions and in professional publications. Even the Quints told the story in a book of their own – or had it told for them, since of all those present in the farmhouse that night they alone had no memory of it.

No one seemed to tire of the story, in spite of the recycling. It *was* miraculous. It *was* unique. And it was contemporary. People, especially in Toronto, tended to remember the evening of May 28, when the first short paragraph appeared in the newspapers, and to recall what they had been doing about that time: watching *Men in White*, a movie about doctors at Loew's, with Clark Gable and Myrna Loy; dancing the new ballroom sensation, the Continental, at the Palais Royale; listening on the radio to the welterweight championship match between Barney Ross and Jimmy McLarnin.

The Dionnes had no radio. Sometimes on Saturday nights they would go to Callander to brother Léon's to listen to *The National Barn Dance* from Chicago, with Uncle Ezra, Lulubelle and Scotty, and the Hoosier Hot Shots. Sometimes on week nights they could not resist dropping over to catch *Amos 'n' Andy*, the insanely popular comic serial that had everybody saying "Holy Mackerel!" and "I'se regusted."

The Dionnes had no radio because they had no electricity. Nor did they have running water. The boys, coming in from the barn, washed their hands in a basin in the kitchen. Flies followed them in through the open door, circling between the food, the manure pile, and the outhouse.

Elzire Dionne's travail began at 1:00 a.m. She lay on a big wooden bed in a bare room just off the kitchen, dimly lit by the mustard glow of a coal oil lamp. Though her body was bloated and her feet so badly swollen that her toes had vanished, she did not complain. She truly believed that she was dying, but she would not ask for help. Her husband, thoroughly alarmed, ran across the field to the two-room log house of her uncle Alexandre, fittingly surnamed Legros – a huge man, amiable in spite of an appearance rendered piratical by a pair of gold earrings and a red bandanna. It was Mme Legros whose aid Dionne was seeking. She was used to helping her neighbours in labour, a service for which she asked no fee. In eighteen years she had lost only one baby, but now it seemed she would lose a mother.

"Auntie," her niece whispered as she walked into the room, "I don't think I'll be able to pull through this time." She asked for a rosary and the two women, in tears, began to pray. Mrs. Dionne repeated aloud the Ave Maria and kissed the feet of the crucifix while her aunt continued to whisper "O God, inspire me in my work," and sensibly put some water on the wood stove to boil.

An hour passed. The pains increased. Dionne set off again, this time to seek out Mme Labelle, the midwife who had assisted at three of Mrs. Dionne's previous confinements. This remarkable woman had borne eighteen children of her own, thirteen without a doctor's help. Married at sixteen and widowed at fifty-seven, she had followed her calling for ten years and had assisted at three hundred births, two hundred without a doctor present. When she was paid at all, she usually received a dollar; but she never refused a case, even though many of the calls came in the deep of the night with the thermometer at forty below.

Her first act on reaching the farmhouse was to fall on her knees with Mme Legros and pray. Dionne, meanwhile, hustled his older children off to neighbours and relatives and brought the eleven-month-old baby, Pauline, down to the kitchen. His wife was worse, her body ice cold. She continued to clutch her rosary, to move her lips in prayer, and to insist that she did not need a doctor. Mme Labelle thought otherwise; she sent Dionne off to Callander to find Dafoe. But as soon as he had gone, Elzire Dionne urged her to try to deliver the baby before the doctor arrived.

She was born just before four o'clock, the tiniest infant the two midwives had ever seen: a grotesque creature with the legs of an insect and a disproportionately large head, bright blue in colour and scarcely human except, oddly, for the large eyes with the long lashes and an appreciable shock of hair.

The baby was so small that Mme Labelle could easily hold her in her palm. She was not breathing. The midwife opened the oven door, held her in front of the heat, massaged her back, and blew air into the collapsed lungs. The baby struggled for breath like a drowning kitten; then from those blue lips there emerged a feline mew, a cry so thin and fragile that it seemed unreal. But there was no time for further ministrations – a moment only to wrap the infant in a scrap of woollen blanket and place her at the foot of the bed – for another birth was taking place. Mme Labelle breathed life into the second child while Mme Legros baptized them both. Neither woman believed the babies would survive for more than a few minutes.

Dafoe had already delivered one baby that night. Now, as he entered the farmhouse, he was faced with an astonishing sight: two babies lay wrapped in tattered woollen remnants on the bed and a third was emerging from the mother. "Good God, woman," said the doctor, "put on some more hot water." He quickly went to work, tying the third child's umbilical cord while Mme Legros scurried about searching for more pieces of cloth in which to wrap her. Now a fourth baby appeared. Dafoe's eyes bulged. "Gosh!" he said and then "Gosh!" again as a fifth followed almost immediately. These last two were still imprisoned in their amniotic sacs – tiny, spider-like creatures, moving feebly in a kind of slow motion behind the translucent walls.

Dafoe ruptured the sacs, gave the babies conditional baptism, and immediately turned to the mother. Elzire Dionne was close to death, her lips white, the tips of her finger's black. The doctor gave her an injection of pituitary to raise her blood pressure and another of ergot to prevent post-natal haemorrhage. At last she was told that she had given birth to five babies. "Holy Mary!" she gasped.

The various narratives of the birth are vague about the whereabouts of Oliva Dionne at this moment. Most agree on two points: he had fled from the room, and he was in a state of nervous collapse that was heightened by the information that in the space of two hours his family had increased from seven to twelve. "My God!" he was reported as saying, "what am I going to do with five babies? It was bad enough to look after one; but how are we going to manage to look after five?" In the days that followed, Dionne continued to worry, publicly, about the heavy financial responsibility.

It was now 5:45. Dionne was clearly in no state to drive a car, but a priest was essential to perform the last rites if Elzire Dionne's condition grew worse. At Mme Legros's suggestion the little doctor drove two miles down the road towards Corbeil to rouse Father Daniel Routhier from his sleep. The priest promised to come as soon as he was dressed. Meanwhile Mme Labelle made a cup of tea and some chicken broth and gruel for her patient. When Dafoe returned, Mrs. Dionne had improved but was not out of danger.

The babies were still alive. Mme Legros had brought from her home a woollen blanket, a bottle of olive oil, some flatirons, and a butcher's basket. In the years that followed, she and Mme Labelle would, for a price, exhibit that basket – or one very like it. The babies were moistened with the warm oil and crammed into the basket, which was set on two chairs directly in front of the open oven. A heated blanket was draped over the chairbacks. Dafoe's advice was to keep the blanket warm and leave them strictly alone. If any of them lived they were to have a drop or two of warm water every two hours; but he did not believe they would live.

By eight, Elzire Dionne's condition had improved enough that Dafoe felt he could go into Callander for some breakfast. Father Routhier, whose car had refused to start, arrived about the same time and, as a precaution, gave the patient extreme unction. Oliva Dionne's brother Léon drove up to the barnyard in his truck to pick up a load of manure. At first when he heard the news he thought it was a joke. Then he roared back to Callander to tell his astonished wife. She leaped out of bed and hurried to the farmhouse to help her sister-in-law. All day long, the kitchen door swung back and forth as the doctor, two nurses, a local reporter and photographer as well as neighbours, relatives, and children, popped in and out along with the flies and mosquitoes. And still the babies lived.

The accounts of what was said and done that day do not always jibe. Everybody remembers that Dafoe walked into the post office and then into the general store to announce: "I saw something this morning that I bet you never saw." It is the kind of remark that a man makes who has just seen a five-legged calf or an albino monkey; to Dafoe, that morning, the quintuplets were mere curiosities that had no chance of survival. Did he also refer to them as "five little French frogs?" It is possible. Certainly the Dionnes, who were fed that story, believed it, and that was the beginning of the breach between parents and doctor.

It has also been said by Dafoe's detractors that he did not bother to return to the farmhouse until five that afternoon. This is not credible. Immediately after breakfast he drove to the Red Cross outpost at Bonfield to try to find a nurse for Mrs. Dionne. De Kiriline had gone on a year's leave, but the nurse on duty, Marie Clouthier, agreed to look in on the mother. When Dafoe stopped by on his return trip, he was gratified to find that Elzire Dionne was out of danger and astonished to discover that the infants were still breathing. Clouthier had other calls to make, but she arrived at 10:30 to find the farmhouse remarkably serene. The midwives had left temporarily. The only attendant was the hired girl. The members of the family were going quietly about their business, relieved that their mother was alive. The nurse made Mrs. Dionne comfortable, reheated the blankets over the babies, and continued on into Callander to see Dafoe.

She told him that the family would need a French-speaking nurse living in. Sister Felicitas at St. Joseph's Hospital in North Bay was called. Sister Felicitas clearly did not believe a word she was told about the five new babies, but she was prepared to supply a nurse anyway. The first French-speaking nurse on the register for the next call was a new graduate, Yvonne Leroux, the daughter of George Leroux, Callander's only taxi driver. A small, pretty twenty-one-year-old brunette, Nurse Leroux had no idea of what awaited her – that in the years that followed her picture would be on all the front pages and in all the magazines, that she would have her own radio program in New York City, that she would turn down two Hollywood movie offers, that she would become the darling of the lecture circuit, and that within a few days she would encounter, on the steps of the farmhouse, the man who would become her husband.

The Sister told her that it was a confinement case in the country, no more. It was Yvonne Leroux's first. She threw a few things into a bag – a thermometer, some cotton wool, a toothbrush, and, because she knew something about rural farmhouses, a hot water bottle. Then she boarded the bus to Callander.

Dafoe, who lived two doors from her family, drove her out to the Dionne homestead, where for the first time she realized what faced her. The babies' arms were no thicker than her own middle finger. It seemed impossible to her that a human being could actually be held in the palm of one hand. It was, she remarked later, "like holding a wounded bird."

The doctor's instructions were simple: keep them warm; feed them nothing but a few drops of warm water from an eyedropper; bathe them occasionally in olive oil; apart from that, leave them strictly alone. That was probably the most sensible advice of all. Nurse de Kiriline was later to say that had the quintuplets been born in a city hospital, they would have expired from too much care.

Yvonne Leroux's first diary entry, clipped and hurried though it is, manages to convey a sense of the conditions – appalling from a medical point of view – with which she was faced:

May 28, 1934. Five premature, scrawny, rickety, hungry mites – five in a basket – a butcher's basket – blankets under & blankets over, shirting & sheeting for wraps. No HWBS, no abs., decent dishes, no screens, doors or cleanliness, and mosquitoes at night & flies in the day. Neighbours trying to be kind but being rather underfoot . . . babies sound like mosquitoes when crying. Straggly arms, legs, large head & abdomen.

She could not afford the luxury of sleep, for any change in temperature brought an alarming reaction from the babies. The slightest increase saw them fighting for breath, their faces flushed. A decrease caused their nostrils to turn blue and their breathing to become alarmingly rapid. They were so tightly packed in the basket that they had to be counted to make sure one or another was not being smothered. All that night and the next day and the following night, Yvonne Leroux sat, sleepless, with the babies in front of the open oven, while the outside world began slowly to realize that something unusual was taking place near an obscure village in the Canadian backwoods.

Dafoe, who had had scarcely any sleep himself, finished his rounds and managed to get to bed around midnight, only to be awakened at four: a long-distance call from Chicago; then another from New York; then Chicago again. The press – or at least the Hearst newspapers – was beginning to sense a story.

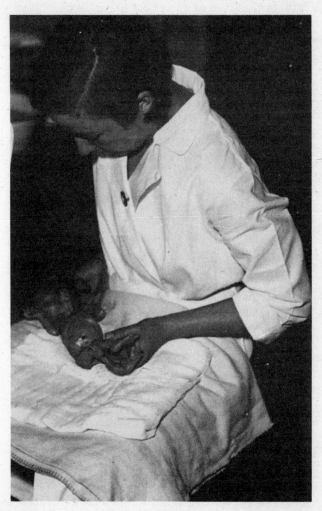

This photograph, made a day or so after the birth, shows Yvonne Leroux in the Dionne farmhouse kitchen with one of the babies whose arms are the size of adult fingers.

Dr. Allan Roy Dafoe, photographed in 1934 in front of his home. Later he became more sartorial. He was never able to find a hat quite big enough to fit him.

Oliva Dionne, photographed in June, 1934 at the Callander railway station where he went each day to pick up breast milk for the Quints. His taste in clothes also changed.

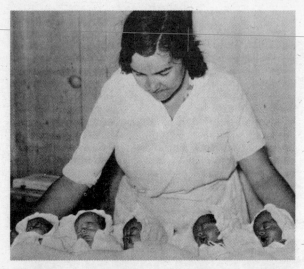

Elzire Dionne, photographed with the quintuplets in June, 1934, after her recovery.

The Dionne farmhouse as it appeared in the summer of 1934.

Oliva Dionne and his five older children: Daniel, Pauline, Ernest, Rose, and Thérèse.

Mme Benoit Labelle, champion midwife. Elzire Dionne's aunt, Mme Legros.

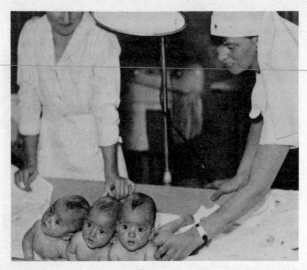

Yvonne Leroux and Mme Louise de Kiriline prepare three of the babies to be photographed in the "rat's nest" after the move to the new hospital.

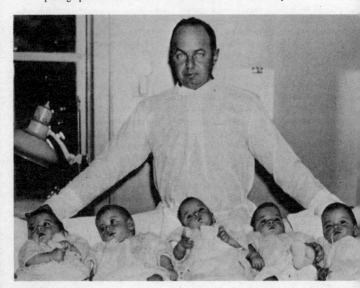

Premier Mitchell Hepburn of Ontario, photographed with the Quints when they were less than a year old. Leroux wrote in her diary that he was terrified of the babies.

The guardianship without Dionne (who refused to be photographed in their company): Dr. Dafoe, Judge Valin, and David Croll. When Croll resigned Percy Wilson took over.

"Quintland" in the summer of 1935, before the playground was built. Crowds rush to see the babies on display on the hospital porch. One pavilion overlooked the scene.

Fred Davis, official photographer.

Will Dafoe, the doctor's younger brother.

Dr. William Blatz, psychologist.

Dr. Alan Brown of "Sick Kids" Hospital.

Shortly after eight the previous morning, Léon Dionne had phoned the thrice-weekly *North Bay Nugget* with an innocent inquiry: would a birth announcement involving five babies cost more than an ordinary one? Eddie Bunyan, the city editor, never found out whether Léon was serious or not, but he had the presence of mind to react. It wouldn't cost a cent, he told Léon. Fifteen minutes later, Dafoe called to confirm the fact that quintuplets had indeed been born. Bunyan immediately assigned a reporter and a photographer to go out to the farm to interview the parents and to photograph the babies. Mort Fellman, then a young reporter, later the editor, was assigned also to call the doctor every twenty minutes to see if the babies were still alive. Bunyan then sent off a one-paragraph dispatch to Canadian Press, which relayed it to Associated Press in New York:

> North Bay, Ont., May 28 – Mrs. Oliva Dionne, residing within a few miles of Callander, nine miles south of here, gave birth to five girls today. All were healthy, said Dr. A. R. Dafoe, Callander, attending physician. Mrs. Dionne is 26 years of age and previously had given birth to six children.

The *Nugget* gave the story a banner headline but, in the words of Mort Fellman, "didn't go into hysterics over it." Nobody was certain the babies would live, and nobody yet realized what the odds were against a mother having *any* kind of quintuplets, identical or fraternal.

The *Nugget* was not alone. The *Toronto Daily Star*, Canada's largest and most aggressive newspaper, thought so little of the story that it didn't bother to put it on the front page but buried it on page 21, along with a report on the impending divorce from a European prince of Barbara Hutton, the Woolworth heiress. Its rival, the *Telegram*, gave the story a two-column headline on its front page but in a minor position below the fold. Its story quoted S. J. Manchester, registrar of vital statistics for Ontario, as disbelieving the report. The following morning the *Times* of London gave the story a single paragraph on page 14. The *New York Times* relegated its brief report to page 21.

There was bigger news in Ontario that day. The Royal Commission on Price Spreads and Mass Buying was about to start hearings in Ottawa; revelations about high profits and starvation wages were expected to make headlines. Gordon Sinclair, the *Star*'s most famous world traveller, was thrilling his readers with a series of reports from Africa, "tales of black magic, sacrificial rites, of strange peoples and stranger customs . . . ." The provincial election campaign was in full swing. On May 29, the new Liberal leader, Mitchell Hepburn, a young onion farmer from Elgin County, arrived in North Bay to continue his attack on the policies of "Honest George" Henry, the Conservative premier.

For Canadians, one of the biggest stories on the morning of May 29 was the defeat of their hero, Jimmy McLarnin of Vancouver, who lost the world's welterweight title to Barney Ross on a split decision. It was this story that Amster Spiro, the city editor of Hearst's New York *Journal*, was looking for when he spotted a small item datelined North Bay. Spiro did not hesitate. He picked up the telephone and called Dafoe, who had just finished answering a similar call from Harry Reutlinger, the assistant city editor of Hearst's Chicago *American*. Shivering in his nightshirt and speaking into the wall telephone at the foot of the stairs, the doctor patiently answered all questions. He had hardly returned upstairs to bed when the phone rang again: a Dr. Bundeson was calling from Chicago to ask if the babies were still alive. Dafoe replied that they were. Bundeson refused to believe it. Dafoe told him to go to hell, hung up, and climbed back up the stairs. As he reached the landing he heard the phone ringing. He hesitated. It was four in the morning. (It was also his birthday.) In the past forty-four hours he had had only four hours' sleep. Should he answer? After a dozen rings he decided he would.

It was Bundeson again. This time he identified himself as president of the Chicago Board of Health and an expert on premature babies; he was also the health editor of the *American*, which had thought nothing of rousing him from his bed on what he suspected was a fool's errand. Now Dafoe's attitude changed and so did Bundeson's. He began to pepper Dafoe with questions and advice. The babies, he said, must be kept warm at all costs; incubators were essential. Dafoe explained that they wouldn't work in a house without electricity. Bundeson said he would try to find an old-fashioned gas-operated model. The other essential was mother's milk; without that the babies had no hope of subsisting. Dafoe explained that Mrs. Dionne was incapable of breast feeding her children. Bundeson promised to try to round up some milk from Chicago donors and send it by airplane as far as possible and then by rail, packed in dry ice.

The two Hearst papers had already decided to pool resources and dispatch a reporter to Callander. The man they chose was Charlie Blake, an experienced newsman who had cut his reportorial teeth covering the Capone gang's activities. Blake scarcely fitted the Hechtian stereotype of the hard-nosed Chicago newshawk; he was young, good looking, soft-spoken, clean-cut, and personable. His immediate assignment was to find an old-fashioned kerosene-burning incubator. It took him all day. Finally, just before train time, he found what he was seeking. It was an odd contrivance, long out of date, three feet in length, two feet high, and about eighteen inches wide – too big for a suitcase, almost impossible to wrap, and awkward to carry – exactly the sort of object that, coming from Chicago, was designed to arouse the suspicions of the Canadian Customs.

In Toronto, on the morning of May 30, Blake was badgered with questions by the inspectors. What on earth was he doing with an 1895 incubator? Blake tried to tell them about the quintuplets, but that only complicated matters; the customs men had not heard of the birth. They began to leaf through records and phone doctors to determine whether the incubator was admissible. Blake fumed. An hour passed. Finally he was allowed to pay $3.75 in duty and bring in the device.

Blake went straight to the office of the Ontario branch of the Canadian Red Cross, whose director, Fred Routley, had been a classmate of Dafoe's at medical school. Routley was persuaded to phone Callander. Dafoe confirmed that he needed the incubator. Blake hired a twelve-cylinder chauffeur-driven limousine for the 240-mile journey north. He reached Dafoe's home just before five on the afternoon of May 30, accompanied by a policeman and a Red Cross official.

The newsreels were ahead of him. In the Thirties they were even more aggressive than the dailies and far more competitive than the TV news departments of a later era. Sometimes they even scooped the newspapers. Fox-Movietone actually filmed the assassination of King Alexander I of Yugoslavia that year. The newsreel editors not only anticipated the big events, they were also flexible enough to dispatch their cameramen at an instant's notice when an unexpected story broke. Movie audiences in 1934 followed Admiral Byrd to the Antarctic, watched the tragic burning of the passenger liner *Morro Castle*, and witnessed on the screen the revolution that overthrew the president of Cuba.

It was no accident that the two cameramen first on the scene represented Pathé and Fox-Movietone, the most innovative of the newsreel companies. Fox, whose chief commentator was Lowell Thomas, had that very year introduced the system of splitting its screen news among departments. Pathé was noted for the speed with which it tied up exclusive newsreel rights; it wanted – and got – the quintuplets.

By the time Charlie Blake reached Callander, the cameramen had their footage. Fox sent its Sault Ste Marie stringer. Pathé had sent its Montreal man, Ross Beesley, by train to Corbeil as soon as the story broke.

The train got into Corbeil about five in the morning. I got some breakfast and then took a taxi to the Dionnes'. I was standing around outside when a car drove up and a chap from Fox got out. He'd driven all night to get there from Sault Ste Marie, Michigan. We knocked on the door but Miss Leroux, the nurse, told us that Mr. Dionne wasn't at home. So we sorta stood around in the front yard and then this car drove up and it was Dr. Dafoe – roly-poly little fella – and he said, Oh, you want to see the children? Come on in. And there were the five little rascals crosswise in a basket. And he said, in the course of the conversation, I don't think they'll be alive tomorrow. He wasn't very optimistic. So we were talking and suddenly the door flew open and in comes Papa Dionne. We didn't know it then, but he'd been at the priest's house in Corbeil. He says, Get out, Get out, Get out! And he started bawling out Dr. Dafoe for letting us in. So we got out; of course there was no electricity, so we couldn't have done anything inside anyway.

We tried to get our cameras on Papa Dionne but he hightailed it back to the priest's house, and we followed in the Fox man's car. Dionne's car was up by the front steps. So we set up our big tripods on the front lawn, ready to shoot when he came out. We thought we had him nailed down now for sure. Shortly after that the priest came out and said, Will you fellas please go away and leave Mr. Dionne alone? But we said, Look, we're on a public street; we have a right to be here. So another half hour went by, and we could see Dionne looking out the window until finally he rushed out and down the steps into his car. We were all set this time, and we cranked away and then scooped up our tripods and rushed over to about six feet from the car and plunked them down again. He couldn't get the car started – looked very excited, and we were cranking away by the side door there when he finally backed away. In the newsreel they had the close-up of him looking startled, and it said, When Mr. Dionne heard the news, this was his reaction. The way they edited it, it came out just about right.

This was Dionne's second joust with the media. On the day of the birth, the *Toronto Star* had asked its North Bay stringer, Art Hill, to interview the father and wire two hundred words to add to the Canadian Press paragraph. Hill's questions embarrassed and angered Dionne. Later he was to insist that he had told the reporter: "The way you talk, people would think I ought to be in jail." But the *Star* reported that he had said: "I'm the kind of guy who ought to be put in jail." The comment was widely quoted and used against him.

Whatever Dionne actually said, it is difficult to escape the impression that he felt, in those first days, a nagging sense of guilt over having brought so much misery on his family. In a male-dominated society – and this did not apply only to Corbeil – it was the father who was held responsible for births. *He* had done it; his wife was merely a carry-all for the children he had initiated. The first words she had spoken to him after the children were born told something about the Dionnes and their attitudes. "What will the neighbours think?" she had asked him. Pregnancy and birth in Corbeil were intimate matters, never discussed or even hinted at. Some months later, when Mme Legros was given a lift by a North Bay driver and asked, casually, whether there might be more Dionne children, she was so scandalized by the question that she immediately got out of the car. "We do not discuss such things," she said. But in the final days of May, strangers invaded Oliva Dionne's home, exploring his private feelings and probing into the recesses of his life.

Dafoe, who was quickly becoming the darling of the media, liked giving interviews. He was never too busy to talk to reporters and was always available by phone. The young medical student with the low marks who had hidden out in the wilderness was now being hailed as a miracle man. His former classmates, his sisters, his old professors would soon be basking in the reflected glory. Dafoe would have been less than human not to have made the most of it.

He was made to order for the press – the homey country doctor with his dog, his pipe, his rumpled clothing and his galoshes, selfless to the point of martyrdom, serenely unruffled by the great events now swirling round him. He seemed to have stepped directly out of the popular radio serial *The Country Doctor*, which Phillips H. Lord, the actor-producer, had created for the NBC Blue Network in 1932.

In contrast, Dionne wanted no publicity. Bewildered, and shaken by what he considered a catastrophe, he was unable to sleep at night. Now he found strangers peering at his wife in her bed and flashing magnesium powder in her face. In the acrimonious struggle that was to come, 90 per cent of the media would be on the doctor's side.

Recovering quickly from its first-day fumble, the *Toronto Star* rushed a team to Callander on Wednesday, May 30. Harry Hindmarsh, its legendary managing editor, believed in covering major stories with entire platoons. One of his reporters, assigned to cover the sinking of the lake boat *Manasoo* in Georgian Bay, was astonished to find twenty-six colleagues on the scene ahead of him.

Hindmarsh's staff was trained in the grand gesture. One had hired an entire train so that he would be first to reach an earlier lake disaster. The paper's expense accounts were princely, its feature writers fiendishly resourceful. One *Star* man even stole an airplane from the rival *Globe*.

To cover the quintuplet story, Hindmarsh sent his top photographer, Fred Davis, a cigar-chewing veteran of the Great War; his chief troubleshooter, Keith Munro; his leading feature writer, Gordon Sinclair, just back from Africa; and a graduate nurse, Jean Blewett, small, pretty, blonde and, of course, highly photogenic. The *Star* was not content merely to cover a story; often it *became* the story. The newspaper tended to write about its own exploits as much as about the news it was reporting.

It used this technique with the quintuplets. On the morning of the twenty-ninth the paper called Dr. William Dafoe, who had already heard from his brother. Dafoe made some suggestions as to the medical and nursing supplies that might be needed in the home. The *Star* improved on his list. Jammed into the back of the newspaper's car were six hot water bottles, six dozen diapers, six cakes of baby soap, a large tin of talcum powder, ten small woollen shirts, five cotton nightdresses, five woollen petticoats, six dozen safety pins, five padded bonnets, fifteen small sheets, five blankets, five coverlets, half a pound of boracic acid, a quart of olive oil, two rolls of absorbent cotton, two tubes of Vaseline, two dozen nursing bottles, six special infant feeders, twenty nipples, and an oval bathtub.

This was not considered enough. The paper purchased an enormous basket, covered it with pink tissue paper, and crammed in an assortment of bramble jelly, jelly powders, biscuits, cream cheese, crackers, cantaloupes, strawberries, tomatoes, celery, sponge cake, and candy. The bill came to three hundred dollars, a tidy sum in 1934 but a bagatelle to a newspaper whose correspondents were sometimes known to include the rental of sleds and teams of malemutes in their expenses. Sinclair, an expense account genius who travelled first class around the world and was invariably pictured in promotional ads wearing a pith helmet, could easily go through a comparable sum in a day or so.

We went to the front door of the Dionne house first. There was no one there, but the door wasn't locked. I think Fred Davis was the first to step inside the door. Mrs. Dionne – she was a big woman with very attractive eyes – was in bed, looking quite motherly. Fred said something to her in English, which she appeared to understand, while I went looking around for Dionne. I found him at the back of the barn.

There was a yearling heifer there, I remember – kind of a nondescript animal, heavily coated with manure. Dionne, I remember, was very depressed about finances. He was convinced he was going to be hard up: it was going to be a hell of a cost to raise those children. I asked him if he'd come around with us to the house and get some pictures but, no, he didn't want to do that. He just stayed back there – wasn't reticent but talked about how his main worry was money. It had been a tough winter for him, and he was feeling kind of down with five new mouths to feed.

Well, we went around to the house, and there was Fred on the verandah. Fred says, She won't go for flash powder. (There were no flash bulbs in those days.) Well, I went in then and I asked her in English if it would be all right if we lifted the babies out in the light. It was an overcast day, you see. There was no sign of anyone else at the time – no Dafoe, no nurse – so we just picked up the five babies and we laid them out in the light and we photographed them. Mrs. Dionne made no objection, but when the nurse we'd brought from Toronto came in she made a hell of a fuss, in French. Are you Catholic? she asked. No. Do you speak French? The nurse again said No, and Mrs. Dionne was furious. She damn near got out of bed. Out! she says in French. Out! The nurse went back on the train that afternoon. I stayed for three days and nights, filing copy from the telegraph office. They had to add extra operators. My stories never carried my by-line because my stuff was still appearing from Africa; but I was seen around a lot, and that caused rumours later.

The early reporters on the scene – Blake, Davis, Munro, and Sinclair – were like prospectors who arrive at a rich strike before the main stampede begins. Three lives were changed that day. Charlie Blake went to Hollywood to write the screen play for the first and most successful of the quintuplet films. Fred Davis became the Quints' official photographer and married nurse Yvonne Leroux. Keith Munro was to become the highly paid business manager of the quintuplets' trust fund. Only Gordon Sinclair suffered, after a fashion. Because he was on the scene in Callander at the time of the country's greatest news story, many people came to believe that he had never actually been to the exotic corners of the globe that he was describing in the same editions of the *Toronto Daily Star*. The myth persisted for more than thirty years that Sinclair had made all those adventures up out of whole cloth. Only his collection of passports stamped with the names of obscure nations, many of which no longer exist, eventually saved his reputation.

FOUR:
The prescience of Ivan Spear

Although nobody put it quite so bluntly, the Chicago Century of Progress Exposition was close to being a magnificent flop. In the glow of optimism that preceded its opening in May 1933, attendance forecasts ran as high as ninety million. But when the great world's fair closed the following November, only twenty-three million had passed through the turnstiles. They didn't exactly throw their money around, either; each visitor spent, on an average, only $1.16. To meet its deficit the fair, designed as a single-season attraction, had to be held over for another year.

What had happened? The fair had been designed to "illustrate man's highest achievements in the interpretation of the forces of nature and their adaptation to everyday use." That may have been the trouble; nobility of purpose is no substitute for showmanship. There were mechanical wonders aplenty: a transparent man; a ten-foot talking robot; an atom-smashing machine; a General Motors assembly line; a gold-plated Packard; a nine-foot mechanical gorilla; and regular demonstrations of a new toy called television, "hailed as the dawn of a new industry no one can venture to predict." But none of these brought the throngs that the fair's organizers had expected.

Nobody could say that the Century of Progess didn't have class. That was where the emphasis lay. The exhibit of paintings mounted for the fair was said to be the most important in history. The ten distinguished designers responsible for the look of the fair made sure that it was "modernistic," a term then being applied to everything from service stations to cruise ships. Comparisons were drawn with the famous Chicago World's Columbian Exposition of 1893, an architectural landmark that helped change the face of North American cities.

Yet for many Chicagoans, the real symbol of that earlier fair had not been the classical lines of the buildings but the pelvic gyrations of a young woman who called herself Little Egypt. The Columbian Exposition lived on in memory because of the hootchie-kootchie dance.

The men who planned the Century of Progress foresaw nothing so tawdry. They might have recalled that the world's fair of 1893 was also held in the depths of a depression and that again in 1933 the mass of the public wanted distraction, not education. To the horror of the exposition's board the distraction was there. It came, not from the Adler Planetarium, which remained half-empty, or from the Panorama of the Dearborn Massacre, which was forced to close for lack of business, but from a farmer's daughter out of Hickory County, Missouri. She was born Helen Gould Beck, but by the summer of 1933 millions knew her as Sally Rand.

For every ten visitors who came to Chicago to visit the Hall of Science, ten thousand came to see Sally, bathed in blue light, twisting and turning her apparently naked body behind two huge fans. A few years before she had been destitute. Now, as she told a delighted Junior Chamber of Commerce, "I haven't been out of work since I took my pants off." The authorities tried to stop her. Haled into court in July for giving a performance described as "lewd, lascivious and degrading to public morals," she easily beat the rap. The publicity boosted her fees to five thousand dollars a week and helped keep the fair afloat.

But when the Century of Progress Exposition reopened the following May, just two days before the birth of the Dionne quintuplets, Sally found she was not wanted. Class triumphed. The midway was banished to a distant corner of the grounds. The Streets of Paris concession, where Sally had performed, was shut down. Two symphony orchestras were hired to counter the cacophony of popular music that had blared from the midway; and the Ford Motor Company was persuaded to install an eleven-acre technological exhibit to attract bigger crowds.

But on opening day the crowds failed to appear. The exposition was, in *Variety*'s candid phrase, "the great fold-up derby." Clearly some sort of sensational attraction was needed to save the day – nothing so vulgar as a fan dance but an act that would appeal to the whole family, some kind of exhibit that prospective customers would simply *have* to see.

It was this very subject that two young Chicago promoters, Ivan I. Spear and Ted Kopelman, were discussing with their lawyer and sometime partner, Luis Kutner, on the morning of May 29. All three had their fingers in a number of promotional pies.

Spear operated the Century of Progress Tour Bureau, a catch-all organization that had no official connection with the fair. Kopelman was promoting a revolutionary new lubricant called Dover Bluebird. Kutner had been connected with a variety of midway attractions, all of them carrying a faint but tantalizing whiff of sex: a Parisian artist's exhibit; a French postcard exhibit; and the so-called Life Exhibit, which purported to show the development of a human being from the embryo stage onward. The lawyer had been stagestruck since his days as a college bandleader. His agent on the campus was the same Leo Salkin who now managed Sally Rand. Kutner had assisted her lawyer at the obscenity trial the previous summer.

Now in Kutner's baronial office, with its dark panelling, leaded windows, leather chairs, fireplace, and grandfather's clock, the three were casting about for an idea that might lure people to the exiled midway. They looked the part of promoters, these three; Central Casting could not have improved on the type – sharp, dapper men in tight-fitting double-breasted suits, with suave features, wavy pompadours, and the kind of pencil-line moustaches worn by the movie stars of the early Thirties. There are fashions in faces, and these men were nothing if not fashionable; they had the sleek Warner Baxter–John Gilbert–Ronald Colman look. Kutner, the sole survivor of the three, remembers Spear as "very colourful, very adept, very resourceful, with piercing eyes and a quick smile." Kopelman was cast in a similar mould, "the same kind of dynamic, exciting guy."

That Life Exhibit sort of intrigued Spear at the time. That was universal, you see. Anyway, as we were talking, I opened the paper and I saw a small squib – quintuplets born in Callander, Ontario. I said to Ivan and Ted, Have you fellows seen this? What? they said. Quintuplets born in Ontario! I've never heard of that before. Whaddya mean, quintuplets? It means five, I said. And we exchanged that word back and forth. And Spear said, Hey! Life Exhibit! Were you thinking that way? It would be a hell of an idea.

Well, within five minutes we crystallized the whole project of a very exciting quintuplet exhibition. We tried to get through to Callander, but we couldn't, so Spear called a newspaper buddy in Toronto. This all took place from my office with great fever, great excitement. We all envisioned a fantastic exhibit at the fair. Then Ivan said, Look, we can come up there to Toronto and drive to Callander; what are you doing, Lu? – come along; we need your help.

So we took an old Lockheed plane to Toronto, and Spear met his newspaper friend. I can't remember the name, now, but we never stop-

ped talking about the idea, planning the exhibit, you know – how big it should be, for example. Ivan says, We've got to get an attending physician. Don't worry about that, I said, I'll get Bundeson. So then we hire this old touring car with a canvas top – no sides to it, a real fantastic thing – and I remember Ivan saying to the driver, Are you sure this car will make it? And the driver says, It's all right; I've had it over twenty years!

So off we go, and all the way we talked about our dreams. We thought we had the hottest thing in the world – if the kids lived; that would be unprecedented. We kept turning it over: Maybe we'll get there too late! Maybe we'll regret coming here . . . maybe we're being too precipitate. But Ivan and Ted would say: No, no, no.

So finally we got to this little farmhouse. There was a priest there, Father Routhier, whom I recall very clearly. Very bland, very nice guy, very concerned about the quintuplets, really. And I remember the look of shock on Dionne's face. So Ivan said to Routhier, We are Chicago exhibitors; we have planned an exhibit for the world's fair; we would like to make a contract to exhibit the quintuplets, subject to medical advice; if we get approval we will arrange for attending physicians to watch over the Quints; and so on and so on.

We spent two hours there. Went to the office of the parish priest down the road a bit and took Dionne with us. Then finally we went into the Dionne home and saw the Quints lying around in a large basket, and they had milk bottles filled with hot water, which were placed between the kids to keep them warm. The nurse, Leroux, was there. She didn't know what to do except to do the best she could. Dionne, he was in shock. Ivan had a cheque made out, and he did a very good thing psychologically. He gave the cheque to Dionne to hold while we drafted the agreement. That was the most money he'd seen in his life. Crappy little farmhouse, by the way; outhouse in the back. I put the contract together, and Routhier had someone type it out.

The contract between the Century of Progress Tour Bureau and Oliva Dionne was actually signed in Orillia. Spear sealed the deal with a one-hundred-dollar downpayment and headed back for Chicago, believing he had tied up all rights to the quintuplets for the rest of the year.

By this time Dionne was being swamped with advice, interviews, and offers. Spear was not the only promoter seeking to exhibit the quintuplets. The manager of Midget City, another fair concession, was one of several who dispatched a representative to Callander.

Outside the farmhouse, strangers began to gather trying to catch a glimpse of the babies. Olivier Dionne drove them off with a pitchfork. His son was taking pills to relieve tension headaches. The neighbours were pestering him with suggestions about the Spear offer. Some told him he would be crazy not to make some money out of the birth; others said that no amount was worth the risk. "What am I to do?" he asked one visitor. "Whichever way I guess, it would be wrong." On May 29, after hearing from Spear, Dionne had asked the doctor's advice. Dafoe's reply was laconic. Make what you can, he told him; there wasn't much chance the babies would live.

Make what you can. That phrase was to serve as an insistent background theme to the melodrama that followed. It was implicit in the actions of all those who, with the best will in the world, sought over the years to serve and protect the quintuplets. Doctor and priest, politicians and press, guardians and parents – all believed that money was the key to the quintuplets' happiness. But it was also the key to their tragedy.

Father Daniel Routhier was certainly concerned about money; the real decision regarding the Spear contract lay in his hands. The forty-four-year-old priest had been in Corbeil since 1930 and had always been an adviser to the Dionne family, who had named a son after him. Now he took on a more intimate role; he would become Oliva Dionne's business agent at a modest 7 per cent.

After the event Father Routhier, removed to another parish, would insist that he advised Dionne to sign the Chicago contract in order to force the hand of the government and of the Canadian Red Cross. He believed that the action would shame them into helping the family financially. But Father Routhier had a further interest. The Corbeil church, consisting only of some cement foundations covered by a frame roof, was insolvent. Routhier's commission was pledged to the church fund. In addition, Dionne had made a vow, according to the priest, "that if he gets any wealth he will build a church in Corbeil."

To his parishioners at Mass, Routhier read in French the following message:

My dear brethren: for me this birth of quintuplets is intended by God.

It is a miracle.

. . . they will live years without being a burden on their parents.

By the generosity of the public doing the will of God, these quintuplets will know no need, they will be better taken care of than any other children, they will make their parents richer than they would ever have thought of.

It is a public and decisive answer of God to those who are preaching and practising birth control.

By this case, Providence is manifesting her existence and God is taking care of all beings whom he is pleased to create.

Under the terms of the Chicago contract, Dionne was to realize 23 per cent of the net proceeds, Routhier 7 per cent, and Spear's organization the remainder. The document's eighteen clauses provided that the entire family of twelve would go to Chicago at the tour bureau's expense as soon as the physician in charge (Dafoe was not named) decided they could be moved without jeopardy. Dionne was to receive a salary of two hundred and fifty dollars a week against his share of the profits to the end of the year. More important was the exclusivity clause: Spear, who called the birth "the greatest human interest story since the Armistice," tied up all photographic, literary, publicity, and advertising rights to the quintuplets until January 1, 1935. The agreement also gave Spear the right to assign his interest to whomever he wished. He lost no time in attempting to do so.

He had two entrepreneurs in mind. The first was C. C. Pyle, a flamboyant promoter best known for his famous 1928 Bunion Derby, a 3,400-mile transcontinental marathon from Los Angeles to Madison Square Garden. In 1934, Pyle was operating the Ripley Believe-It-or-Not Odditorium at the fair. It was Spear's notion, apparently, that the quintuplets would fit in easily with the various deformed human creatures – scaly, dog-faced, and reptilian – who formed the core of the exhibit.

Before Pyle could act, however, an even more successful showman leaped in with an offer. Sally Rand's manager, Leo B. Salkin, was prepared to put up forty thousand dollars in cash against a guarantee of $125,000 or 25 per cent of the net profits obtained from exploiting the children. Spear was too greedy; he held out for $300,000. By the time he was ready to accept the lower figure, Salkin had cooled off. The entire venture had become too controversial.

Meanwhile, more reputable entrepreneurs were persuaded that the Quints could somehow be put on display. Rufus C. Dawes, the distinguished president of the Century of Progress Exposition, announced that the five babies would be welcome as an attraction. Elwood Hughes, general manager of the Canadian National Exhibition, promptly followed by inviting the parents to bring them to Toronto. "We are not out to make it merely a money proposition," Hughes said. "We want it to be dignified and fitting." That word "dignified" would turn up again and again in future commercial overtures.

The five human mites, struggling for life in the Dionne farm-house, could not have been moved ten feet that month without endangering their lives. By June 2, the two smallest, Emilie and Marie, were close to death. The statistics from Toronto's Burnside Hospital, taken over a four-year period, showed that nine of eleven babies weighing less than three pounds at birth failed to survive. The largest of the Quints weighed only two and a half pounds. The smallest, Marie, weighed one pound eight and a half ounces, and none was more than nine inches long.

The quintuplets were at least two months premature. In such cases, strict medical procedures are mandatory. Constant warmth is essential; the surrounding temperature cannot drop below eighty degrees Fahrenheit for an instant. Because of their low resistance to infection, premature babies must be kept away from anyone with even the slightest head cold. No one should be allowed to handle a premature baby without donning a clean gown and face mask and scrubbing up with soap and hot water. Oxygen is usually necessary because the babies' lungs are often inadequately developed and lethal cyanotic attacks can occur that make twenty-four-hour vigilance essential. Feeding is critical. Without human milk, survival is unlikely. As a medical article under Dafoe's by-line was later to state, "The things that are not done for these babies are almost as important as the things which are done. The premature infant is frail, does not stand handling and must be left undisturbed most of the time. Unnecessary manipulation and over-treatment may be as damaging as neglect."

Given these requirements for survival, it is not surprising that Dafoe held out little hope for the five Dionnes. The mother's milk promised by Bundeson did not arrive from Chicago until fifty-two hours after their birth. Another nine hours elapsed before Blake's primitive incubator was put to use. For the first twenty-seven hours the babies were given no nourishment except a few drops of warm water from an eyedropper. Then, early on the morning of May 29, Dafoe, still groggy from his nocturnal telephone calls, extemporized with a formula of cow's milk (seven ounces), sterilized water (twenty ounces), and corn syrup (two ounces). Yvonne Leroux fed the babies from an eyedropper, a few drops at a time, at two-hour intervals.

When the smallest babies, Marie and Emilie, began to turn blue around the sides of the mouth and nose, Dafoe would dose them with two drops of rum diluted with ten drops of warm water. The alcohol never failed to revive them. When Dafoe was asked some time later why he had used rum instead of brandy, he replied that no one in that part of the world could afford brandy. He made do with what he had.

When Marie Clouthier returned on the afternoon of May 29 from the Red Cross outpost, Dafoe sent her out to find some mother's milk. She managed to get two ounces from nursing mothers at the North Bay hospital. This was rationed carefully to Marie, Emilie, and Cécile, the three smallest. Bundeson's milk supply arrived by train the following morning, packed in dry ice and frozen solid. Dafoe mixed it with water and fed it to his charges. The Chicago incubator had been made to hold one baby, but the quintuplets were so tiny that Yvonne Leroux was able to cram the three smallest crosswise into the makeshift nest. Annette and Yvonne remained in the butcher's basket.

In Toronto, members of the Junior League were hustling about in their own cars collecting breast milk from nursing donors. The milk was pooled at the Hospital for Sick Children, boiled, bottled, refrigerated until evening, packed in ice, and shipped by train to Callander. The initial shipment, the first of one hundred and twenty, arrived on Thursday morning, May 31. By October, when they were switched to cow's milk, the children had consumed more than eight thousand ounces. These shipments, unique in history, were credited with keeping them alive.

But breast milk alone could not save the children. That same Thursday night, Dafoe, peering into the window of the incubator, realized that Emilie and Marie were fading fast. He rummaged about in his bag and found a two-inch hypodermic syringe and a small piece of rubber tubing, which he fitted over the end. Yvonne Leroux was in a state of collapse; she had been without sleep for forty-eight hours. Marie Clouthier, arriving from Bonfield to spell her off, suddenly realized what Dafoe intended to do. She was aghast; he was planning to give the two weakest babies an enema.

"Doctor," she warned, "if you do that it will kill them."

"If I don't," said Dafoe gruffly, "they'll die."

He performed the operation successfully and then fed each baby ten drops of rum. Clouthier was convinced the rum saved their lives.

Yvonne Leroux was able at last to get some sleep. As night fell and the family vanished upstairs, Marie Clouthier was alone with the kerosene lamp, the sleeping mother and nurse, and the five babies, clinging to the slender thread of life. It gave her an odd feeling as the night closed in. Over the measured breathing of the sleeping women she became aware of the nocturnal rhythms of the northern spring – the unending chant of the frogs drifting across the swamps and above that an unaccustomed cry, plaintive and haunting: the call of the whippoorwill. She had never heard it before but would always remember it and when, on occasion, she caught it again on a spring night, her mind would go back to the lonely hours of June 1, 1934, when she sat in solitary vigil in the sleeping household and willed the tiny creatures in the incubator to hang on to life, at least until dawn.

Is it possible that there were seventeen people crammed into that farmhouse? That is what the record shows: two parents, Oliva Dionne's sister Alma, ten children, two nurses, the grandfather, and Mme Legros, who moved in after Nurse Leroux commandeered her stove. Early on Friday, Dafoe realized that a strong hand was needed to bring some order out of the anarchy. Flies and mosquitoes were buzzing and flitting through the unscreened doors, along with a stream of visitors – neighbours trying to be helpful, newspapermen, and promoters – and the members of the Dionne family themselves. A single basin in the kitchen, filled with water from a pump, was used by children coming from the outside privy and others coming from the barns. Clouds of dust from the increasing traffic on the road outside filtered through the windows. The temperature had risen to ninety degrees Fahrenheit. Thérèse Dionne, aged four, had a bad cold and by Friday was running a fever. Dafoe insisted that she be moved out of the house, in spite of the protests of her parents. It began to look as if the babies might have been safer in a Congo village of mud huts.

Dafoe needed Louise de Kiriline. He traced her through the Red Cross in Toronto.

"I want you to get on the job as soon as you can," he told her on the telephone.

"I'll leave in half an hour," she replied. She arrived that same Friday evening, and Oliva Dionne, whose control of his family had been steadily eroding, now found that he was no longer master in his own home.

De Kiriline took over and ran the household, brooking no protest from parents, relatives, or friends. She arrived to find mother and babies crammed into a dark room with a single tiny window, next to the summer kitchen. Immediately she set about reorganizing the entire main floor of the farmhouse.

She pre-empted a small parlour, twelve by fourteen feet, next to the larger living room. This would be the babies' nursery. She pushed the upright piano, the marble-topped table, and the other furniture into the living room. She pulled down the red plush curtains and replaced them with clean sheets and muslin netting. She scrubbed the floors, walls, and ceilings with Lysol (whose maker would later, gratefully, sponsor Dafoe's radio broadcasts). She appropriated a big dining table and placed it in the centre of the new nursery as a changing table. She had Olivier Dionne build shelves to hold medical supplies and feeding equipment and then, after the babies were moved, attacked the living room. Here were boxes and cartons of gifts, sent to the family by well-wishers, unopened and stacked to the ceiling. De Kiriline opened them all, threw out the useless presents or stowed them out of sight, and arranged all the useful supplies on shelves. She designated the living room as a combined rest room, dining room, and office for the nurses, who were now three in number, including Pat Mullen, a relief nurse sent by the Red Cross. They would be organized into overlapping shifts of twelve hours each, for she decreed that two must at all times watch over the babies.

De Kiriline then took over the kitchen, arranging for a constant supply of hot water for the incubators and of wood for the stove. More people were jammed into the house: an extra nurse, an orderly, and two maids, one for the nursing staff and another for the Dionne family, who were relegated to the second floor of their home. In the midst of this whirlwind of activity nobody bothered to consult or even to communicate with Oliva Dionne or his bedridden wife, an oversight which Louise de Kiriline was later to regret publicly.

The family's attitude was very hostile. They felt that they had been ousted and, of course, they were. But then, they didn't realize that if they had stayed down there the babies wouldn't have lived. I would say for myself that I was thrown into a very difficult situation without experience, and I don't think I was up to it properly. You know in hindsight it is much easier to say how you would have handled the situation. Mind you, my concern there, of course, was just to keep the babies alive – just to do that. Now, I think, I would take much more time with the parents – realize much more their feelings. But I was too taken up just keeping the babies alive, to the detriment of my relations with the family. I really was quite brusque.

Years later, de Kiriline remarked, drily, that "the babies survived in spite of us." The "us" covered a great deal of territory. The press continued to present the picture of five infants, struggling for life in the care of a simple country practitioner named Allan Roy Dafoe. But behind Dafoe, always in the shadows, stood a back-up team whose expertise and facilities were the equal of any in North America.

Early on the morning of May 29, Dafoe had called his brother, William, the Toronto obstetrician, to seek his advice. The call was long and detailed. For the next several months no day passed in which that call was not repeated. Dafoe usually phoned his brother around six in the evening and sometimes more than once. Behind Dr. William Dafoe stood the formidable figure of Dr. Alan Brown, the crusty, brilliant head of the famous Toronto Hospital for Sick Children. Brown, one of the inventors of Pablum, was also one of the best-known baby doctors on the continent; he, as much as anybody, steered the quintuplets past the shoals and reefs of an uncertain babyhood.

Dafoe's intimate relationship with the *Toronto Star* really began with his brother, who advised the newspaper on what was needed at Callander immediately after his brother's call. It was a relationship that would put the newspaper squarely in the Dafoe camp and two of the *Star*'s top men – Fred Davis and Keith Munro – in the quintuplets' employ. The *Star* was also beholden to William Dafoe for the design of the incubators that it had constructed and shipped to Callander with the usual fanfare. The Toronto doctor had dug up a picture of a Tarnier's incubator from an old copy of *Cook's Obstetrics*. From this he had a draughtsman make careful plans. The first of the incubators reached Callander, courtesy of the *Star*, on Sunday, June 3. It was big enough to hold four of the babies; little Marie remained in the original Chicago device.

That same Sunday, William Dafoe arrived in Callander, bringing with him an eighty-gallon iron cylinder containing a mixture of 95 per cent oxygen and 5 per cent carbon dioxide. For the next several months all the babies received regular "oxygen cocktails," as they were called, administered directly; the mixture kept the quintuplets alive until their breathing apparatus was fully developed. Until now, it had been possible to stimulate the heart and lung action of Yvonne and Marie only by regular doses of rum. Marie's heart had almost stopped during the early morning hours of June 2. Yvonne's condition was, if anything, worse. She alone did not waken and cry at the two-hour feeding periods and had to be coaxed to take her milk. Even rum produced little reaction. But after the oxygen treatment, Yvonne threw off her torpor and began to improve. The treatments – which had been developed through the Great War – produced an almost instantaneous effect, bringing the babies' breathing to normal a few moments after application.

Almost everybody remarked on the contrast between the Dafoe brothers. The younger man was handsome, impeccably tailored, and sophisticated. At college he had been a top sportsman – outstanding at hockey, lacrosse, and soccer – and he still had the trim body of an athlete. His war record was excellent: three years in the Canadian Army Hospital Unit and six months as a sub-lieutenant in the Royal Navy. Unlike his brother, he had seen a good deal of the world. He had done graduate work in obstetrics in Edinburgh and had continued his studies in various European centres. Now, in addition to his practice, he lectured in obstetrics and gynaecology at the University of Toronto.

The *Star* now felt it had a corner on the story. Fred Davis had driven up with the new incubator and had promised to deliver three more. But when he went out to the farmhouse to take some photographs, he found his way barred by Olivier Dionne, armed with a pitchfork. "Get away from there; get away," cried the grandfather. Ivan Spear's contract gave him exclusive rights to all photographs of the quintuplets and their family.

The controversy over the Chicago contract had by now reached such a pitch, however, that Dionne was doing his best to repudiate it publicly. The Quints had become the biggest domestic news in North America. Hundreds of thousands of newspaper readers breathlessly awaited the daily medical bulletins describing their progress. This was real life soap opera – far more intriguing than *Just Plain Bill*, *Myrt and Marge*, or *Poor Little Cinderella*. Would the new incubators arrive in time? Would tiny little Marie fight off the grim shadow of death? Would kindly, selfless Dr. Dafoe defeat the wicked promoters from the evil city? Would fame go to the heads of the parents? In the continuing serial, the doctor was the hero while Oliva Dionne, the father who was not allowed in the same room with his children, found himself cast in the unaccustomed and bewildering role of the heavy.

FIVE:
Guardianship

"What will the neighbours say?" Elzire Dionne had said to her
husband when she was told that she had given birth to five babies.
Then, as she later recalled, she added these words: "They will
think we are pigs."

And some people *did* think they were pigs. Large families were
not fashionable in the Thirties, at least among the Anglo-Saxon
population. The average number of children per Canadian family
dropped from 2.31 in 1931 to 2.06 a decade later. But rural French
Canadians had much larger families. At the beginning of the Depression they had an average of 3.55 children per family while the
figure for the larger Ontario cities was only 1.7. Large families,
especially among the poor, were felt to be more than a little vulgar
and also, given the cost of welfare, an unnecessary public expense.
People who had more than three children were thought by many
to be ignorant, unfeeling, priest-ridden, or sex mad.

The notorious Millar Stork Derby, which was reaching its final
stages in 1934, did nothing to allay the suspicion of the sophisticated that childbearing was somehow indecent. The derby was
conceived by a wealthy Toronto sportsman and lawyer, Charlie
Millar, who, having no close relatives, turned his last will and tes-
tament into a series of practical jokes. Millar left racetrack shares
to opponents of betting and brewery stock to temperance advocates. But the bulk of his considerable fortune was earmarked for
the Toronto mother who, in the ten years following his death in
1926, would give birth to the largest number of children. Obviously Millar considered childbearing on this scale to be
outrageous, and, as he had expected, his legacy was roundly con-
demned as obscene. The attempts to break it in court centred
around the argument that the will was encouraging immorality, a

clear indication of how some people felt about any form of sex, in or out of wedlock. But the will resisted all attacks and by 1934 there were several well-publicized mothers in the race. It was pointed out that had Mrs. Dionne lived in Toronto, she would have won handily.

Sex in the Thirties was plain dirty; childbearing, at the very least, was vulgar and, at the worst, obscene. Canada not only banned *Spicy Stories* and *Gay Paree*, with their innocent photographs of unsmiling bare-breasted women and their once-over-lightly attempts at risqué pulp fiction, but it also impounded all copies of the April 11, 1938, issue of *Life* magazine because it dared to carry a photograph of a baby being born. In Chicago, the very mention of obstetrics was enough to cause the board of censors to give a "pink ticket" (for adult viewing only) to the second of the quintuplets' movies, *Reunion*. Even a suggestive tone of voice could be considered indecent. The National Broadcasting Company barred Mae West from its microphones for life, not because of what she said on the Charlie McCarthy program but because of the way she said it.

Nor was the stage secure from the censor. In Toronto a month before the quintuplets were born, a hullabaloo was raised over Robert Sherwood's hit play, *Reunion in Vienna*. Police forced a series of script changes that seem laughable today: the word "bathroom" was deleted; an eight-second kiss was reduced to five seconds; the word "damn" was excised; and a love scene was toned down.

Sex was something to be sniggered at. Children giggled over Mae West jokes and Little Audrey jokes:

> *Little Audrey's mother asked her to buy some groceries at the Safeway but little Audrey laughed and laughed and laughed because she knew there was no safe way.*

After 1934, there were jokes about Papa Dionne:

> *Papa Dionne visited the Royal Winter Fair and asked to see the prize bull. "Listen," he was told, "it's no problem. The prize bull just asked to see you!"*

In the eyes of many, Dionne was a kind of freak, a superstud. In Chicago in 1935, he was followed into the men's room of the Congress Hotel dining room by the curious who wanted to catch a glimpse of his penis, which was widely believed to be of legendary proportions. Even before the details of the Spear contract were made public he was, to many, an unsympathetic character because of "what he had done" to his wife. Some of the letters that poured into the Callander post office, addressed to Dafoe, were positively vehement.

> I want to suggest you sterilize Dionne, and thus prevent another such catastrophe. . . .

> Don't you think it would be a good idea to sew the mother up so she cannot have more children?

Inherent in many letters was the feeling that some government action should be taken:

> Isn't there something you and the authorities can do to get [Mrs. Dionne] and her ten babies away from that brute of a man? . . . He isn't safe to run at large. . . . If he lived here he would have been tarred and feathered. This whole community is up in arms over it all. . . . Couldn't he be compelled to be sterilized or something done . . . ?

Dafoe actually included that letter, from Grand Rapids, Michigan, in an article that was to appear under his name in the *Journal of the Canadian Medical Association*. It was deleted only after William Dafoe wrote to the editor to advise that it be dropped because "the newspapers would probably descend upon it, and undoubtedly this would lead to further trouble with the parents."

Dionne was aware of these attitudes – some of the letters went directly to him – and it increased his sense of isolation and bitterness. Sometimes, as Mrs. Ken Morrison remembers, he would come into the store to buy some groceries and hear the tourists whispering about him.

He was standing in the store one day, and some people came in about where the candies are; and they were asking questions about him, talking about his "litter" and all that sort of thing. I couldn't get them to stop, you know, saying things like that. So I wrote on a piece of paper, Mr. Dionne is right behind you and he's listening. Oh, they went out of that store so fast! Visitors – I didn't know them – from the States, maybe, or they could have been commercial travellers. The Quints would be a few months old at the time. You know, we didn't like that sort of thing. I mean, what would you do if you heard that? If people came in and said things like that? It was terribly embarrassing. He just felt like a pig, you know – that he had too many children.

He resented people making remarks, and we did, too, and we didn't allow that kind of talk when we heard it.

After the news of the Chicago contract was released by Father Routhier, the feeling that the authorities should take some decisive action became widespread. The story of the deal with Spear was published almost simultaneously with the *Toronto Star*'s report, under an eight-column headline, that Marie was near death. A wave of public indignation followed. Dionne was seen as a callous, grasping man, perfectly prepared to risk the lives of his children by renting them out to a carnival showman. This idea – that he didn't care about his offspring – proved difficult to shake, once it registered in the public's mind. More than forty years later, Dr. William Dafoe's widow, in the course of an interview, remarked that she "didn't think children meant much [to the Dionnes] at the time. They had so many of them, you know."

Certainly, Oliva Dionne had signed a contract to exhibit his babies. It contained an escape clause, however: the doctor had to consent. Immediately the news was published, Dafoe, who had originally told Dionne to sign, began to assert his authority. "As long as I'm boss there will be no trip for these babies," Dafoe announced. "The father can go if he wants to, but not the children." Dafoe was rapidly establishing control over the quintuplets, and the word "boss" appears more than once in his pronouncements. He had already made it clear to de Kiriline who was in charge. He called himself Boss Number One; she was to be Boss Number Two.

Dionne and Routhier had renounced the contract and mailed back Spear's cheque within twenty-four hours of the meeting in Orillia. Dionne's contention was that no document dealing with the future of his children was valid unless agreed to by both parents – and Elzire Dionne had refused. But Spear did not give up easily. In mid-June, he and Kopelman returned to North Bay with two lawyers to try to reason with Dafoe. The doctor told them that if the contract went through, "you've got to find another doctor, you've got to get other nurses. Either I'm going to take care of the babies my own way or not take care of them at all." Dafoe had read the newspapers and was well aware that the public would not stand for his resignation. Spear decided to sue the doctor, the Dionnes, and everybody else involved for breach of contract, but the trial was two years in the future. In Chicago the faltering exposition, deprived of a new attraction, decided to go with the old: Sally Rand was allowed to return. This time, she danced behind two gigantic translucent balloons instead of fans, and thus the Bubble Dance was born.

What happened next was unprecedented. The Government of Ontario stepped in, removed the quintuplets from the control of their parents, and placed them under a board of guardians that did not include either Elzire or Oliva Dionne. Such a move would be unthinkable today. Those who did not live through the Thirties (and a few who did) find it hard to understand that any democratic body could take a step that now seems callous and unjust. But it is important to make clear that all those involved, including, perhaps (and briefly), the parents themselves, were sincerely convinced that what they were doing was in the best interests of everyone.

The public wanted the government to act for the sake of the babies' safety. From Callander, Dafoe was reporting that he was being plagued by a succession of promoters and showmen. At one point it was rumoured that the children would be made wards of the Children's Aid society, but as John Brown, the superintendent for the region, explained, he could not legally interfere because "as far as we are aware they are being well cared for and are in no danger of being neglected."

Still the public wanted decisive government action; that was, after all, very much the mood of the time. People now tend to forget the extent to which authoritarian figures who moved efficiently and swiftly were admired in those days. Mussolini was widely looked up to for efficiency with train schedules. Hitler was admired because he was "doing something." Huey Long, the near-dictator of Louisiana, was seen as a presidential possibility, and Father Coughlin, the expatriate Canadian who advocated his own special brand of authoritarianism by radio, had an immense following. R. B. Bennett, before his defeat in 1935 by Mackenzie King, was applauded by a large section of the business community when he urged that revolutionaries be crushed under "the iron heel of ruthlessness." Even the comic strips developed authoritarian heroes to fit the period: Tarzan, the Lone Ranger, Mandrake, Alley Oop.

In an era when the entrenched leadership seemed unable to lead, the voting public turned to men who promised decisive action. In province after province, governments toppled during the mid-Thirties as political Mandrakes with names like Pattullo, Aberhart, Duplessis, and Hepburn took command. Mitchell Hepburn's Liberal victory on June 19, 1934, was a stunning upset – the greatest sweep in the party's history; and it was largely due to the personality of Hepburn himself.

He was just thirty-eight, a cherubic-looking farmer who resembled the Campbell kids who romped through the soup ads of the period. He won because he had the ability to move people and because the "little man" (to use an overworked phrase of the day) believed that Hepburn was his protector. He pictured his opponents as spendthrifts, supported by financiers who bled the ordinary man while driving about in fancy limousines. One of his most telling election promises was that he would sell every government limousine as soon as he took power. "My sympathy," he said, "lies with those people who are victims of circumstances beyond their control, and not with the manufacturers who are increasing prices and cutting wages at the same time." He won sixty-six seats out of ninety, and his first act was to offer moral support to the "hunger marchers," an army of unemployed men converging on North Bay and heading for Toronto to publicize the need for higher relief payments.

The Dionne issue was made to order for Hepburn. With a single stroke he could make himself the protector of innocent babies, and at no political cost. The impact of the government's action was so strong that Senator David Croll, who was then Hepburn's minister of welfare, believes to this day that the Hepburn Government was completely in charge from the moment of the quintuplets' birth. In fact, Hepburn did not take office until the babies were more than three weeks old.

Yes, I was Minister of Welfare, and I had representatives across the province; and I vividly recall the morning my secretary came to tell me that one of the supervisors had called in and said there was a report that somebody had given birth to five children up north. Well, we got a lot of muddied reports. I said, We'll see what happens; let me know if there's anything further. Later that day or the next day, in came the supervisor—I think it was Alf Gray who was looking after it—and he asked me what to do and I said, Do what's necessary—whatever they require. Next day they confirmed it, and the press had already gotten hold of it; but the doctor kept insisting, Don't get excited about this . . . it won't last. Well, anyway, our man went up there, but they had everything the doctor wanted so there was nothing we could do. Next thing I remember is the reporter from Chicago coming up there with the incubators, and then we said, Well, hell, if they need incubators this is our job not his; let's go up and do what has to be done. So we got incubators. The doctor was told to order what he wanted. We got in touch with his brother and I left it to him.

Well, nothing happened. Everything was normal. The family was just like any other family that needed looking after—just hoping to keep them alive. And then there was the Chicago world's fair, and the next thing that came to me was a report that the father had made an agreement with somebody to exhibit the children. At that moment I got very busy. The doctor said, You must stop this; they certainly won't live – not a chance. But how could you stop it? They were the father's children. What could you do?

Well, there was a man in my department called Cummings, the deputy minister; he was an Englishman, bright as bright could be. And he came up with the idea to take them over in the name of the Crown. He said, You have a right to do that; you represent the Crown; you are the guardian. I walked in and saw Mitch and told him the situation. I said, You know this is a Catholic family and you can't take children away from Catholics – particularly someone like myself;* you're in real trouble. He says, I don't care what trouble you're in. You're in charge, and you do what has to be done.

Hepburn was concerned. He was a very human being on these things, you know. Of course, he hit the roof over Chicago. If they hadn't done that it would have been much more difficult. . . . When the people woke up to the fact that they nearly dragged them down there, it shocked them. Dafoe was a good guy, a good family doctor. . . . We supported him from the beginning. What did I know about it? Nothing at all. Whatever Dafoe said – if he said it was nine o'clock in the morning, it had to be that way.

"Vanity," wrote Conrad, "plays lurid tricks with our memory." Croll is clearly confusing the guardianship of 1934 with the later Guardianship Bill, which went before the legislature the following spring and made the quintuplets wards of the Crown until their eighteenth birthday. But that was in the future. The details of the original guardianship were released on July 27 by Hepburn's attorney general, Arthur W. Roebuck, who announced that he had obtained a judicial order removing the quintuplets from their parents' authority – so defeating the "perfidious contract." Roebuck in making the announcement could not resist a bit of post-election politicking. He declared that "when exploiters from American cities come to Canada to pull this sort of racket they need not think that the attorney general's department is going to stand idly by. The lives of children are a bigger concern in Canada than profits of an exploitation or promotional undertaking." These were noble words, but in the light of what was to come they have a sour flavour. Within a year, the quintuplets would form the centrepiece of the most lucrative promotional undertaking in the province's history.

*Croll is a Jew.

Dionne's counsel, H. R. Valin of North Bay, echoed the attorney general's remarks, declaring that Roebuck's appointment of four guardians was the most satisfactory thing that had happened, for both the parents and the babies. He described the Spear contract as outrageous: "Plainly it was drawn up by men very clever in the use of the King's English and putting hidden meaning into innocuous phrases. . . . If the contract were carried out the Dionnes would be dragged from one show place to another and would have as much liberty as a prize cow. Certainly it would kill the babies."

The four guardians – who were to serve for two years – were W. H. Alderson, chairman of the emergency commission of the Ontario Red Cross; Dafoe's closest friend, Ken Morrison; Dafoe himself; and Olivier Dionne, the quintuplets' grandfather. Alderson, Dafoe, and Morrison were strong Liberals; it would have been unthinkable in those partisan times to allow a Tory on the board. Croll had just fired 140 members of the Ontario relief department who belonged to the opposition party. It was a measure of Dafoe's political muscle that the only Conservative inspector who was not fired was his friend James McCluskey, the big Irishman who administered relief in the Nipissing area. The North Bay Liberal Association had demanded his dismissal, but Croll announced that he alone would be retained "for his splendid work in handling the Dionne Quintuplets' case."

Valin told the press that Dionne was fully aware of what he was doing. Later, when the controversy grew bitter, Dionne was to insist that he was forced to sign the guardianship papers when Dafoe and the Red Cross threatened to cut off the supply of breast milk, which was now coming from Montreal as well as Toronto. Dionne's statement is simply not credible. It is more probable that the government pointed out to Dionne that under the new arrangement he would no longer have to worry about supporting the quintuplets. The costs of keeping the babies alive were staggering, and although the Red Cross was paying the bills for the nurses and assistants as well as the medical supplies, there was no guarantee that this would continue. It is not inconceivable that somebody – Alderson or Dafoe – asked Dionne how he could afford to foot the bill for such items as breast milk. At all events, he signed his children away.

There were now, in effect, two Dionne families under a single roof. That would soon change. On July 31, four days after the guardianship was announced, the government revealed that it planned to erect a separate building for the quintuplets and their medical and administrative staff – but not for the other members of the family. Then, on August 4, the *Toronto Star*, which had been biding its time, was able to boast that it had made special arrangements with the new guardians to publish "the picture scoop of the year," a full page of photographs of the quintuplets taken in their home. With Ivan Spear out of the running, Fred Davis had negotiated an exclusive one-year contract on behalf of his paper, prohibiting anybody else from taking pictures of the Quints. The *Star* retained Canadian rights and sold off world rights to Newspaper Enterprises of America (NEA), an American syndicate. Davis left the paper and settled down in North Bay as the official photographer of the quintuplets, producing over the years thousands of pictures of the five children. He did not, however, have a contract to photograph the rest of the family; that would be negotiated the following spring by the *New York Daily News*. As a result, the quintuplets were never shown after 1935 with their parents or their siblings – only with the doctor. For the rest of the decade, as far as the public was concerned, their father was Allan Roy Dafoe.

The move to the new quarters completed the physical and the psychological splits in the Dionne family. It does not seem to have occurred to anyone at the time – to civil servant, politician, editorial writer, man on the street – that the new building could also have housed Elzire and Oliva Dionne and their other children. On the contrary, the public mood was clear: it was important that the quintuplets be separated from their parents and given a "civilized" upbringing. Certainly this was Dafoe's attitude, and Dafoe's word was law. The last thing he wanted was interference. The doctor's son who had once been bossed around by his parents and younger sisters was now totally in charge. In a speech to the New York Academy of Medicine later that year he revealed something of his attitude: "These children," he said, "are the only ones I have ever had with whom I could do what I liked. With the ordinary baby that you look after the mother or father object, the relatives object, and you cannot do as you like with them."

One can sympathize with Dafoe, whose sole interest at the time was to keep the babies alive. He had no faith in the Dionnes' ability to understand the simplest principles of preventive medicine. He made no public statements at the time, but in 1941, near the end of his life, he had a conversation with a North Bay newspaperman, Bruce McLeod, who quoted it a decade later. "Dionne wouldn't believe anything he couldn't see," Dafoe said. "I tried to explain to him about germs – why diapers and bottles had to be sterilized. His babies were dying of dysentery and he wouldn't believe it because I couldn't actually show him the germs. How could anybody talk sense to a man like that?"

Never before had a hospital been built for a single family group. This one would cost five thousand dollars and would be rushed to completion by early fall. In addition, the government promised to straighten and surface the road from Callander and to erect a pole line through the bush to bring electricity and telephone service to the quintuplets' new home. The contractor was one Dan Barker, introduced during an address to a gathering of Liberal ladies as "a Liberal stalwart." The structure, when finished, would be named, not after the family, but after the doctor. It would be the Dafoe Hospital and Nursery.

Beyond question, the hospital was necessary if the quintuplets were to survive. Conditions in the storey-and-a-half farmhouse, where as many as twenty-two people were living and working, were unbelievable. In their heated glass prisons, the infants clung to life. "It seems funny to think that a quarter of an ounce can mean so much to anyone," Yvonne Leroux wrote in her diary. "But when the babies lose an ounce or over we get nearly frantic. They weigh so very little that every little bit counts enormously."

The nursing staff also had the mother to contend with. Elzire Dionne could not understand why she was not allowed to get up and go about her housework three days after the birth, as was her custom. The nurses managed to keep her in bed for almost two weeks. When she insisted on getting up, she developed a temperature and phlebitis in her right leg and was forced back to bed. Her father-in-law chopped a square hole in the wall of her room so that she might peer into the makeshift nursery, but she was not allowed to touch her own children, let alone cuddle them; that would have meant certain death – a truth she found difficult to accept.

In the second week in August (a fateful one for the world, for it was also the week that Adolf Hitler took total power in Germany) a series of alarms shook the household and made it obvious that conditions in the farmhouse were becoming intolerable.

First, there was a kidnapping scare; Yvonne Leroux surprised and routed prowlers trying to enter the living-room window. The Lindbergh case of 1932 had touched off a rash of similar crimes; within a week the snatching of John Labatt, the Ontario brewery king, would shock the country.

Next, there was a fire. Nurse de Kiriline overturned an alcohol lamp and as the flames crept toward the incubators, smothered them with her body. She was hospitalized for several days with bad burns.

Then there was the problem of a non-malignant tumour on Marie's leg. Dafoe feared that if it broke, the baby might bleed to death. A Johns Hopkins radiologist arrived at the crowded farmhouse and performed, without charge, an operation to retard the growth.

Finally, there was a whooping cough epidemic in North Bay. Dafoe placed the Dionne household under virtual quarantine. Visitors were banned, and for a time it was believed the Dionnes would be evicted from their own home. This didn't happen, but it was clear to the family that they occupied their farmhouse on sufferance. Mrs. Dionne could not do what she and other French-Canadian mothers had always done – show off her newest children to the various aunts, uncles, and cousins in the neighbourhood. The kitchen, which had been her domain, was now under the absolute control of the nurses, who pre-empted the stove and the new kerosene refrigerator. She was a supernumerary, and it was clear that the situation could not continue much longer.

The new refrigerator was one of several hundred gifts still pouring in from commercial and private donors: dolls, dresses, bedpans, dollar bills, cheques, gold necklaces and bracelets, baby buggies, diapers, and food – everything from a chest of silverware and dishes from General Rafael Trujillo, the Dominican strong man, to a smoked ham from a well-wisher in Ohio. One nine-year-old girl in Rhode Island sent a five-cent piece for the Dionne Hospital Fund with a note saying she "would love to send more but Daddy only works three days to keep us five going." There were more gifts than the family could use, and Mrs. Dionne would call in her friends who also had large families, take them up to the room where the presents were piled, place a heavy trunk over the trapdoor to prevent strangers from invading her private quarters, and invite them to help themselves.

Letters from all corners of the world were choking Dafoe's mailbox at the rate of more than a hundred a week. The doctor was inundated with medical advice, most of it useless, some of it grotesque. The American Goat Milk Record Association urged that the Quints be reared on goat's milk, while a Chicago veterinarian suggested that a lactating Yorkshire sow would solve all the feeding problems: "Her milk could be obtained by pumping, or else by preparing a place in the house where the babies [could] be directly suckled."

All sorts of suggestions were made to solve the problem of intestinal toxaemia: watermelon juice, blackberry root, horsetail plant, sassafras, knot weed. Except for insulin, there was no such thing as a miracle drug in those times. People still depended on homemade nostrums handed down from generation to generation. (The boy heroes in the funny papers – Elmer, Skippy, Perry Winkle,

Freckles, and even Desprit Ambrose – were perennially threatened by their comic-strip parents with doses of sulphur and molasses.) It is not surprising that Dafoe was offered a solution of "Sheep's Dung Tea" as a cure for the "Blue Spells" and, from a Mrs. Greensman of Bridgeport, Connecticut, an equally offensive panacea for all ills: she had, she said, saved a baby's life by giving her one drop of blood from the mother's afterbirth, dissolved in a little warm water.

As the Dafoe Hospital neared completion, hundreds of cars continued to bump along the tortuous road that linked Callander with the farmhouse. Undeterred by large signs marked NO ADMITTANCE, strangers trampled the shrubs in the Dionne garden and did their best to elude the guards and peer through the window for a sight of the famous five. One Alaskan prospector who had not visited the outside world for years spent his holiday travelling from Nome to Callander just to see the babies. He was refused permission but managed to talk Dafoe into pulling one of his teeth and then insisted that the doctor accept a one-dollar fee and give him a signed receipt "to show the folks back home."

The parade of showmen and promoters arriving in Callander died away after the provincial police threatened to impound the car of two Pennsylvania lawyers, but the knot of strangers standing on the road outside the farmhouse continued to grow. Some tried to bribe their way in; others adopted ruses or disguises. Two women went so far as to dress up as nuns. This only served to feed the family's suspicions of the outside world. "It's hard to know who to trust," Olivier Dionne declared that summer. "I guess it's best not to trust anybody. We were always living a quiet and simple life and now suddenly to have visitors arrive from all over Canada and the United States – it's tormenting."

On September 1, with the new hospital still unfinished, the quintuplets experienced the worst crisis in their lives. Yvonne's temperature shot up to 103 degrees that day. On September 2 it was worse, and by then the others had fevers which quickly climbed to 105. Dafoe had ordered that every used diaper, no matter how slightly soiled, must be boiled every day. This instruction had not been carried out; worse, it was found that two hundred diapers had been piled in open boxes in a fly-infested shed near the barn. The result was an outbreak of intestinal toxaemia. Although reassuring reports were issued to the press, the nursing staff did not believe the babies could survive.

On September 14, the day of the official opening of the still-uncompleted hospital, there was no certainty that the quintuplets would be alive to occupy it. Yvonne Leroux wrote in her diary:

"Grand opening. Parents did not attend. Babes still sick. Three smallest ones look dreadful. They are waxen and faces drawn. Blood group tested by Dr. W. Dafoe. My blood tests same as theirs and would likely be used if transfusion performed."

A week later, the situation was no better. Cécile's temperature exceeded 103 degrees. All the babies had lost weight. Dafoe was now convinced that if they remained in the dark and stuffy Dionne parlour they would die; what was needed was a prescription of fresh air and sunshine. He decided he could wait no longer; he would move the five babies into the unfinished hospital that day.

"In spite of everything," Leroux noted on September 21, "no supplies, no furniture, no electricity, Doctor has decided babies must go over to the hospital. We prepared all morning and all day yesterday, taking over babes' clothes, blankets, medical supplies, preparing room as much as possible before the babes came over."

Louise de Kiriline devised a five-foot-square padded box, dubbed a "rats' nest," that would hold all five infants in front of a sunlit window. The quintuplets were each fed their regular diet of mother's milk, given an oxygen cocktail, bundled into warm blankets, and then driven in heated cars through a blinding rainstorm one hundred yards across the road to the new building.

The effect was miraculous. Within a day their temperatures started to drop and their complexions lost the blue-green pallor that had made them resemble tiny corpses. Within a month Dafoe had their day cots moved out onto the front porch, where the sun and air turned their cheeks so rosy that he felt able to announce publicly that they had attained a normal life expectancy. On October 19, Pathé News, which now had exclusive rights to film the babies, arrived with a truckload of six-volt batteries to make the first quintuplet short subject. The medical crisis was over. The family crisis had just begun.

SIX:
Manhattan merry-go-round

In the first week of December 1934, when the quintuplets were almost six months old and well out of danger, Allan Roy Dafoe was persuaded to take a holiday. The Liggett company, which operated a chain of drug stores, offered to bring him to New York to speak at a public meeting at Carnegie Hall. Later he would go on to Baltimore as a guest of the Johns Hopkins Hospital and then to Washington for an audience with President Roosevelt.

In less than six months, Dafoe had become the world's best known and most popular doctor. His picture appeared regularly in the magazines and newspapers with the quintuplets, and every word he uttered seemed to find its way into print. He did not force himself on reporters, but he was unfailingly polite with them. Usually he conducted them into his book-lined study, where he answered their questions with his customary bluntness. He was a disarming interview subject – modest and self-effacing, gruff and generous and always patient. It is not easy to conjure up the nimbus that enveloped Dafoe – the awe and reverence in which he was held. It is a measure of his stature that on December 4, Dr. Elmer Lee, a noted New York child specialist, announced that he had placed the little doctor's name before the 1934 Nobel committee as a candidate for the prize for the year's outstanding medical achievement.

In an interview with Gordon Sinclair of the *Star*, Dafoe poohpoohed the Nobel idea. Sinclair reported that the doctor's income was lower than it had ever been; that he had been paid only seven hundred dollars for his work with the quintuplets – less than the nurses; that his car had been stolen, his telephone bill had tripled, and his postage bill had soared to fifteen dollars a month. Years later as a television panellist, Sinclair would develop a reputation for asking public figures how much money they were making, but apparently he did not think to ask Dafoe how much the Liggett company was paying him for the Carnegie Hall speech. It was a remarkable amount – three thousand dollars – the equivalent of more than two years' annual salary. In addition, the drug company picked up all the expenses for the doctor and his entourage. Dafoe's public image was always that of a self-effacing GP who didn't give a hoot about money. That image was never tarnished. The press, which must have come to realize that Dafoe was making a tidy fortune from his sudden fame, never bothered to explore the subject. It was as if the media had determined in advance what role the doctor was to play on the front pages. In less than a decade Dafoe would become a well-to-do man, but the public continued to view him as a simple country practitioner of even less modest means.

Alan Brown of the Sick Children's Hospital had chosen his senior intern, Dr. G.P. Hamblin, to replace Dafoe in Callander during the doctor's absence. Hamblin was selected over two others because he was the only man available who could afford the fifty-dollar licence to practise; it had been a present from his grandmother. The experience was for him "a joy and a delight," not so much because of the quintuplets, who required a minimum of attention, but because for the first time the twenty-eight-year-old Hamblin realized what it was like to be a general practitioner in a one-doctor community. He never forgot it.

The train got into Callander from Toronto early in the morning. It was still dark when Dafoe met me and took me up to his house with the sleet freezing on the wooden sidewalks. He took me into his living room; a lot of comfortable chairs and three or four walls lined with books, mostly paperback, I think – detective stories, Maupassant – and we sat up there until Mrs. Little got up and got our breakfast ready. By that time there was a knock at the door and a man came in, and Dafoe said, Well, lad, here's your bag. I'd brought my own bag, but he wouldn't let me take it; he gave me his bag. He said, Now there's a father in there, his wife's in labour; so here's your first case. Off I went – and it wasn't daylight yet!

This young girl was only about sixteen or seventeen and it was her third pregnancy. The family lived way back in the bush somewhere, and when they first consulted Dafoe he had arranged for them to be brought into a vacant log cabin on the edge of town. So I delivered my first baby by candlelight. I opened the bag and found a long pair of forceps, which I never got around to using. He didn't even have a pair of scissors, and there wasn't any string or ties for the cord. In those days they had big hot ranges in the kitchen and next to it a box of wood in which they also put their bags and ties and paper. I rummaged around in that and got some twine and sterilized it in boiling water. Later, when I went back, I said to Dafoe, You don't have any stitching material. And he said, I've never put a stitch in in my life – it makes it tough on the next one!

I think he took me out next day and introduced me to the girls. It was always quite a chore for me to get there because they were working on the road. The car dealer in North Bay would give me a car from the used car lot and of course it was a clinker; then I'd have to go and get another one. The road was closed to normal traffic, and I'd have to wait until they filled in the holes and let me over. They got to know who I was. Every day I checked the babies' weights and chatted with Mme de Kiriline. Looking after the babies was more a publicity thing. But afterwards I thought what a big investment I had in my education and career; if anything happened to those babies I'd have had to become an engineer or something, I'm afraid. I never even saw Papa Dionne, but one day I was out to the hospital and a woman was standing looking through the glass into the nursery, and I was told by one of the girls that was Mrs. Dionne. I had the feeling they didn't want to present me because she might say something nasty or critical. The fight was on, you see, but I didn't see any of that. I was only there for ten minutes a day.

I did a lot of house calls. There was no other way because the people didn't have any vehicles. I'd usually get a call on the phone fourth hand. They were all marvellous people. Two things impressed me. One was aging: in the first few seconds you had to size them up as to how old they were relative to your own age. I was twenty-eight and I'd figure, Well, he might be forty-four or forty-six, and then I'd discover he was younger than me. The other thing was that as poor as these people were, they were clean. But I hardly saw a cotton sheet on a bed; they'd be sacks, washed and sewn together. Sometimes you'd have to climb a ladder into the top part of a one-storey house where the sick person would be, and you'd find two or three beds up there. There was no point sending a bill. They were all on welfare. I didn't even keep a record. When Dafoe came back he just handed me over the hundred-dollar cheque which he got every month from the Ontario government for indigent work.

To Dafoe, the contrast between the flickering kerosene lamps of East Ferris and the blazing candlepower of Broadway must have been overwhelming. Overnight he was swept from the backwoods hamlet that had been his home for twenty-five years to the continent's most glittering metropolis. It was as if he had been transported through space and time to a distant world. Yet, in all his days in New York, the little doctor never so much as lifted an eyebrow at the wonder of it all or expressed the slightest surprise over what he was shown. It was this refusal to be dazzled by big-city sophistication that charmed the big-city sophisticates. "He arrived," the *Herald-Tribune* reported, "with an air of inability to be amazed at anything anymore."

The New York of 1934 was a fantasy as much as it was a city. It exists today only in the black-and-white movies of the Late Show – movies such as *Forty-Second Street*, *Broadway Melody*, and *Gold Diggers of 1933*. Far more than Hollywood, New York was Mecca to millions who had seen it only in the terms of the establishing shot of Times Square (with the flashing Chevrolet sign) that so often followed the main title. On Sunday nights those same millions, tuning in to *Manhattan Merry-Go-Round*, heard Ford Bond introduce the program that "brings you the bright side of life, that whirls you in music to all the big night spots of New York town." And every night, close to midnight, anyone tuning in to the Red or the Blue or the Columbia or the brand-new Mutual network could hear the clatter of glasses and the chatter of crowds as the cheerfully optimistic music of the great bands, playing in the leading hotels and the new "nightclubs," leaked from the Philcos, the Spartans, and the Capeharts. *We're in the Money*, the bands played. *I've Got a Pocketful of Dreams....*

The nightclub, which replaced the speakeasy after the repeal of the Eighteenth Amendment, was not yet a year old. Half a dozen new ones were scheduled to open in Manhattan that Christmas season. One of them, the Congress, advertised itself as the world's largest, able to seat twenty-five hundred. Few Americans had ever seen a nightclub or had more than a hazy idea of what one was like. The radio music, the movies, and the newspaper accounts conjured up a fairy-tale image of champagne bubbles, half-naked dancing girls, faultlessly dressed waiters, soft blue lights, and the glitter of diamonds.

A delicious air of minor sin hung over the city, but it was not the tawdry or violent sin of a later era. There were no porno shops or blue movies on Times Square, and one could wander anywhere without being mugged. A few adventurers were experimenting with marijuana, which the *World-Telegram*, at the time of Dafoe's visit, called "a crime provoking drug . . . [which] promotes degeneracy and insanity in its addicts. . . ." But booze, legitimate for the first time in fifteen years, was the real attraction. People could not get over the thrill of walking into a bar and ordering a mixed drink without having to announce that Joe had sent them. In the

Lounge Cafe of the Waldorf, the customers were stealing the new cocktail picks at the rate of twelve hundred a week.

That Sunday morning, while Dafoe was being whisked from Grand Central Station to the Ritz Carlton, ten thousand people poured through the doors of St. Patrick's Cathedral, where at all seven Masses they were asked to shun all motion pictures and plays proscribed by the newly formed Legion of Decency. When asked to stand and take the pledge, none remained seated. Of thirty plays and musicals on Broadway, only four were on the approved list, but, given the glittering Broadway schedule that season – it reads like a list of Who's Who in the Theatre – one doubts that all of the suppliants at St. Patrick's were able to keep their pledge. Ethel Merman, Tallulah Bankhead, Katharine Cornell, Bob Hope, Henry Fonda, Edith Evans, Sybil Thorndike, Eva Le Gallienne, Alfred Lunt, Lynn Fontanne, Leslie Howard, and Jane Cowl were among the stars whose names appeared in lights off Times Square.

Sunday night was party night for theatre people. The undisputed queen of the party givers was Elsa Maxwell, a dumpy little woman with the face of a Pekinese and the voice of a bullfrog. On that particular Sunday night she was hostess at a Turkish soirée mounted at the Waldorf-Astoria to honour Cole Porter on his birthday. The anniversary cake was fifteen feet high and the guest list was as glittering as the candles. The Fritz Kreislers, who arrived early, were reported to have left early – early being 2:30 a.m. But George Gershwin, then composing *Porgy and Bess*, was still on hand at five. This was not the only party to hit the society pages the next morning. In Washington, Eleanor Roosevelt held a masked ball at the White House for the wives of the Washington notables who were attending the all-male Gridiron Dinner. First prize for the most ingenious costume went to a group of five ladies who came dressed as the Dionne quintuplets.

The saviour of the quintuplets was, at that time, taking his ease on the estate of George Gales, the Liggett president, at Locust Valley, Long Island. His day had been long and exhausting, but he did not show it. The Toronto train, with the Dafoe party aboard – it included Dr. and Mrs. William Dafoe and James McCluskey, the relief officer – pulled into Grand Central at 8:10 on an unseasonably cold morning. Gales was on hand to greet the Canadians, accompanied by his vice-president and a crowd of minor executives together with the usual clutch of reporters and eight large patrolmen and a sergeant from the Seventeenth Precinct.

Breakfast had been laid on in the five-room Louis XVI suite on the ninth floor of the Ritz Carlton. Then the doctor and his party were driven south to the ferryboat *Knickerbocker* for the obligatory trip to Staten Island, so that Dafoe might view the New York skyline, dominated in those days by the Empire State Building, just three years old. The ferry was the largest vessel on which Dafoe had ever travelled.

Next the doctor was whisked up lower Broadway's windswept canyon to the city hall, preceded by his eight-man motorcycle escort, sirens wailing. Pedestrians, recognizing him immediately, waved and cheered. Looking across from the city hall at the sunlight striking the needle of the Woolworth Building, Dafoe remarked that he wouldn't mind a ride on the subway. His wish was granted at once, and the entire party, including the detective assigned by the city as his personal bodyguard, boarded the BMT, where the photographers snapped the little doctor clinging to a strap. He was asked, of course, what he thought of the New York subway system. "Very convenient," replied Dafoe in his blunt fashion.

By two that afternoon the doctor's suite was packed with more than thirty reporters and six newsreel cameramen. Dafoe, looking a little nervous, filled his pipe and faced the press for forty minutes, a "droll, elfin little man" in the words of young Dorothy Kilgallen. It was noticed that his brother stood right behind him, coaching him in his answers. Dafoe gave the same perfunctory and laconic replies to the same questions that had been asked earlier that day. Somebody asked him about birth control; he refused an opinion. A woman reporter asked him if he thought New York mothers spent too much time in nightclubs. "I don't know anything about that," said the doctor. "Up north they don't do that. Up north all they do is have big families." Then he turned to face forty-eight thousand candlepower of lights and, as the cameras turned, briefly discussed the health of the quintuplets. The press was spellbound: here was a man who didn't seem to give a hoot about money and wasn't the least impressed by big-city glamour. The *Times*, in an editorial next day, remarked in its weighty fashion that "there is an unmistakable touch of awe in the presence of an affirmation of life at a time when all the world over human life has become so cheap and so incidental."

This was only a prelude to the events of the following day, for after Dafoe's Carnegie Hall address, the city would be his. On Monday morning he rose at five. Elsa Maxwell's party was still in full swing; Princess Barbara Hutton Mdivani was dancing with Prince Serge Obolensky while Dafoe was strolling about the Gales estate waiting for the others to rise. At ten he was back in the city with his motorcycle escort leading him on to the Empire State Building whose president, the former New York governor Al Smith, took him up to the observation tower to observe the Manhattan panorama from still another vantage point. The Happy Warrior, his trademark brown derby squarely on his head, asked Dafoe what the "quintriplets," as he called them, looked like when they were born. "Like rats," said Dafoe. This seemed to disturb his brother. "Like kittens," William Dafoe suggested. "No," repeated Dafoe stubbornly, "like rats." The press changed the word to "puppies."

The doctor, looking across the ocean of office buildings, spotted the Goodyear blimp suspended above the city and expressed a desire for a ride. This was quickly squelched by his brother, who felt he was, in the phrase of the day, "too air-minded."

That night, Dafoe donned the new dinner jacket he had bought in Toronto, tucked a white handkerchief into his breast pocket, left for Carnegie Hall, and in the space of a few hours managed, to quote the *World-Telegram*'s headline, to WIN HARDBOILED BROADWAY ON HIS FIRST NIGHT OUT.

The word "hard-boiled" crept more than once into the newspaper accounts of Dafoe's visit to the big city. New York reporters liked to describe themselves as hard-boiled and their city as hard-boiled. "Manhattan took him to its hard-boiled heart," Dorothy Kilgallen reported. But the truth is that Broadway and Manhattan were slushily sentimental, and so were the sob sisters, gossip columnists, editorial writers, and newshawks who regularly went into ecstasies as each new celebrity made his siren-howling advance up to the city hall. At times, Dafoe's conquest of New York sounds remarkably like the script of *Nothing Sacred*, the Hollywood screwball comedy made a couple of years later, in which Fredric March, the hard-boiled reporter, brings Carole Lombard, a small-town girl with a supposedly incurable disease, to Manhattan as a publicity stunt. The press conferences, the nightclub and Broadway scenes in the movie have an astonishing similarity to what the *New York American* in large headlines called DR. DAFOE'S TRIUMPH.

Dafoe's triumph was a brilliant coup for the Liggett company's publicity department. The drug firm had issued three thousand tickets for the speech on a first come, first served basis. Twenty thousand New Yorkers vainly clamoured for admission. When the doctor walked out on the stage – a diminutive figure, with his closely cropped grey blond hair and his neatly trimmed moustache – even the press tables shook with applause. It was remarked that no other man except Toscanini had ever held a Carnegie Hall crowd so spellbound.

Dafoe spoke for forty minutes, retelling the story of the quintuplets' birth, quietly and without flamboyance. It needed no embroidery. The audience, leaning forward in their seats, gave him the accolade of absolute silence. Nobody so much as coughed. Dafoe, by his very lack of pretension, had scored a hit.

The doctor then showed slides of the five babies and their parents. When Oliva Dionne's picture flashed on the screen, the audience burst into laughter.

There followed a two-reel motion picture of the children filmed in October by Pathé News. It was the second movie Dafoe had ever seen.

What he really wanted to see was one of the fabled New York nightclubs. Off he went, followed by his private detective, his entourage, and a covey of newspapermen, to the Paradise Cabaret Restaurant at Forty-ninth and Broadway, where Sally Rand was featured, "direct from her sensational success at the Chicago World's Fair." In addition to the two-hour floor show and the music of Will Osborne's orchestra, the supper club's patrons were treated to a full-course dinner, all for a total cost of one dollar and fifty cents.

William Dafoe was uneasy about his brother's visiting a nightclub; it scarcely fitted the image of the humble rural practitioner. At the very least he hoped Roy would not be singled out by the management. That, of course, was impossible. The master of ceremonies, Nils T. Grantlund, better known to radio and vaudeville audiences as NTG, turned a spotlight on the party and introduced the doctor as "one of nature's greatest heroes, now and forever." Dafoe wanted to stand up and thank him, but his brother persuaded him to stay seated. It was noticed that the doctor got more applause than Sally Rand. After her bubble dance, she performed especially for him the fan dance that had made her famous. The chorus line was trembling with awe in the presence of the little country doctor. Grantlund told the press that Dafoe had caused ten times more stir among the girls than had Douglas Fairbanks.

Soon after Dafoe's arrival, Walter Winchell of the *New York Mirror*, the town's leading gossip columnist, strode into the nightclub. Just the day before he had pulled off one of the great scoops of the Lindbergh kidnapping case by revealing details of a clue, dealing with a section of the ladder employed in the crime, that helped send Bruno Hauptmann to the electric chair.

The columnist attached himself to the Dafoe party and stuck with it the rest of the evening. Of all the paeans composed to Dafoe during his New York visit, none was quite so fulsome as his. Through his Sunday night *Jergens Journal* (named for a sponsoring hand lotion) and his widely syndicated column, Winchell commanded an audience of millions. He could sneer or he could gush, depending on his personal whim. With Dafoe he gushed. "I'm nuts about that doctor," he said. "I thought I knew a lot about blessed events . . . but now I've met a man who knows ten times as much. . . . He thrilled the devil out of me. I mean it. We've never seen a man like that in New York. Everybody I know is selfish. Why, I read in today's paper that he helped one woman through seventeen confinements without one cent of pay. I can't get over him."

Sally Rand, clad in an ermine wrap and a black toque, joined Dafoe at the crowded table and stayed to chat for half an hour, reminiscing about the days, ten years before, when she had had to sleep on benches in Central Park. The two engaged in some light banter. Sally suggested that in return for the bubble dance, Dafoe give her a prescription for quintuplets. "Impossible," said the doctor. "If you want quintuplets, you'll have to come to the north country."

When Sally returned to her act, Winchell whispered in the doctor's ear: "Doc, she's really a nice girl."

Dafoe, without turning his head, murmured: "Nice ass, too."

It was clear from his conversation that Dafoe had no clear idea of how a nightclub worked. He wanted to know whether people threw parties like this one every night and seemed surprised when Winchell explained that this was a show that took place three times every night of the week. The following day Winchell devoted his entire column to the doctor.

That Tuesday afternoon, Dafoe attended a five o'clock tea given in his honour by William Randolph Hearst, Jr., who was anxious to publish a series of articles under the Dafoe by-line. In addition to the usual socialites, all of Hearst's stars turned up – Winchell, Damon Runyon, O. O. McIntyre, Gilbert Seldes, Hendrik Willem Van Loon, and the legendary Arthur Brisbane, the most cynical editor in New York, who had been charged just the previous month with the impossible task of beefing up the faltering *Daily Mirror* and overtaking the *News*.

Brisbane had also just completed his annual task of naming the outstanding woman of year. He chose Mrs. Dionne over Mae West because, he said, though Mae West had given birth to a school of acting, Mrs. Dionne had given birth to a real school. It was a typical Brisbane remark. Hated, feared, and envied by his colleagues, he was on the eve of his seventieth birthday and his production was still incredible. With the help of his ever-present Dictaphone he churned out five hundred thousand words a year for his thirty million readers – the biggest audience of any journalist in the world. Hearst paid him the staggering sum of two hundred and sixty thousand dollars a year, and Brisbane invariably started a conversation by announcing that fact.

Those conversations were notoriously short. It was remarked by some of his colleagues at the tea party that afternoon that no man on earth had held the editor's attention for more than half an hour. Dafoe broke the record: they talked for thirty-five minutes. Brisbane produced a pencil and started taking notes at a furious pace. That concluded, he strode over to his gossip columnist, whose daily outpourings he considered so much gibberish. "Winchell," he said, "I've got a story that's never been written." Since the story had been written over and over again, one wonders whether the great editor ever bothered to take time off from his dictating to read his own paper.

That evening, the eight screaming motorcycles led the party to the Winter Garden to see the 125th performance of *Life Begins at 8:40*, the biggest musical in town. The show-stopper was a hilarious dance routine in which Ray Bolger made sport of the recent heavyweight fiasco in which Max Baer had easily disposed of the gigantic but totally inept Primo Carnera. Never having heard of either Baer or Carnera, Dafoe had no idea of what the skit was all about. He was taken backstage during the intermission to be photographed with Bolger and his co-star, Bert Lahr, but during the second act he strayed out of the theatre, to be discovered by his frantic bodyguard strolling alone up Broadway.

By the time he left New York for Washington, most of the major columnists had devoted their pillar of type to the doctor. Hendrik Willem Van Loon, whose more serious work included such best-sellers as *The Story of Mankind* and *Van Loon's Geography,* set the general tone in the *Mirror*:

> Suddenly we remembered that we are merely a city and there are an awful lot of people living in the wilderness, which for most of us begins just west of Manhattan Junction, and we were made to realize that some of the finest gentlemen dwell right in the heart of that wilderness.
>
> That is what you have done for us, and I for one am mighty grateful.
>
> I can't say that I am very much interested in your quintuplets . . . a father without a job and a mother whose only purpose in life seems to have been that of breeding the largest possible number of children within the shortest possible space of time – that combination is hardly likely to furnish the world

with a fresh crop of geniuses. The French Canadian undoubtedly possesses certain virtues which make him worthy of the Almighty's mercy. But I doubt whether the assembled I.Q.'s of your five little charges will ever surpass that of a single little Chinaman or Batak baby.

But that is neither here nor there. You are the hero of the occasion and not those five squealing little savages.

Since, for the moment, there were no channel-swimmers or flagpole-sitters or other heroes upon whom the multitude could bestow its favors, the quintuplets were dragged in to give a little relief to lives that otherwise would have expired from sheer boredom.

Dafoe's odyssey had now taken on some of the trappings of a royal tour. In Washington he was tendered a reception by the Canadian embassy and granted a two-minute audience with the president. Roosevelt stretched it to more than ten. When Dafoe told a press conference that no woman's life was complete unless she had had a baby, nobody rose to take issue with him. On he went to Baltimore and Johns Hopkins and then, in spite of his brother's demurrals, returned to New York by airplane. The doctor sat up with the pilot, listening to the radio chatter from the ground. Suddenly a voice broke in, asking for him by name. It belonged to Lyman du Pont, head of the largest chemical concern in America, wishing him the best of luck from Wilmington, Delaware.

A second round of sight-seeing and receptions followed. At the invitation of New York's chief of police Dafoe even presided at a line-up to witness the questioning of a self-confessed murderer. He agreed, cheerfully, to anything and everything. "Sure, why not?" he'd say when another excursion was suggested. The recurring phrase became, for a time, part of Manhattan's slang; and when a letter addressed simply to *Sure, why not?* was sent to Canada, it found its way with little delay to the Dafoe home in Callander.

Society women began to phone him to plead that he remain in New York to look after their babies. Dafoe, of course, harboured no such ambitions. New York to him was impure, not morally but medically. His reaction to it foreshadowed a later, pollution-conscious age when he declared that "the smoke-saturated, germ-laden air of a great city is not to be compared to 'the breath of life' which my little girls have drawn from the first in cool, clean, invigorating Callander, Ontario." The air of New York, Dafoe declared, was pregnant with poison and the noise in its streets could cause a form of shell shock to a delicate nervous system.

He returned to his home on a Sunday night (accompanied by a

Hearst feature writer who was ghostwriting a series of articles under his name), just in time to catch Walter Winchell's weekly broadcast, much of which was devoted to him: "You lovable doctor, sitting beside your fireplace and smoking your pipe, keep being happy – and by that I mean: *keep being you!*"

Could he continue to be himself after the circus of Manhattan? One old comrade detected a difference. Louise de Kiriline found that the old one-to-one relationship had changed.

He changed completely from the country doctor that I had known. He was quite different. He treated me and other people differently. He became, well – stuck-up. He became, I think, a prisoner of his own publicity. I was never the same with him after that, and we had worked so closely together. I think his brother had a great deal to do with that. You see, Dr. Dafoe and I, we had been completely equal, but when Dr. Bill Dafoe came, he influenced him to treat me as nurses are usually treated by doctors – and that's not as an equal. . . .

The big change came after he had been to New York. I think that was when he fully realized the extent of the publicity he had had. I never recognized him after that. It was the end of our intimacy. I think he just gave way – I don't know, it might have been quite unconsciously – but it went to his head, and he became a mean person in a way that I had never seen before. I had started to write a book about the care of the babies, and I went to Dr. Dafoe and asked him to write a foreword. When he heard about this book – well, it wasn't so much him as all those around him, but they immediately started to write a book for Dr. Dafoe, and that book was ghostwritten so quickly that it came out before mine and therefore, of course, spoiled it completely.

And yet the remarkable thing about Dafoe is not that he changed – the events of that manic year would have warped the psyche of a messiah – but that, outwardly at least, he changed so little. There is no doubt that he enjoyed being boss. He had originally come to Callander to be the supreme medical authority in a small bush community. Now his authority was recognized throughout the world, and it was certainly felt in the nursery. He had hobnobbed with the great and the near great. He was on intimate terms with Mitchell Hepburn, who arrived in January and was photographed nervously holding one of the babies. In his letters to the premier, the salutation was always the intimate "Dear Chief." Dafoe had only to lift a finger to get anything he wanted; politically, it was impossible to deny any request. But if power corrupts, he was less corruptible than most. His intimates

undoubtedly noticed subtle changes, but to the world at large he remained the same lovable doctor of the Winchell broadcast.

In February, 1935, John F. Coggswell, in a series of three long display articles, turned the pages of the *Boston Sunday Post* purple with his praise of Dafoe: " . . . anyone's vocabulary is lacking in enough adjectives to do him justice – modest, wise, genial, friendly, cheerful, charitable, courteous, kindly, reputable, ethical – they all apply."

That June, the *Ella Cinders* comic strip featured a long series about a country doctor whom it called Dr. Dale but who bore an uncanny visual resemblance to Dafoe. Ella discovers Dr. Dale in a small town after he has saved the life of a child bitten by a spider with a serum that he has developed and tested on himself. She calls a newspaper in New York which brings Dr. Dale to Manhattan, where he receives a Dafoe-like reception before returning to his humble practice.

A year later, the *St. Thomas Times Journal* could report that "fame and publicity haven't gone to his head a bit. It is his unaffected personality that has made him loved by thousands, yes millions of people on this continent." The same year, Charlie Blake wrote: "There is probably no greater personality in the world today."

No human character could live up to this adulation. Though the press continued to present Dafoe as both hard-working and poor, the time was quickly approaching when he would be neither. Unknown to the public, he was amassing a fortune from commercial testimonials and had all but ceased to keep up his private practice. By 1938, when he had virtually nothing to do, he was, to quote the later words of his secretary, "the laziest man I ever met." But there was one change in Dafoe that was obvious to all who had known him in the old days. He was no longer the weary country doctor, old at fifty, nagged by rheumatic pains, irregular meals, and improper rest. The birth of the quintuplets had given him new life. The pains vanished; his brow was smoothed; his eyes sparkled; and he looked younger and more vigorous than his years.

Celebrities came and went in the Thirties, but Dafoe's hold on the public's imagination never slackened. Wherever he went – and he enjoyed travelling to the big American cities – his expenses were paid and he was treated like visiting royalty. He would soon have his own daily newspaper column and a tri-weekly radio program. He would become a perennial guest star on the big network shows. "Of all my radio interviews this man's was the finest," Rudy Vallee declared, in an unconsciously revealing statement. "He is a natural showman, and many a professional would do well to ape his timing." In 1939 Dafoe was the only Canadian asked to give a paper before the prestigious *Herald-Tribune* forum in New York. The other invited guests included Franklin D. Roosevelt; Madame Chiang Kai-shek; Lord Halifax, the British foreign secretary; and Edouard Daladier, the premier of France.

In October 1940, on one of his innumerable trips to New York, Dafoe was still able to generate the same kind of electricity that had marked his first tour. On the drive down people recognized him at every stop – the border customs officials, service station operators, students at Cornell, innkeepers in the Catskills, and the taxicab drivers, waiters, bootblacks, and general public in Manhattan. He was again given a police escort, and the town's elite, from a former governor of New Jersey to a vice-president of the Chase National Bank, were delighted to be asked to a lunch in his honour.

Dafoe's prestige stood almost as high among the members of his own profession, who always flocked to hear him, jostled for invitations to private luncheons, and showered him with honours. From the viewpoint of the average GP, this was no less than his due. By the end of the Thirties he had made an entire continent aware of the dedication, low pay, exhausting work, and sacrifice of the rural practitioner. More than a decade after his death, Clark Kinnaird, the head of King Features Syndicate, summed it all up in a one-sentence epitaph: "He fostered the whole country doctor literary, movie and radio industry and his story should be told."

SEVEN:
The spectre of Chicago

Oliva Dionne and his wife were not on hand to greet Dafoe when he returned from New York shortly before Christmas, 1934. They were photographed with him, however, for a publicity shot – Dafoe dressed as Santa Claus and the parents holding the five children. It was the last of its kind. For contractual reasons, the Dionnes would not be shown again with the quintuplets until 1941.

A few days before the Yuletide, the Quints made their first Christmas broadcast, which consisted of an announcer's comments, some words from Dafoe, and a babble of baby voices. The original idea came from the Columbia Broadcasting System, which entered into an agreement with the guardians; but Hector Charlesworth, chairman of the Canadian Radio Broadcasting Commission, announced that such a broadcast, which would have to originate through the facilities of a Canadian station, was illegal. Only the CRBC could originate such a program. Dafoe refused to allow a live broadcast at 8:15 p.m. but agreed to let the CRBC make a recording, which could also be used by the American network. Columbia refused. It had never broadcast a recorded program; custom dictated that everything originating on the networks be live. It was an awkward arrangement – senseless to a later generation raised on electronic tape – but it did contribute a feeling of tension, a kind of electricity, a delicious sense that something totally unexpected might happen that no canned program could emulate, and it helps to explain the enormous hold that radio had over people in the Thirties. But the Dionne quintuplets did not gurgle for CBS in the Christmas season of 1934.

On Christmas day, all the Dionnes made their way through a heavy blizzard to dinner at the Dafoe Hospital. More than one hundred gifts arrived, mostly clothing, toys, candy, and rag dolls. The quintuplets were not allowed any candy, and because Dafoe, for sanitary reasons, decreed that they could not play with anything made of cloth, the dolls were distributed to the other children.

It must have seemed to the family that Dafoe carried his (or Dr. Alan Brown's) fear of germs to ridiculous lengths. He stubbornly resisted the idea that the other children might play with their new sisters. On January 21, 1935, the three girls and two boys were allowed to look at the quintuplets through the observation windows, but that was all. "We cannot allow children to enter the nursery, because they are such germ carriers," the doctor declared. Adults, apparently, were immune to germs, especially if they were VIP's. On that same day, Mitchell Hepburn visited the hospital with two members of his cabinet, David Croll and Paul Leduc, his minister of mines. All three donned white smocks and were photographed with the children. "Quite the most remarkable sight I ever saw," said Hepburn. *He was scared of the babies and hardly knew what to do with them*, Yvonne Leroux wrote in her diary.

Meanwhile, Oliva Dionne had acquired a brace of business managers. These were Leo Kervin, who operated a resort hotel at French River and was reeve of his township, and brother Léon, the service station operator, who would act as Kervin's assistant. They were to receive 40 per cent of all moneys realized by Dionne from promotions associated with the quintuplets. On February 4, it was announced that their first venture would be a series of stage appearances in Midwestern American cities.

I wasn't on that trip but Leo, my husband, went. Mr. Dionne was completely lacking in a business way; he needed somebody to sort of guide him. It's so long ago now, but I do remember when it happened. They had written up a little statement for her to make. She was to come on the stage and be introduced as Mrs. Dionne, and it just said how thankful she was for all the help they had gotten from Chicago and the rest of the world. Just three or four sentences . . .

Oh, yes, there was a fuss. Well, of course, Oliva was a poor man, and his whole ambition was to get his hands on money; anybody who couldn't wangle that for him just hadn't his interest at heart, according to him. So when this Chicago thing came up he said, Well, they're not talking about babies now, are they? And he did need money; definitely. In the sense, mostly, I guess – not that he was hungry or anything like that – but that he knew the Quints were making money and he sort of envied the fact. Maybe I shouldn't use that word "envy": that they were wealthy in their own right, or becoming so. And he was still in the same rut as he always had been in. And he tried to find a means or tried to grab at a means of improving that. So that's why they went. Besides, what's wrong with adults going on the stage? The press made an awful fuss over it, but, you know, they weren't going to die as a result of it. It was a good experience for them. She was well coached as to what to do and she did it very nicely, apparently, and the people certainly gave her a good clapping. Of course, the press didn't see any good in anybody else profiting by the birth of the Quints. Probably the press wouldn't have ridden Leo quite so hard if they'd known more about him. They thought he didn't know what he was doing. But he'd gone to school with Oliva Dionne in Callander. He had a friendship with him. . . . Leo was a close friend of Dr. Dafoe's before all this, you know – a very close friend. But anybody who was on Dionne's side was not a close friend of Dr. Dafoe's after he got involved with those Quints. . . .

The tone of the press coverage of the Dionnes' tour to Chicago, Detroit, and other Midwestern centres contrasts sharply with that accorded Dafoe in New York. Where Dafoe's treatment had been reverential, the Dionnes were given the kind of tongue-in-cheek reporting that, while never specifically malicious, could not be described as sympathetic. Certainly the story had its moments of comic relief. Max Halperin, who engineered the exclusive theatrical tie-ups, could have been typecast as a vaudeville promoter in a Hollywood movie. The spectacle of him standing helplessly by while the Dionne entourage, invoking the all-expenses-paid clause in their contract, calmly ate their way through his profits is high farce. But there was human interest, too, and not a little pathos. In North Bay, the *Nugget* protested the press coverage of the tour by newspapers that "for unknown reasons . . . have gone out of their way to make Mr. and Mrs. Oliva Dionne . . . appear in a ridiculous light."

The *Toronto Star* had great fun with Halperin, who told the paper that he had found beautiful satisfaction in his glorification of motherhood. "It sort of gets you here," he said, thumping his heart with his fist; his other hand, according to the *Star*, was in his pants pocket. The paper reported that Halperin smoked thirty-five-cent cigarettes and used such words as "colossal" and "terrific" to describe anything "even when he is referring to the freshness of his breakfast eggs." Certainly Halperin talked promoterese. He said such things as "the American people want to meet this wonderful little mother," and he was always coming up with "superb sensations," such as his plan, never realized, to have the Dionnes awakened on Sunday morning in Chicago by the voices of one hundred choir boys, massed outside their hotel door.

The Dionnes, along with Kervin, Léon Dionne, and a cousin, Mrs. Joseph Rochon, left Toronto on the 9:40 train to Chicago on the evening of Monday, February 4. It was their first trip away from home since their honeymoon in 1925. Coming directly from Corbeil to the raucous capital of the American Midwest, they must have found the contrast even greater than Dafoe's discovery of New York. The newspapers that week lived up to the rough-and-tough reputation of the so-called Chicago school of journalism. Mayhem dominated the front pages. As the Dionnes stepped off the train into the arms of a gaping crowd that morning, Helen Straub had been tabbed as the chief suspect in the murder of her husband, whose bullet-riddled body was found in the basement of a fashionable club. The following day, mobsters gunned down Thomas E. Maloy, a labour union leader, as he was riding in his automobile on a street on the South Side. The trial of Bruno Hauptmann was entering its final week, and the newsreels, which would be appearing on the screen between the Dionne performances, were advertising "Ten Dramatic Minutes. Actual Court Room Talking Scenes! HEAR BRUNO GIVE HIS ALIBI TESTIMONY. . . . HEAR WILSON'S TERRIFIC ATTACK. . . . SEE AND HEAR BRUNO SNARL: 'STOP! STOP!' "

Max Halperin had spared no expense. The presidential suite of the Congress Hotel, where every U.S. chief executive since Grover Cleveland had spent at least one night, had been completely overhauled for his charges. The suite contained four bedrooms and two parlours overlooking Lake Michigan, furnished with Louis XVI pieces and decorated with ponderous gold mirrors.

At the press conference that morning, the Dionnes announced that they would like to see a nightclub: "We have heard so much about them. They are gay, no? We are so wanting to see one." Dionne also expressed a wish to see Amos and Andy in action and was disappointed to learn that they were absent on a southern tour. His wife had only one desire: to meet Cardinal George Mundelein of the Chicago archdiocese of the Roman Catholic Church.

The session with the newsreels was an ordeal. The Dionnes spoke so softly that their memorized speeches were scarcely audible over the buzz of the cameras, which were supposed to have caught the couple eating breakfast in their bedroom. (They had eaten hours before, but it was easier to conceal the bulky microphones among the dishes.) The glaring lights gave Mrs. Dionne a headache. "I'm fed up," she told her husband in French and walked out, Dionne trailing behind her and the photographers shouting, "Aw, come on – just one more shot."

The pictures that appeared the following day showed the couple looking glum. The Dionnes shared the back picture page of the tabloid *Times* with the usual gaggle of murder suspects and heart-balm aspirants, all captioned in searing type: "WOMAN HUNTED AS CLUB SLAYER." "QUIZ PALS IN SLAYING OF MALOY." "SIFT WILD SEX CULT OF WIDOW." The papers depicted the parents as bumpkins. The report in the *News* began with the words: "A French Canadian farmer with a collar several sizes too large for him and his buxom wife, a dimpled woman on whom greatness has been thrust . . . came to Chicago today bewildered by it all." The report went on to describe Dionne as "a mild appearing man with a Charlie Chaplin mustache and not much chin."

Halperin had brought the Dionne party into town a full three days before they were to appear on stage at the Oriental in order to build up publicity for the theatre. Dionne sheared a sheep at the stockyards, lunched with executives at the Saddle and Cycle Club (where Helen Straub's unfortunate husband had been murdered two days before), and then was taken on a shopping expedition with his wife. Crowds milled about the couple and followed them down State Street. The crush of the curious became so heavy that it was impossible for them to buy gifts for the children. One middle-aged woman rushed up to Mrs. Dionne crying, "You're a wonderful woman"; a policeman stopped her when she tried to kiss her. As the Dionnes were hustled into a limousine, waitresses and shop girls ran out onto the rainy windswept streets and pressed their faces against the window to catch a glimpse of the couple.

But there were other reactions. When Dionne was taken into a restaurant and introduced as the father of the famous Quints, the waitress backed away. "Stay away from me! Don't touch me!" she said. That night, before she fell asleep from exhaustion, Elzire Dionne cried and told her husband she wanted to go home. But home was almost three weeks away.

The press was fascinated by the party's appetite for confections. It was reported that they consumed sixty bottles of ginger ale and innumerable dishes of strawberry shortcake during the first two days in Chicago. On Wednesday, February 6, when they were taken to a nightclub, "Dionne watched the showgirls as long as there was nothing else to do but as soon as the toasted club sandwiches were brought, he didn't give them another look until he finished the last lettuce leaf and bread crumb." A reporter urged him to give his opinion of Chicago nightclubs – a stock question, apparently, for visiting firemen that season. He replied: "If I talk, maybe I get into trouble, eh?" Photographers began to flash their cameras and to urge Dionne to smile; he had difficulty in managing more than a sickly grimace. A trio of blonde showgirls surrounded him and asked him to hold up a magnum of champagne as a symbol of the city's night life. Dionne clutched the bottle gingerly and looked sadly across at the squad of snapping cameramen. In New York, Dafoe's natural reticence had been greeted with hosannas; in Chicago, Dionne's shyness became the subject of merriment.

The words "DIONNE QUINTUPLETS" dominated the Oriental Theatre as display advertising. It required a second look to note the words "Mother and father of the famous" appearing in much smaller type above. The accompanying vaudeville show was described as "a whirlwind of stage fun." In addition to the Dionnes' appearance, it featured a new ballet starring the Trudi Pickering Dancers, a comedy act, Red Donahue and His Mule, and the famous Eddie Peabody, master of twenty-eight musical instruments. There was also a Warner Baxter movie, *Hell in the Heavens*, and a newsreel – all for twenty-five cents admission.

The Dionnes spent the morning of Friday, February 8, preparing for their opening that afternoon. In her suite, Mrs. Dionne was given a new finger wave, immediately dubbed "the Dionne," as well as a massage and a manicure. Her husband had his hair trimmed and slicked back. Tailors and dressmakers followed with a suitable wardrobe. Mrs. Dionne, who liked gaudy hues, brightened at the sight of a flowing silk dress combining her favourite colours, violet and raspberry red, but was persuaded to appear in a quiet brown. Her dress size, forty-six, and her weight, two hundred pounds, were duly reported. The rehearsals at the theatre went on until noon. The Dionnes, very nervous, prepared to go out for lunch. The manager ordered them back and fed them sandwiches.

In the darkened theatre, the whirlwind of stage fun was already in progress. A trained mule kicked the blackfaced comedian, Red Donahue, into the orchestra pit. As the laughter subsided, the footlights winked out and a Pathé News feature, telling the story of the Quints, flashed on the screen. The pit band struck up *Baby Your Mother Like She Babied You*, and as the film ended the footlights went on again and the band switched to *O Canada*.

Eddie Peabody began to introduce the members of the Dionne party. "They are not actors, folks," he warned the audience. "They are just pioneers, frontier people." Mrs. Rochon was led on first through the blue curtains, then Léon Dionne, who made a deep bow, straight from the waist. A momentary pause followed. Then came the announcement: "Ladies and gentlemen: the world's most famous parents!" A ripple ran through the audience as Oliva and Elzire Dionne emerged into the blazing light. Peabody asked Mrs. Dionne to step forward. She gave Mrs. Rochon a last, desperate look and stepped up to the microphone. All she could manage was a faint "Merci beaucoup." Her husband, in a blue serge suit, red tie, and new shoes purchased in Chicago, quickly went through his memorized speech: "Mrs. Dionne and myself are glad to have the opportunity to thank the people of the United States for their interest in our babies." The audience applauded, and the Dionne party moved toward the exit. There was a mix-up in cues and the Pickering girls came on a moment too soon. The party struggled to make its way through a swirl of scantily clad dancers to the dressing room. The first show of the day was over for them. There would be four more.

In the dressing room, they received a stunning surprise. A United States marshal shouldered his way in and handed an official document to Elzire Dionne. She took it and burst into tears. It was a subpoena, intended for her husband – the marshal had thought "Oliva" was a girl's name. Ivan Spear was suing the Dionnes and fifteen other defendants, including Dafoe, the guardians, NEA Service, and Pathé News, for one million dollars for breach of the original contract, which had given him exclusive rights to the quintuplets' pictures and publicity.

Dionne was shaken. A million dollars was an incomprehensible sum. For the first time he was making a little money. Would it now be eaten up in a lawsuit?

All that week the Dionnes lived from noon until midnight in the stuffy theatre dressing room. Did they ever ask themselves what they were doing there – a family of farmers from the dark back country plunged suddenly into the not-so-glamorous world of show business? Did they ever discuss the caprice of nature that had fixed upon them, of all people, to blink in the spotlight? It is doubtful, for that was not their way; besides, it was God's will. The worst thing about show-business life, they quickly learned, was that it was boring. Mrs. Dionne, entranced by the showgirls, begged to be allowed to remain in the wings to watch them dance. During the movie, she played solitaire and hummed hymns while her husband chain-smoked. Her public shyness masked a tough inner fibre. She seemed so soft, so docile, so timid. But when the make-up man tried to apply greasepaint to her face, she threatened to walk out. Inwardly she was a tigress, as the nurses at the Dafoe Hospital would discover.

Mrs. Dionne was glad to leave Chicago. She preferred Detroit, perhaps because there were fewer reporters to greet the party. The *Toronto Star* was now describing the tour as a "nine-day wonder," in sharp contrast to *Variety*, which reported that the Dionnes were a sure-fire attraction.

The Canadian paper made sport of the way the Dionnes ate into Max Halperin's expense account. It reported that "at almost every meal they stowed away huge helpings. Conversation at the table wasn't allowed to interfere with the serious business of eating, the only phrases being 'pass the salt' and 'hand over the bread.' " And again in Detroit: "Mrs. Dionne said she was hungry on arriving and immediately had a breakfast of tomato juice, a double order of oatmeal, scrambled eggs, boiled eggs, bacon, ham, wheat cakes, toast, tea and coffee. Through her interpreter, Georgiana Rochon, Mrs. Dionne explained she was on a diet." What the *Star* had described, of course, was breakfast for five persons, not one. The *Star* went on to quote Halperin as declaring that the Dionnes were steadily eating him into the red; the promoter had thought the living-expense clause in their contract would be an easy one because they were "simple country folk."

If the *Star*'s report of the Dionne stage tour had not been so detailed, if the emphasis had been different, if the tone had been more sympathetic, if the parents themselves had made friends with the reporters, then the events that followed might have taken a different course. But that was not the paper's style. Of their arrival in Detroit it wrote: "They received a civic welcome from the mayor, Frank Couzens, and then went on to the furious business of making money. . . ." Dafoe had been paid three thousand dollars and expenses for a forty-minute lecture in New York, and no one suggested that he was venal; but then Dafoe had been wise enough not to mention his fee, and besides, he had been in the *Star*'s camp ever since Fred Davis signed on as the Quints' personal photographer.

The news from Chicago produced a public outcry against the Dionnes, led by the premier himself, who called it "cheap American publicity."

"It's nauseating to Canadians, it's disgusting, it's revolting," Hepburn said of the parents' stage appearances. "It's a disgrace. It's cheap, and we are going to try to save the children from such humiliation if possible. I deprecate to the fullest extent the Dionnes going on the stage when in fact they have no value in such a position except as parents of the quintuplets. I will be very much disappointed if the American authorities allow such a thing. I know we wouldn't allow it here. It is a reflection on the Canadian people." Nobody questioned this remarkable statement or asked the premier how, in a free country, any government could prevent a man and his wife from appearing before an audience and saying hello and thank you.

"One thing you can be sure of," Hepburn added. "We will protect these children from anything like that. We'll protect them even if it takes an act of the legislature to do it."

Spear's lawsuit had fuelled Hepburn's rage; an American promoter was, in effect, daring to sue his government! In Hepburn's mind, and in the public's, all the old memories of the infamous Chicago contract came flooding back. *Chicago!* Its image in the Thirties was the worst in North America. If New York was paradise, Chicago was perdition. If New York was Fred and Ginger, Chicago was Cagney and Raft. It is possible that if the Dionnes had commenced their vaudeville tour in another city, say Indianapolis, there might have been less fuss. But Chicago – the home of Al Capone, site of the St. Valentine's Day massacre! The babies were to have been exhibited in Chicago; now the parents were being exhibited in Chicago. The two incidents became confused in the public's mind, and this confusion increased over the years so that after four decades, Senator David Croll would "remember" details from the early spring of 1935 and believe they took place in the early summer of 1934, "after Chicago," as he put it. For it was Croll, the youngest cabinet minister in Hepburn's government, the immigrant newsboy who had risen to become mayor of Windsor, who as minister of welfare was charged with drawing up the new legislation that would protect the quintuplets from the wiles of American promoters.

Dionne, meanwhile, was making statements to the American press that served to exacerbate the situation back home. "We have been treated worse than strangers," he declared in Indianapolis. "When outsiders come to the hospital they are shown the babies, but when we go there we are made to feel that we are intruding. The nurses won't even say good morning. After all, we're just the parents."

In Detroit, Dionne had engaged a thirty-three-year-old Windsor lawyer to intercede on his behalf in an effort to regain some parental control and also to get a share in the money accruing from testimonials and commercial contracts. The lawyer was Paul Martin, a committed and ambitious Liberal, then on the threshold of the career that would send him to the United Nations as secretary of state for external affairs and to the office of the Canadian high commissioner in London (but not, to his disappointment, to the prime minister's residence in Ottawa). Hepburn at first refused to see Martin and declared that "the babies aren't going to be put on exhibition to the detriment of their health if this Government has anything to say about it." It was a popular statement. The assumption that Dionne wanted control of his own children for no other reason than to exhibit them was not questioned.

Before the Dionnes returned home, the government gave notice that it would introduce a bill in the Ontario legislature extending the guardianship until the age of eighteen and putting the quintuplets under direct control of the government through David Croll's department. Croll was about to fill the same role as that of the Lord High Chancellor in *Iolanthe*.

The first guardianship, of two years' duration, had been designed to protect the quintuplets' health. The second, of seventeen years' duration, was to protect their finances. The old guardians were paid off: Alderson of the Red Cross received the handsome sum of $2,500; Ken Morrison, $1,000; Dafoe, $500; and Olivier Dionne, $400. The new board of guardians would consist of Croll, Dafoe, Oliva Dionne, and later Judge J.A. Valin of North Bay, a respected Ottawa-born French Canadian who spoke scholarly accentless English. A short, impeccable figure with a close-cropped moustache, Valin was, of course, a staunch Liberal. He was also approaching senility. Since Dionne intended to boycott all meetings of the guardianship and Croll, in Toronto, was not an active guardian, Dafoe was in effective control of the quintuplets. The main task of Croll's department would be to control the quintuplets' business affairs.

With Martin at his elbow, Dionne issued some conciliatory remarks about the Hepburn government and declared that he was willing to give a written guarantee that he would not exploit the children. Martin in a diplomatic letter to Croll, his Windsor colleague, agreed with most of the provisions of the new legislation but asked for more money for his client. Hepburn was not mollified. "Their only thought is to make money," he told the legislature. "And our only concern is that those five babies shall be reared as normal, healthy girls. This bill is going through, and we're going to break those contracts. . . . The Minister of Public Welfare is right when he says that these babies will not be sandwiched in between a sword-swallower and a bearded lady in some Chicago show."

The government continued to use the spectre of the Spear contract as its main ammunition in forcing the new law through the legislature. "These children are our own royal family," Croll declared. "To ballyhoo them under a tent would be an insult to the babies and parents." Spear, of course, had long since given up any idea of exhibiting the babies; what he wanted was damages under the clause in the contract that allowed him to exploit them photographically. But the public believed, in spite of Dionne's protests, that if the law did not go through, the quintuplets would be spirited away to a Chicago freak show.

Hepburn was determined to push the bill through as quickly as possible. It was actually Number 68 on the order paper, but it was the first to reach committee stage. The debate on March 15 was stormy; the Opposition did not object to the bill itself – only to the fact that the minister of welfare, David Croll, would be in charge of the financial arrangements. The Conservative members demanded that the quintuplets come under the Official Guardian of the province rather than a department of the government. Hepburn, his face red with anger, was having none of that: "In spite of everything which the Opposition says, this bill is going through the House today without another i dotted or another t crossed," he said. Before the final vote, the house was in an uproar. Charges of "liar" and "hypocrite" were levelled and withdrawn. One member offered to punch another in the nose. Hepburn's explanation for the quality of the debate was probably correct: the Conservatives were about to go into convention to choose a new leader, and every candidate wanted a chance to speak.

In the midst of all this hullabaloo, a new alarm was raised. Croll charged that an American newspaper syndicate was "trying to cause a turmoil." There was truth in this. Lillian Barker of the *New York Daily News*, a flamboyant Southerner, had arrived at the Dionnes' door and been admitted. She enjoyed an immense advantage over her colleagues in that she spoke excellent French. She swiftly made friends with Mrs. Dionne, whose biography she would later write, and almost immediately sewed up picture rights for the family in the farmhouse for her paper's syndicate. For several years she remained firmly in the Dionne camp. The *News* was just as shrill in its coverage of the long dispute over the custody of the quintuplets as its rivals in Dafoe's corner.

Miss Barker's presence certainly did not help the tensions rippling through the Dafoe Hospital. "There is a terrible undercurrent of everything hateful going on," Yvonne Leroux noted in her diary at the time. Whether or not Barker masterminded the next incident is not known, but it does bear the earmark of a facile journalistic mind. On March 18, the Dionne parents made the gesture of physically moving into the hospital. The press was alerted well in advance. "What a mess," Leroux wrote. "The Dionnes moved in today. He & She came over with trunks and walked in & sat down. They had a crowd of followers. Newspapermen, relatives & managers – the followers had to stay out. The Prov. police were down & talked to them and after a while they decided to go back home. The trouble is that all this emotional upset is a terrible strain on us & the babes sense it and become difficult to handle."

That was March 18. A few days before, David Meisner had been sentenced to fifteen years for his part in the kidnapping of John Labatt. On March 23 – just two days before the new guardianship act was signed by the lieutenant-governor – provincial police in Toronto were told by a Chicago informant that a plot was afoot by promoters to snatch the famous five and run them across the border out of provincial jurisdiction, either by plane or by car. "We are scared stiff," Yvonne Leroux wrote, "and go about praying. We have arranged a system whereby if I do get surprised during the night we will all be awakened and since everybody is on edge they all sleep lightly. I carry a large butcher's knife with me when I go down to the furnace or anywhere else where the bells aren't handy, as the staff consists of Mme. de Kiriline & Laurence, the cook, who sleep on the 1st floor – and Lise who sleeps in the basement & myself who does night duty."

The next day she noted: "The kidnap plot is verified and supposed to be serious. Will know for sure tomorrow. All through this the babies sleep quietly, play, and eat well and thank God don't realize as we do. The anxiety and suspense is making us nervous old hens. After the lights go out we go in & count the babies every fifteen minutes."

The following day a police guard was placed on the quintuplets, outside lights were installed, and a high wire fence was built to encircle the entire nursery compound. The quintuplets were now legally under the direct control of the Ontario government for a period of seventeen years and two months. Almost everybody felt that they were the luckiest babies alive. That was what every mother in those gloomy days wished for her children – that they would not have to endure the same uncertain future that was plaguing the adult generation. The sentiment was brought home forcefully that month. On March 16, a group of jobless took possession of the police station in New Toronto and announced to the chief of police that they were "laying their babies on his doorstep" because the municipality was refusing to issue relief vouchers.

The *New York Sun* put it all into an editorial, the day the bill became law:

> One thing only is sure. Of all the babies in the world, they are the only ones who need not worry about their future so far as it concerns material things. Emperors may abdicate, thrones may fall, dominions may secede, republics may crumble, but whoever and whatever exercises sovereignty will see to it that proper food, clothing and shelter are found for the Dionne quintuplets.

Of no scion of a royal house, of no pride of a millionaire's nursery, can the same be said.

Canadians breathed a sigh of relief. *Their* babies were safe. The enthusiasm of the public for the new law is reflected in a sampling of the premier's mail from that time.

From Wm. F. Sparing, Detroit: "The whole world thanks you for your most wholesome Christian interest in the Dionne quintuplets."

From J.F. Dostal, Colorado Springs: "The parents . . . do not possess the will power to resist the temptation of modern commercialization. . . ."

From Bill Fry of the Dunnville, Ontario, *Chronicle*: "The parents need guardians just as badly as do the Quints."

Dionne got similar letters ("If you had your way, the children would be dead") and so did Dafoe: "Your government must be the best in the world to take and keep these babies. The parents are most abominable, ungrateful, bad tempered and unworthy!" These might be considered the work of cranks were it not for the fact that the same general attitude was expressed by a large section of the press.

The popular assumption was that a generous government was laying out the taxpayers' money to support the quintuplets. The government, however, had no need and no intention of laying out a penny. The money would come from the quintuplets themselves. The fees for the guardians, the doctor, nurses, police guards, cooks and orderlies, together with the cost of running the hospital, the equipment and furniture, the telephone bills – even the public washrooms soon to be constructed for the comfort of the curious – all these expenses would be borne by the rapidly growing trust fund from commercial endorsements, photographs, and motion picture rights being negotiated by the department of the Honourable David Croll.

EIGHT:
The men behind Dafoe

On the first anniversary of the quintuplets' birth, May 28, 1935, the entire third floor of the Empire Hotel in North Bay was reserved for the news media. Canadian Press, Associated Press, United Press, Hearst, NEA Service, the CRBC, and all three U.S. radio networks were represented. According to Evelyn Seeley of the UP, the Dionne saga was "the greatest sob story any newspaper person ever covered." In spite of the chain-letter craze that had mesmerized the continent and disrupted postal services everywhere, mail and gifts poured in for the famous five. (Fred Allen in a letter to the U.S. postmaster general, James A. Farley, remarked that "the only five people in the world today who can start a chain letter and come out even are the Dionne quintuplets.") All the networks carried a special birthday broadcast during which Dafoe spoke and the quintuplets were heard to gurgle. The parents did not attend. "We don't consider it an honour to be invited by pure strangers to visit our own children," said Oliva Dionne. "We can't go to church because they are trying to steal our pictures for their own good and profit."

Government officials, Red Cross representatives, and the new board of guardians attended the birthday celebrations. Across the road, Dionne was building a new porch for his farmhouse. A showman offered to replace the house and pay him ten thousand dollars to exhibit the original home. Dionne turned him down. Croll also offered to build a new house and restock the farm. Dionne turned that down, too.

That night the press gave Dafoe a testimonial dinner. Every speaker stressed the manner in which the doctor had co-operated with the news media. NEA Service had arranged for a suitable number of telegrams from American celebrities – sixty in all – to be read aloud. Many of them helped promote the perennial jokes and catchphrases with which the stars of radio and screen were associated: *"Come up and see me some time"* – Mae West . . . *"Congratulations. Wanna buy a duck?"* – Joe Penner . . . *"I'm your greatest fan"* – Sally Rand . . . *"I have five girls myself. What I'm looking for is a doctor who will bring me boys"* – Eddie Cantor . . . *"Congratulations on your interesting chapter in the great novel called life"* – F. Scott Fitzgerald. The list that NEA selected to congratulate Dafoe gives a fair idea of Who was considered Who in the mid-Thirties: Harold Ickes and Frances Perkins of the Roosevelt cabinet, Oscar of the Waldorf, Paul Whiteman, Admiral Richard Byrd, William Green of the American Federation of Labor, Al Smith, Phil Baker, Al Jolson, Miriam Hopkins, Claudette Colbert, Joel McCrea, Carole Lombard, Ernst Lubitsch, Loretta Young, Fredric March, Ronald Colman, Marlene Diétrich, Gary Cooper, and Frank Black.

At the farmhouse, Elzire Dionne was recounting her life story to Lillian Barker. Leo Kervin announced that the book would embarrass the government but that "it may be possible to tone it down if an adjustment were to take place immediately." Croll was having none of that; the government, he said, had no intention of buying off the Dionnes. Kervin's days as Dionne's business agent were numbered. (Dionne had already fired Paul Martin, his lawyer.) A few months later Kervin broke with Dionne, charging that Dionne had fallen into the hands of "a group of chisellers."

Through all this squabbling, the five children slept and played peacefully. The nurses displayed them daily on the hospital porch, holding them up, one by one, for the crowds to see. If one was sick, the nurses held up the same baby twice; nobody could tell the difference.

They were unique – just how unique, the world was only beginning to learn. Almost all the quintuplets born in history have been fraternal, developed from two, three, four, or five eggs. The Dionne babies were developed from a single egg. Dr. Norma Ford of Toronto, the internationally known geneticist, studied all the fifty-three authenticated cases of quintuplets born over the previous three centuries and could find only two other instances of identical births. Fraternal quintuplets were to become more common following the development of the fertility drugs, but the world has yet to see another set of five identical babies. Such a birth has nothing to do with heredity or a family tendency toward multiple births (the Dionnes had no such history). It is entirely a matter of chance.

The Dionne quintuplets captured the world's record for group survivors. Until that time, the record had been held by one of five children born to a Lisbon mother in 1866; the child survived for fifty days. The Lyons quintuplets, born in Kentucky in 1896, also survived briefly; the youngest lived for four days, the eldest for fourteen.

The five Dionne babies were unique in other ways. They not only looked alike but they also shared some curious and rare characteristics: a fusion of the second and third toes, something that is found only once in a thousand cases, and an identical fold of skin at the outer corner of both eyelids, common to Mongolians but found in only a tiny percentage of Caucasians. All had asymmetrical faces, the mouth slanting down diagonally from left to right. The patterns of all ten palm prints were also highly unusual.

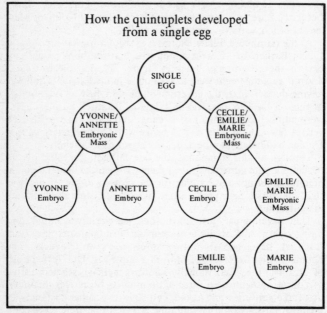

How the quintuplets developed
from a single egg

SINGLE EGG

YVONNE/ANNETTE Embryonic Mass

CECILE/EMILIE/MARIE Embryonic Mass

YVONNE Embryo

ANNETTE Embryo

CECILE Embryo

EMILIE/MARIE Embryonic Mass

EMILIE Embryo

MARIE Embryo

Each belonged to blood type "O"; all had the same eye pigmentation and pattern (medium brown, flecked and bordered with grey), the same dark curly brown lashes, the same light brown eyebrows, the identical shade of reddish brown hair, the same clear, rosy complexion.

The original egg had twinned within the mother and then each twin had twinned again, producing a set of embryo quadruplets. But one of these four eggs had twinned a second time, so that five embryos were produced.

The first twinning produced two embryonic masses: the Annette-Yvonne mass and the Cécile-Emilie-Marie mass. The second twinning produced separate embryos for Yvonne and Annette and also separated Cécile from the Emilie-Marie mass. The final division separated Emilie from Marie. It was also thought possible that a sixth embryo might have been formed because Dafoe reported that the mother had had pains at the beginning of her third month of pregnancy and had passed an egg-sized object, which could have been Cécile's twin.

The final split that produced Emilie and Marie gave as well a mirror set of twins. Emilie was left-handed, and her hair whorl ran clockwise. All the others were right-handed with counterclockwise whorls.

To a considerable extent, the social and physical characteristics of the quintuplets related to their embryonic development. Yvonne, the first born and the largest at birth, was to become leader of the five – the elder-sister figure, mature, stable, serene. Annette, who shared her embryonic sac, was socially aggressive, more rebellious and more assertive than the others. At the other end of the scale, little Marie, the last born, was the slowest to develop but also the most affectionate – the baby of the group. She and Emilie, the mirror twins, tended to play together. Cécile shared characteristics of both the original embryonic masses.

For example, it was not surprising, when the children at the age of four ran a play beauty parlour, that Yvonne was the manicurist and Marie her customer, Annette the hairdresser and Emilie her customer. In the same way, the champion skiers were Yvonne and Cécile, and both wanted to be leader among the skiers. Marie, the last out of bed each morning, depended on Emilie to wake her up and find her clothes for her. Yvonne liked to tell stories – usually tall ones; Emilie on the other hand liked to listen to them.

The quintuplets' upbringing was as unique as their prenatal existence. No other children in all history have had a remotely similar experience. After they were removed from the farmhouse, the five little girls lived in a hospital for nine years, cared for by a succession of white-clad nurses. Their parents and their brothers and sisters never slept under the same roof; they were more like visiting uncles, aunts, and cousins. For the first year of their lives – the most important in all child development – they were *never* out of sight of one another; they lived in one room, slept in one room, were fed and bathed together. Until a new playground was added to the hospital, they were almost like Siamese twins.

They existed in an adult environment. The only children they knew were each other. They were more than two years old before they were permitted a brief romp with their brothers, Ernest, aged ten, and Daniel, aged four. At that point, September 30, 1936, the two boys had not really laid eyes on their famous sisters for two years. For the first five years of their lives, except for one ten-minute ride around the grounds in their father's car, the quintuplets never left the hospital playground, not even to visit the house in which they were born. They were totally ignorant of the outside world and had no idea of the way other people lived. The only glimpse they had of a different existence was when they visited the hospital kitchen – an enormous treat for them. They were slow to learn bladder control because their five commodes were on the verandah; that excursion, too, was a delight to be savoured and stretched out. Within themselves they formed a tight little community. As far as they were concerned, life simply meant five people. They could not bear to be separated from each other. Thus they developed a peer relationship far earlier than most children, and the subtle differences between them became accentuated as the years went by.

Each quintuplet, for instance, adopted a favourite colour: mauve for Yvonne, green for Annette, blue for Cécile, rose for Emilie, and yellow for Marie. When the quintuplets were five and able to talk, Annette drew her sisters' attention to a particularly brilliant sunset and their nurse, Mollie O'Shaughnessy, recorded their comments:

> Annette said, "My, isn't Emilie lucky with her colour all over the sky, all red and pink." Then Yvonne spoke up and said, "Well, Annette is lucky, too, because her colour is in all the trees and all over the ground in the summer and on some of the trees in winter." Then Marie said: "Well, I am not jealous because my colour is in the sun and the moon." Cécile piped up and said, "Well, my colour is in the sky all day long, except when it rains." Then Yvonne spoke again and said she guessed her colour was a rather hard colour to find, but it was in the little flowers that had gone to sleep for the winter.

Dafoe was to write in a medical journal that after the first year the care of the five babies was no different from that given any well-cared-for child. If that were true, one might well ask: Why the hospital? Why the isolation? Actually, no children in the first nine years of their lives were cared for in quite the same protective way as the Dionne quintuplets.

Dafoe was fanatical about germs. When the quintuplets were

two years old, the Key quadruplets from Texas came to visit them. The doctor barred these guests from the nursery for fear the Quints might catch something. Pets were also taboo. Other toddlers might cuddle kittens and puppies, but not these five. The rules laid down for the Twentieth Century-Fox crew making a feature movie in August, 1936, were equally strict: nobody was admitted to the porch without special permission; no one could handle the babies except Dafoe and the nurses on duty; everybody admitted near the babies must spray nose and throat; anyone with a cold was banned; anybody entering the nursery must wear a white robe, face mask, and soft-soled shoes. Everything possible was done to prevent the quintuplets from suffering the usual childhood diseases. When the elder Dionne children came down with measles, Dafoe barred Oliva Dionne from the nursery; in a much-publicized caper, Dionne crawled through a drainpipe to get to the hospital to see his children. Not everybody agreed, however, with Dafoe's decree regarding measles, mumps, and chicken pox. A good many paediatricians were coming to the conclusion that children gain immunity from many diseases by mingling with those who have already had them.

But was this really Allan Roy Dafoe, the country doctor who, in the old days, had to be persuaded by Louise de Kiriline to wash his hands before treating a patient? The instructions may have been Dafoe's, but the iron hand behind them was that of Dr. Alan Brown, the tyrant of the Hospital for Sick Children in Toronto, a baby doctor with a towering international reputation. It was said of Brown that he had greater clinical ability than any other man on the continent, and his management of the great hospital tended to prove the assertion. He terrified almost everybody. The official history of his own hospital does not spare him: "A short, pudgy, pugnacious, swaggering doctor who . . . never had any doubt in the world but that in all things he was dead right."

Brown's performance at the Sick Children's Hospital, after a long apprenticeship in New York, Munich, Berlin, and Vienna, was a Toronto legend. Within a year he had cut the infant death rate in half. He was a brilliant diagnostician. It was claimed that he could tell if a one-year-old had been a premature baby. He was also known for some strongly held prejudices. He did not believe that anyone needed tonsils. A GP once asked him: "At what age do you take tonsils out?"; to which Brown replied: "Not before the umbilical cord is cut."

He bullied the middle-class mothers who brought their babies to him, for he was strict about diet and feeding; but they kept coming back. He had no small talk; it was the babies he cared about, not the parents. He could properly take credit for the early pasteurization of milk in Ontario. But Brown thought cow's milk overrated. "It's for calves," he used to say. Mother's milk was what was needed.

To the public, Brown was best known for heading the medical team that created two popular commercial products: a nutritious biscuit for children baked under conditions that preserved its vitamin content and later manufactured as McCormick's Sunwheat Biscuit; and, in 1932, the precooked cereal known to the continent as Pablum. Thanks to Brown and his team, the Sick Children's Hospital collected more than a million dollars in licence fees from the international sales of the two products.

This, then, was the man whom Dafoe consulted regularly and who, more than anybody else, was responsible for the quintuplets' physical care. It was certainly Brown who allowed the children no candy or ice cream, who insisted on a diet so strict that it could not be broken even for a turkey dinner on Christmas Day, who watched the weight charts with a hawk's eye, checked the milk formulae, ordered their tonsils out, and was ready at any moment to make a rush trip to Callander, as he did at three o'clock on the morning of April 23, 1935, when Dafoe called his brother Will in Toronto to report that Marie was ill and that her ears were troubling her. The two Toronto doctors lost no time in reaching the hospital to examine the smallest of the quintuplets. They reported that nothing was seriously wrong, but Oliva Dionne refused to believe Brown's diagnosis, as he would refuse to accept all future medical verdicts regarding the children. "I don't believe any man until I see him," he said. He insisted that two doctors of *his* choice from North Bay also examine Marie. Dr. G. W. Smith and Dr. J. E. I. Joyal dutifully arrived and confirmed Brown's assessment.

Brown had little patience with most parents; with the Dionnes he must have had even less. Mrs. Dionne's approach to child rearing had little in common with his. She believed in plump babies, and she fed her other children on thick soups, rice, potatoes, quantities of well-cooked vegetables, fresh bread, and unpasteurized cow's milk. She was horrified at the diet Brown had prescribed for the quintuplets. In April 1935, she publicly charged that the children were not as robust as they ought to be and blamed it on "scientific feeding." She said she wanted to see the girls get more substantial food and more liberal helpings at mealtimes. She claimed they were being forced to eat a "greenish mush" (which was actually mashed fresh fruit with oatmeal) that was leaving them hungry. She prescribed soup made from fresh meat, mashed potatoes covered with gravy, carrots, rice, and all the milk they wanted. And she couldn't understand why they were given only a single slice of bread for lunch. One can guess Brown's reaction. Dafoe, in a public statement, explained that the quintuplets' weight was being kept at a low level to increase their resistance to disease.

The turnover of nurses at the hospital began on June 1, 1935, when Louise de Kiriline left, to be replaced by Cécile Lamoureux. Over the next six years the quintuplets would have thirteen more surrogate mothers, all of them clad in white and all of them used to working with sick patients in hospitals rather than with healthy children in a nursery. Nurses are used to doing everything for their charges, from feeding them to washing them. Though they tried not to and were warned not to, the consensus is that they did far too much for the Dionne babies.

De Kiriline's departure was touched off by a row with Mrs. Dionne. The two parents were entertaining cousins from Montreal and had decided, after Sunday dinner, to take them across the road to look at the quintuplets, who were asleep on the porch in their perambulators. De Kiriline appeared on the porch, stood at the head of the short flight of steps leading to the walk, and, as the party approached, cried, "Don't you come up these steps!" Then, it was reported, she slammed the door in their faces. The story made headlines; the following week, de Kiriline quit.

"Miss Lamoureux has taken over," Yvonne Leroux noted in her diary. "Let us leave it at that. She is very excitable and so excites the babies very easily." Miss Lamoureux lasted a little more than six months.

The most phlegmatic of nurses would have been hard put to endure a prolonged tour of duty at the Dafoe Hospital. The isolation of the building, the growing tension between two opposing cliques, and above all the terrible fear that something might happen to one of the quintuplets contributed to an anxiety that drove some to the edge of a breakdown.

It was difficult not to take sides in the growing controversy. Although the nurses tried to remain impartial, and a few succeeded in gaining the confidence of both the parents and the doctor, most of them ended up in one camp or the other. This was less Dafoe's doing than it was the Dionnes'. Oliva Dionne had embarked on a campaign to have his children returned to him, and he meant to fight with every psychological weapon at his disposal. His initial tactic was obstruction. Although he refused to attend any of the meetings of the guardians, he made it his business to raise an outcry when anything, no matter how slight, seemed to be affecting the welfare of the quintuplets. He was constantly demanding additional medical examinations, a change of nurses, more precautions. In addition, he was writing highly publicized letters to everybody from the Pope to King Edward VIII, demanding that his children be returned to him. The effect of his constant surveillance on the nursing staff was the creation of additional tensions.

Leroux wrote in her diary on April 28, 1935: "Will this foolish turmoil never stop? The parents are suspicious of us and in general everybody seems upset." Another entry, more than a year later, speaks for itself. "July 25, 1936: Mr. & Mrs. Dionne were over. Cécile fell & hurt her eye. Parents perturbed but are seeing that even if parents are there children hurt themselves anyway. It's the first time Mrs. D. has been over since May 29. . . ."

For the nursing staff, and later for the teaching staff, the hospital came close to being a prison. The single phone was not connected with the outside world but only with Dr. Dafoe's office in Callander. Dafoe could take and relay occasional messages to the nurses; they could not phone out. Boyfriends had difficulty reaching them. Only Yvonne Leroux had no problem in this regard: Fred Davis became her steady companion and later her husband.

There was a feeling of claustrophobia brought on by the fact that everybody who worked at the hospital was locked in. A policeman unlocked the doors and a guard unlocked the gate in the high wire fence for those who wanted to leave the premises. For the ones without cars – and scarcely anybody had a car – the isolation was most pronounced because the only bus service to Callander was the one that arrived twice a day for the showings of the children. Nor were the nurses encouraged to walk out or to mingle with the community, as Cécile Michaud discovered.

We had to be careful who we talked to and where we were seen. We never did frequent a beverage room, because we could have been publicly accused of being seen inebriated some place, which no doubt we wouldn't have been. We avoided going to any of those places.

We had to be cautious who we spoke to. If we went out through those crowds, if anyone talked to you, you just ignored them. They'd question you about the Quints and quote you, and it would get to the newspapers. We had to watch that all the time.

When we went out of the grounds, our name was put down and the time we left the grounds. And when we came back the time was logged by the guards. And they'd put down any visitors to your residence: the time they came, the time they left, and how many and who they were. After two years, I'd had it. We were under constant pressure from the family, the board of governors, the public – everybody. So

Dr. Dafoe told me, I know you've been wanting to leave; I think what's going on with the parents, they're going to try and make it tougher for you, just like they did with the other nurses. So I gave a month's notice.

The parents, they had a resentment toward the nurses, which was a normal thing, I guess. They accused us of taking the children's affections from them because we were with them constantly. We didn't interfere when the parents came around, but even though we didn't, they'd run to us normally. We were with them, took care of them, bathed them, fed them. We were constantly with them; and you couldn't help but love them, they were so affectionate. We'd put them in bed at night, and they'd grab you around the neck and kiss you. At times we had to be a little severe: they'd climb out of their cribs and get into each other's cribs – well, just like normal children.

I remember the first afternoon when I came. They were just ready to eat in their dining room. We had to sit down at those little tables. They were all looking at me in awe because I was still dressed in street clothes. They told them that I was going to be living with them. You could see the twinkle in their eyes! I was just enthralled with them. They were so much alike. I thought, My goodness, it isn't possible that I see them in person – those five girls! They were just beautiful. But then they were into their tricks right next morning. Ooh, they were enjoying it! They made right up to me that day; they didn't show any strain. You know how babies get shy – they won't come near? Well, they made right up to me. And that first night when they were put to bed and I was in my street clothes, I went along with the other nurse, Miss O'Shaughnessy, and said good-night to them, and they grabbed me round the neck and kissed me, just like they did her. It was amazing. I thought, I've been accepted so far by the girls, and that's all I need because they're the ones I'm gonna be concerned with. I thought, I'll stay for the summer. And the longer I stayed, the better I liked it. I enjoyed it. So I stayed two years.

It did something to me when I left because I loved those little girls. I hated to leave them. I didn't tell them I was leaving them, either, because one nurse, Louise Corriveau, when she left there was an awful reaction. They cried for days. That's why I didn't tell them. They thought I was coming back. It's just as well I did leave because it would have been another shemozzle, like they had with Mme de Kiriline.

Leave-taking was just as hard on the nurses as it was on the little girls. When Yvonne Leroux left in December 1936, she could hardly bear it; the quintuplets, whom she had nursed and mothered since the first day, were like her own children. That, in fact, was why she decided to leave: she was becoming too attached to the babies. When she returned for a visit some months later they greeted her cheerfully, but on a second visit a short time after that, she found that they had almost forgotten her; and that, too, was almost too much to bear. She never went back to the Dafoe Hospital.

In the summer of 1936, after the horseshoe-shaped playground with its observation gallery was opened, the visiting public could enjoy the spectacle that charmed the nurses. The play area was designed in consultation with Dr. William Blatz, the innovative and controversial director of the Institute of Child Study at the University of Toronto – a pioneer in the new science of child guidance. To Blatz, the quintuplets, landing virtually on his doorstep, must have seemed sent from Heaven especially for his benefit. No social scientist had ever been faced with such a unique and intriguing challenge. At his famous nursery school, St. George's, the first in Canada and one of the first on the continent, he was limited to the study of children of upper-middle-class professional and academic families that were advanced enough, or eccentric enough, to show an interest in the education of pre-school children. But here he had children who sprang from a totally different background; and not only that: there were five of them, all alike. Moreover, they were confined in a controlled environment, twenty-four hours a day, away from their parents. For Blatz's purposes, the conditions were close to being perfect. It is perhaps significant that in Blatz's popular version of the results of his studies, *The Five Sisters*, there are, in all those 205 pages, only four passing references to the parents and siblings.

Blatz moved in aggressively in April, 1935, immediately after the new guardianship was established. He had Dafoe's blessing – the doctor's "Sure, why not?" attitude extended to innovative behavioural techniques as much as it did to nightclubs, airplanes, and unorthodox surgery – but not Brown's. In the words of one of Brown's colleagues, "Blatz really took over from Brown, pushing him out of the picture." The two brilliant but strong-willed scientists were natural antagonists. Brown was interested in the physical welfare of the quintuplets, Blatz in their social welfare. Brown used to grumble about Blatz's "damn foolishness" and was irked because Blatz, who did not work under him, never asked his permission to perform tests or make observations. As these increased, Blatz more than Brown was seen to be the man in charge.

"To suggest that Dr. Blatz was a controversial figure is to be guilty of understatement," the Senate of the University of Toronto once declared in a jocular accolade. It went on to call him a

118

"general all-round disturber of the intellectual peace." That he most certainly was. Most people considered his doctrines dangerous and unworkable, and cited his own family as evidence. In the early Thirties, persistent rumours circulated about "the four bad Blatz boys," who were said to be holy terrors. But there *were* no bad Blatz boys. Blatz had no sons, only a daughter.

His views, which seem slightly old-fashioned today, were thought to be radical by all but an academic minority. Almost everything he advocated ran counter to the socially accepted methods of child training. He believed in discipline but was opposed to hitting, frightening, bribing, coaxing, or lying to small children. Long before Dr. Brock Chisholm made his controversial statements about the Christmas myth in the mid-forties, Blatz was telling his charges – including the Quints – that Santa Claus was a pleasant fiction. In 1932 he debated in *Maclean's* magazine the question "To Spank or Not to Spank." Blatz, of course, was against spanking. It says something about social attitudes that his opponent was a judge of the Court of Family Relations. Blatz was also opposed to classroom competition, report cards, penny banks, and the reward and punishment system. What he did advocate was a strict minute-by-minute routine, inflexible and unchanging, in order to give young children a sense of security.

In the early Thirties, the whole nursery school concept was foreign to most Canadians. The idea of removing young children from their parents during daytime hours ran counter to prevailing attitudes; to many it meant the end of the sanctity of the home. Some, in fact, believed it to be a form of child neglect. Today, the school that was once considered dangerously unrestrained is thought of as overstrict by the advocates of a more permissive society.

In place of corporal discipline, Blatz believed in guidance. The child was to be nudged "gradually toward successful control by the simple device of making little of his outbursts and, when he was ready, recalling his efforts to the situation at hand." The real secret of discipline, Blatz believed, was "to *expect* a child to fit into a routine rather than to worry about how to make him do it." Children who acted in a socially unacceptable manner – who were too boisterous at meal times, for instance – were separated from their fellows until they calmed down. Blatz had an isolation room built into the quintuplets' nursery: "If, during play, the child was boisterous, she was removed to the isolation room where she could be as boisterous as she liked; but since the 'over-social excitement' (as boisterousness is sometimes called) was largely to attract social attention, it lost its point when she indulged in it alone."

The isolation room was as much a part of the quintuplets' lives as the farmhouse kitchen was for their brothers and sisters across the road. Mollie O'Shaughnessy once heard Emilie in the bathtub, talking to a cake of soap : "Soap – where are you gone? Now soap, you don't want to listen to Emilie. Very well, when I find you I am going to put you in the little room to play by yourself. That's not very nice, is it?" And, on another occasion, when Emilie heard frogs outside, croaking in the night, she asked her nurse: "Why don't you put them in the little room for talking in their beds?"

Blatz planned the quintuplets' routine on an almost minute-to-minute basis. It did not vary from the moment they rose ("the blinds are raised at 6:30 and on getting up the children go directly to the toilet, are washed, assisted to dress and have their hair done") to the moment they retired at 6:30 ("Each child says good-night to her sisters and the staff and proceeds to bed . . . "). Blatz divided the quintuplets' day into twenty-seven segments, listing such activities as "drink of water" at 8:45 a.m., "putting away toys" at 10:45, "relaxation routine" at 11:30, and "directed play" at 4:30.

To enforce this system he had a team of teachers (one of whom would become his second wife) working with the quintuplets. Wherever possible, the nurses – Mollie O'Shaughnessy was one – were sent to St. George's school for several weeks of training before coming to Callander.

Oh, yes, I went down and took a course there. I thought perhaps Dr. Blatz was a little severe. I don't think he wanted you to show too much love toward the children. I don't know why he thought that; he didn't like to emote too much himself. Suppose, for instance, one of them wakened up through the night with a nightmare: he didn't want you to make too much of it. But, of course, being human and so forth, you told them what it was, and you explained it to them and took them into bed with you until they calmed down; and then you took them back to their own bed and told them everything was fine. . . .

The theories of child rearing developed by Dr. John Bowlby, the child-training prophet of his day, and published by the World Health Organization in 1951 were, of course, unknown in the days when the quintuplets were young. Bowlby was to write: "What is believed essential for mental health is that an infant and young child should experience a warm, intimate and continuous relationship with his mother (or permanent mother substitute – one person who steadily mothers him) in which both find satisfaction and enjoyment." Bowlby argued that even bad parents do a lot for their children and that "young children thrive better in bad homes than in good institutions." Twenty years later Bowlby's theories in their turn came under critical analysis by those who had studied the rearing of small children by the multiple parents of the Israeli *kibbutzim*. Blatz was simply doing his best for the Dionne babies according to the most up-to-date research available at the time, and much of what he did had the advantage of sound common sense. For instance, it was the job of his deputy, Dorothy Millichamp, to try to get the nurses to enjoy helping the children learn to do things for themselves instead of acting as handmaidens or ladies-in-waiting to royal infants. This was not always easy or possible.

Of course, it was necessary to have nurses at the beginning rather than teachers, and I expect Dr. Dafoe was more comfortable with them. It was set up as a hospital in the beginning for the care of very frail babies, and the atmosphere tended to remain "hospital." The nurses didn't always understand. They are the hardest students to take into pre-school education, you know. Their training is the opposite – their goals, their philosophy, their values. Nurses, you see, are used to taking care of sick children. It was always hard. For instance, the Blatz system does not encourage or even allow for any form of competition; but the nurses would, on occasion, use competitive discipline: Yvonne can do it, why can't you? And they were very anxious that the babies eat, because you see the weight charts were being published in the newspapers, so that to lose a meal was quite serious from the nurses' point of view. I'd go away and arrive back and find the babies flipping their bacon up to the ceiling and just having a whale of a time, but not eating. Sliding out of their chairs and so on. We'd have to begin all over again with a program that would get the children back on the track, which meant small servings and not appearing to care whether they ate or not. And then they would eat. But they'd tend to pile it on the plates and try to push it into the children; and, of course, they got all the normal reactions from over-anxiety.

The babies could be very frustrating; when one screamed, they all screamed. They really were, I guess, spoilt more than they were disciplined. The whole lot of them would take their kiddie-cars and run them into the wall and scream until somebody turned them around. One day, I remember, I decided to do something about this: I sat down in the playroom with a book and pretended to read. They all ran into the wall and screamed. I just sat and sat until they gave up. They'd decided it wasn't worth it. I remember looking at my book afterwards and it was upside down.

The nurses used to sing to the children. Marie got to the point where she would scream if they stopped so they had to keep on singing. Things like that, you see, build up so easily if the children are learning. They learn that sort of thing as well as any other.

I remember Cécile used to suck her thumb. One day Dr. Dafoe, as he passed her, tapped her hand. For the next two weeks the whole five children sucked their thumbs. It just made them conscious – they all started thinking about their thumbs. And it was just a man's act as he went by.

In addition to prescribing and supervising a routine for the babies, Blatz had the nurses make careful minute-by-minute behavioural observations. For example, they checked every emotional upset between the twenty-second and thirty-eighth months of the babies' lives, listing and analysing a total of 1,434, of which 1,301 were defined as "anger" and 133 as "fear." Marie and Annette showed anger more often than the other three; Emilie was least prone to emotion. Fear responses were about the same for all except Marie, who manifested fear more frequently than the others. Social success, social aggressiveness, self-control, non-compliance, rebelliousness, affection – all of these were noted, graded, and reduced to graphs and charts. Yvonne, the first baby born, ranked first throughout the entire testing period. Emilie and Marie, the two smallest, were consistently fourth and fifth. Annette and Cécile interchanged between second and third.

Blatz also recorded the quintuplets' language peculiarities. The first words of the average child, he noted, are "mama, dada, tata, bye-bye and mum," these being the easiest sounds to pronounce. The quintuplets' first words were "mamma, papa, tantan, dotteur and tittat." Blatz wrote that the five children were probably "the first on record who have included 'doctor' in their first vocabulary." It was not surprising. Nurses and teachers came and went. The visits of the parents and siblings were sporadic. The only regular daily visitor to the nursery was Allan Roy Dafoe.

The quintuplets were late in talking. Premature babies generally are, but in this case there was a second reason. The five little girls were able to communicate with one another without speech – in Blatz's words, "as a flock of birds may do" – by employing a multitude of gestures and cries that amounted to a private language. At three, their spoken vocabulary was no greater than that of the average two-year-old. But they understood each other and they knew their names. Sometimes when even their own father confused them, the child involved would thump her chest, shake her head in exasperation, and point to the proper sister. On occasion, all would point. It was difficult even for the teachers to tell them apart. As one remarked, "You were always in the position of not knowing if you'd taken the same one to the toilet five times or if you'd taken them once each."

The Blatz program for the quintuplets, which was hotly criticized by the Dionne camp, has always been defended by his followers. Pre-school education is now recognized as a way to counter cultural deprivation and institutionalism. Without Blatz, the hospital would probably have been more like an institution than it was, for the idea of children actually playing inside a hospital was then quite new. Dorothy Millichamp believes neither the minds nor the personalities of the quintuplets would have been fully developed if Blatz had not intervened. Like almost everybody else involved with the Dionne quintuplets – doctors, nurses, politicians and public servants, parents and neighbours – Blatz acted from sincere motives. Everybody tried to do his best for the babies according to his lights, given the astonishing conditions of their birth, the public's intense interest, the temper of the times, and the knowledge then available.

The basis of the Blatz system was the idea that children should be encouraged to fit happily into the adult society for which they were destined, adapting to the world as it was and not as it ought to be. But the adult world that Blatz contemplated for the quintuplets was not the old Norman world of the Corbeil farming community. If Blatz's method of child rearing was considered advanced for its time, it was certainly light-years away from that common to the Roman Catholic community of which Oliva and Elzire Dionne had always been a part. What would happen if, suddenly, the quintuplets were removed from Blatz's control and given a traditional rural Catholic upbringing?

"It would be a tragic circumstance if an attempt were made to incorporate into their training a rigid discipline of old-fashioned obedience and conformity," Blatz wrote of the quintuplets. He was, perhaps unconsciously, referring to the way in which the children of Corbeil were raised. His own attitude was experimental and critical, but the church to which the Dionnes belonged was not noted for its acceptance of change or experiment. The end product of the Blatz method, ideally, was the independent child – outgoing, exploring, questioning. The Corbeil concept was that children should be docile, compliant, and obedient to parents, church, and society. To Blatz, human nature was malleable; it could be moulded by good or bad influences. The Catholics of Corbeil believed in redemption, certainly, but they also believed in original sin; human nature was essentially bad. Thus children needed to be trained through punishment, fear, and repression.

The Dionne quintuplets were brought up very much as royal children are, and the consensus in 1936 was that they would continue as royal children for the rest of their lives. Although Dafoe and the government paid lip service to the idea that they would at some future date be reunited with their family, the date was always so vague that it is hard to believe it was realistically contemplated. Blatz himself wrote, with studied imprecision, that "it has always been in the minds of the guardians that some day there will be a closer relationship with the family." But he added, prophetically, "To reconcile such a situation will require the best of judgment and the happiest of arrangements."

The quintuplets received none of the practical training that was the birthright of every child born in Corbeil. Although Fred Davis was continually photographing them with toy brooms and dustpans, they were never taught the rudiments of housekeeping. Their siblings practically lived in the Dionne kitchen, but the quintuplets at the age of nine could not even boil water. They knew nothing about sewing, knitting, or mending clothes. Shopping was as much a mystery to them as astronomy. They had never handled money and had no knowledge of prices or costs, for they had never been in a store. Royal children can overcome such handicaps because they remain royal, surrounded by servants and equerries who handle mundane matters. But how long could the Quints remain in seclusion? It clearly did not occur to anybody involved in their welfare that whether they were reunited with their family or not, the day might come when they would need to go out into the world, unprotected and unescorted.

Equally serious was their total lack of experience in social relationships. No effort was made to introduce the quintuplets to other children or to adults who were neither nurses nor teachers. In fact, such contact was discouraged, partly, at least, because of the continual fear of "germs," and partly, one suspects, because of an unvoiced belief that the quintuplets were too special to be exposed to coarsening contact with mere mortals.

Blatz's own program for the quintuplets was to ease their isolation gradually after the age of five, when an "ideal modern school" would be set up in Callander for the Quints, their siblings, and other local children. At that time, too, they were to be allowed to choose clothes that were not necessarily identical down to the last hair ribbon. Until that time he was satisfied to go along with the prevailing rule that all five must be dressed alike because, in his assistant's words, "the public demanded it."

It is easy with hindsight to wonder why the public's wishes should have mattered at all, but it is not so easy to fathom the intensity with which the average man and woman identified with the quintuplets. The proprietary interest was fierce; these were *their* children. It was, as Dorothy Millichamp recalls it, "an unbelievable psychological phenomenon. The mail was extraordinary. 'What are you doing to *my* babies?' people would write. They had a really possessive feeling towards the children. It was frightening. If the Quints lost an ounce of weight the letters would come flooding in: 'What have you done?'"

The public demanded that the identical five be dressed in identical fashion. That was the way all twins were dressed in the Thirties; only a handful of behavioural scientists were beginning to suggest that it might be better if they were allowed to express more individuality. One of these was Dr. Alfred Adler of Vienna, the founder of the school of "individual" psychology. No more impressive figure existed in the field. Adler, who had made the terms "inferiority complex" and "masculine protest" part of the jargon of the times, was usually mentioned second in the great triumvirate of Freud, Adler, and Jung. In March, 1936, he published an article about the quintuplets in *Cosmopolitan* magazine that brought down upon him a tornado of protest but that now seems remarkably prescient:

Treating the quintuplets alike in every respect induces a uniformity which is not conducive to the development of the individual. It would be wise to dress the five children in different colors, give them different toys and even different food. They should find playmates outside; they should have frequent contacts with their brothers and elder sisters, and as little fuss as possible should be made about the fact that they are quintuplets. Every manifestation of their nascent individuality should be encouraged. This may be enough for the present; the future requires more drastic changes.

Psychologically, the separation from their family is not an asset for the quintuplets. Papa and Mama Dionne and the five other children, three girls and two boys, live across the street from the nursery built to harbor the quintet. The parents may visit and see the quintuplets every day, but their influence and their privileges are restricted. . . . Some of the crumbs from the board of the quintuplets fall upon the parental table. Nevertheless, the difference in status between the quintuplets and their family tends to create psychic tensions. The Dionnes are poor relations of the rich quintuplets. The conflict between parental authority and the authority of the guardians may also induce emotional disturbances at some future time.

The quintuplets live like the inmates of a model orphanage, and a certain emotional starvation is inseparable from institutional life. There are other drawbacks. Family life fosters various mental faculties. It develops, for instance, the centres governing speech. Conversation is more restricted in an asylum than in a family. As a result many children brought up in orphan asylums suffer from inadequate vocabularies. This difficulty may be overcome in the case of the quintuplets but it should not be ignored.

Life in a glass house is not conducive to normal human development. Five little guppies living in a fish bowl may not be distracted by constant exposure. But babies are not fishes. Children accustomed to being exhibited are never happy unless they elicit attention. . . . There is danger ahead. It may be conducive to their well-being to bring up each separately in some trustworthy family. This is the procedure advocated by enlightened sociologists in the education of orphans. Separated from one another, living, so to speak, *incognito*, Yvonne, Annette, Cécile, Emilie, and Marie could approach their problem normally and solve it effectively. The interests of science could still be served by watching their growth and development unobtrusively.

This was the advice later to be followed by Franco Diligenti, a well-to-do Argentine textile manufacturer, who became, in July of 1943, the father of fraternal quintuplets. But the public was outraged by Adler's article. The press of Canada made slighting references to his phrase about "guppies in a bowl." Adler, it was suggested, had denigrated the entire nation. Dafoe revealed that the famous psychologist had visited the hospital in his absence, armed with a letter from the Ontario Department of Education, but had been refused admission. The result, said Dafoe, was that "he was sore when he found the rules were real rules and he couldn't break them no matter who he was."

Adler was startled by the reaction and bedevilled by the controversy. "In city after city," it was reported, "people jump at him from doorways, wait for him in hotel lobbies and buttonhole him at dinners asking: 'Do you really think that the quintuplets ought to be separated?'"

Such a course was not conceivable in the spring of 1936. Apart from everything else, the quintuplets were an incredible commercial success. They had transformed the town of Callander, given a boost to North Bay and a transfusion to the Ontario tourist industry. They had acted as salesgirls for scores of domestic products, starred in a motion picture (with two more in the planning stage), buttressed the fortunes of a photo syndicate, and brightened the lives of hundreds of thousands. They were more than five toddlers; they had become a national treasure. Separate them? Doom them to obscurity? It would have been easier to halt the relentless flow of Niagara.

NINE:
"A little filthy lucre..."

By May of 1936, the Dionne quintuplets' bank account had reached a quarter of a million dollars. A year later it had risen to six hundred thousand dollars. By the end of the decade it amounted to just under one million dollars. This was net profit after all expenses were paid: hospital upkeep, staff salaries, nursing care, police protection, the shepherding of visitors, new construction – a total of more than sixty thousand dollars a year.

It is important in this context to review the value of a dollar in the decade of the Depression. In 1934, one Canadian dollar would buy almost as much as five dollars in 1977. That is the conservative estimate of federal statisticians. But for many people a dollar was worth a good deal more. Wages might be low, but so were taxes. Those with jobs took almost all of their pay home.

A whole range of popular items was much cheaper than the five-to-one ratio suggests. Admission to a motion picture in a Famous Players theatre in 1977 had risen to $3.75. In Toronto in the mid-Thirties it varied from twenty cents to fifty cents. Most matinees cost a quarter or less. Children paid as little as a nickel and in the third-run houses on Saturday morning saw two features, a serial, a newsreel, and a cartoon and sometimes got a free lollipop. *Maclean's* magazine, which now sells for seventy-five cents, was also a nickel; so were the *Saturday Evening Post*, *Liberty*, and *Collier's*. *Time* and *News-Week* sold at a tenth of their 1977 price.

Do the statisticians take into account that you also got more for your money in those days? Chocolate bars sold for a fifth or less of their 1977 price, but they were also much larger. When the double-dip ice cream cone made its appearance, the price remained at five cents; nor did it rise when the *triple* dip was invented. Milk shakes cost a dime but filled three glasses and sometimes three and a half. Winola, at a nickel, offered twelve ounces of counterfeit Coke instead of the customary six.

Food dollars, in many cases, stretched farther than the five-to-one ratio. Coffee was thirty-five cents a pound. You could buy a live lobster for twenty cents. Sirloin steak sold for as low as nineteen cents a pound, a prime rib roast for seventeen cents, a shoulder roast for as low as seven cents, and butchers invariably threw in odd bones and bits of shank "for the dog." Three-room apartments in a respectable district in Toronto rented for twenty dollars a month. Eight-room houses were advertised for as low as twenty-five dollars a month. On the other side of the country, in Oak Bay, a fashionable suburb of Victoria, British Columbia, you could buy a six-room frame house on two lots for three thousand dollars. In 1936, the Quaker Oats company ran a contest in which entrants were asked to write a one-hundred-word essay on the subject "Which of the Dionne Quins Would I Adopt?" The prize was a "wonderfully romantic" brand-new six-room "Dream Home" designed by a leading architect and featured in *Architectural Forum* magazine. It could be built, the ads said, for eight thousand dollars.

Then there were the bonuses. Sweet Caporal cigarettes contained "poker hands," which could be exchanged for premiums. Everybody who lived through the era remembers the prizes in the boxes of Cracker Jack and the free china at the movie theatres. It was the era of the Free Sample. To this day there are people who treasure the little aluminum porridge dish featuring the Dionne quintuplets that one cereal company distributed with every box of rolled oats.

For anybody with a reasonable job, then, life in the Depression was not necessarily gloomy. The trouble was that so few had reasonable jobs. On the production line the average annual wage was less than a thousand dollars a year. Unskilled labourers made about half that. The Royal Commission on Price Spreads, which began its hearings the day after the quintuplets were born, uncovered a series of horror stories, some of them involving Eaton's department store, which many considered to be one of the more enlightened mercantile enterprises in the country. In 1933, a woman working for Eaton's was expected to do enough piecework to take home $12.50 for a forty-hour week; but to achieve that was a near impossibility. Mrs. Annie Wells found that it took her four to five hours, working at top speed, to produce a dozen voile dresses. For that she was paid $1.15, or nine and a half cents a dress; they were sold for $1.59 apiece.

Even in the union shops in Toronto, male garment workers

made as little as ten dollars a week, and in the non-union shops as little as six, if they could work full time. The non-union hourly rate was as low as fifteen cents. In Montreal it went as low as ten cents for men and eight cents for women. In rural shops, women earned as little as four cents an hour. For some people, then, a dollar could mean a day's wages or even two or three days' wages.

It is no wonder that money became an obsession. People sang about it – hopefully: *Oh, Baby, what I couldn't do-oo-oo/With plenty of money and you-oo-oo;* wistfully: *We're in the money!/We're in the money!*; and sometimes with false scorn: *I'm no millionaire/But I'm not the type to care,/ Cause I've got a pocketful of dreams.* History's most successful commercial game, Monopoly, sprang from a period when people got a thrill out of playing millionaire, even though the money was all play. Politicians sprang to prominence because they promised hard cash to the voters. Howard Scott, the founder of Technocracy, got an immense following when he proposed a scheme that promised an annual twenty thousand dollars for every able-bodied citizen over twenty-five willing to work four hours a day for 165 days a year. Millions believed Dr. Francis E. Townsend, whose famous Townsend Plan promised two hundred dollars a month to everybody over the age of sixty. In Alberta, William Aberhart was swept into power in 1935 on the pledge that he would give everybody a monthly payment of twenty-five dollars through a new economic system known as Social Credit.

As every film buff knows, far more motion pictures in the Thirties dealt with rich people than with the victims of the Depression; everybody enjoyed living vicariously. Radio giveaways, which were invented in that era, needed to hand out only a few silver dollars (as *Dr. I.Q.* did) to be wildly successful.

The greatest fad of all during the decade was the dime chain-letter mania, which began in Denver in April, 1935. The net profit in this, the most plausible of all get-rich-quick schemes, was $1,562.50, provided that nobody broke the chain. Before the craze died, the U.S. post office, which ruled the letters illegal, had sent between two and three million of them to the dead-letter office. In Canada a law was swiftly passed to outlaw them, but not before the nation's post offices had been glutted. Fifteen hundred dollars does not loom as large today, but for many people in 1935 it represented as much as two years' wages.

It is understandable that for millions, money seemed the solution to most problems, and for millions it really was. *In spite of the trouble that money brings/Just a little filthy lucre does a lot of things*, the song said. People believed it because it was true. Rich people might suffer marital discord and shoot their paramours, as the papers were forever reporting, but at least they knew where their next meal was coming from. They had a roof over their heads, warm clothes, a fancy car, and enough ready cash to afford a trip to those faraway places where people met their lovers in the popular songs: the Isle of Capri, the Beach at Bali Bali, Blue Hawaii, Treasure Island, and A Perfume Counter on the Rue de la Paix.

The Depression, wrote Hugh MacLennan, the Canadian novelist, "bred a generation determined to give its children the good things it had lacked and spare them the harsh disciplines it had known." The solution for *their* Quints, as the public saw it, was to allow them to make as much money as they could as quickly as possible. Theirs was to be a goldfish-bowl existence. They could never live a normal life. Dr. Dafoe himself had said that more than once, and Dr. Dafoe was to be believed:

> They can't live the normal life of ordinary individuals so there isn't any point in bringing them up as ordinary children. They must have the special training of Royalty, to give them reserve and stamina and calm acceptance of the interest and curiosity of the multitude. They must learn to be looked at, talked about, written to and studied, without losing their sense of proportion or their ability to enjoy life. And because they will always have to buy their privacy and pay dearly for it, as all people in the glare of publicity must do, we are trying to build up sufficient funds to make it possible for them to have peace and freedom as the years go by.

Implicit in this statement was the assumption that the quintuplets would continue to be on display for the rest of their lives – that they would, in effect, remain forever as cute little babies, playing together for the entertainment of the public. Nobody, apparently, contemplated a time when they would grow up, marry, separate, eschew publicity, and vanish from the front pages as many other instant celebrities had done. Dafoe was as big a celebrity as they; he, too, was never free of the glare of publicity. But he had not found it necessary to "buy" his privacy. If anything he had more peace and freedom after he made headlines. Yet his statement went unquestioned, perhaps because it provided the rationale for the Quintuplet Industry.

Within a few months of their birth, and for another decade, the country became used to paintings and photographs of the quintuplets, advocating a bewildering variety of commercial products:

The list of commodities that paid to use the quintuplets' names may well be the longest in the history of advertising endorsement. It runs to more than two score – every kind of product from Pure-test Cod Liver Oil and Musterole Chest Rub to Remington Rand Typewriters. The Quints even received three hundred dollars in royalties from a song called *Quintuplets' Lullaby*, which sold some twenty-two thousand copies.

This was the smallest sum the trust fund received. General Motors, in 1939, paid fifteen thousand dollars just to use a picture of the five sisters in their automobile advertising. Corn Products Refining (Karo Syrup) paid fifteen thousand dollars a year for the babies' endorsements. Aluminum Goods Manufacturing Company, which paid on a royalty basis, delivered twenty-four thou-

Dafoe in New York

Surrounded by the Manhattan press in his Ritz Carlton Hotel suite, the famous country doctor answers questions laconically. Brother Will is right behind to coach him in his answers.

Left: With Al Smith atop the newly opened Empire State Building. To the Happy Warrior, the famous children were "quintriplets."

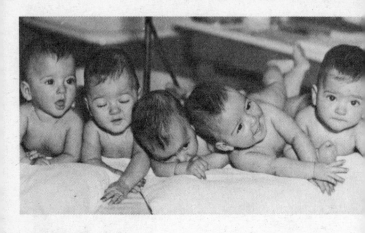

Quintuplets' Progress
At nine months *above:* Emilie, Annette, Marie, Cécile, and Yvonne. At about two years, *below.* At three years, *above right;* and just under the age of six, *below right.*

134

135

The quintuplets' cuteness was legendary. These photos help explain the enormous hold they had on the public. *Above,* Yvonne (left) and Emilie in a pose the press could not resist. *Below,* Mitch Hepburn, the Premier, is upstaged by one of the two-year-olds.

The crowd entering the new observation gallery, *circa* 1936. Queues were lengthy, but admission was free and hardly anybody complained though some burst into tears.

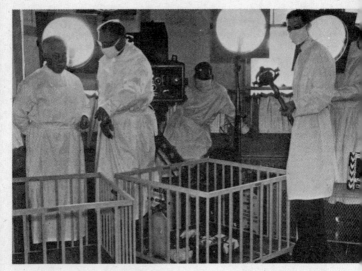

Twentieth Century-Fox's camera crew prepares to film *The Country Doctor*. Dafoe (left), terrified of germs, insisted on masks and gowns for the entire company.

Off to see the Queen in June 1939, with nurse Mollie O'Shaughnessy, *left*, teacher Gaëtane Vézina, and nurse Louise Corriveau, *right*. The siblings were frozen out.

SEPTEMBER 2, 1940 **12** CENTS

A few of the covers from magazines of the Thirties featuring the quintuplets. The babies made the covers of *Life* and *Look* on two occasions. They were perennial subjects for the Hollywood fan magazines along with Shirley Temple.

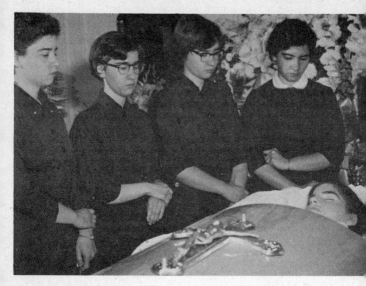

At Emilie's funeral. *Left to right:* Cécile, Marie, Yvonne, Annette.

Elzire and Oliva Dionne on their fiftieth wedding anniversary. The surviving quintuplets, estranged from their parents, sent a card but did not appear.

sand dollars to the fund in 1935, thirty-one thousand in 1936, and another thirty-one thousand in 1937. McCormick's Biscuits, in 1936, paid fifteen thousand dollars in royalties to the fund. The Quints received 25 per cent of the gross from each Pathé movie short, usually between twelve and fifteen thousand dollars. NEA picture service, which had paid ten thousand dollars a year for the first two years, jumped the price to an annual fifty thousand dollars at the beginning of 1937 as a result of spirited bidding. One of the most lucrative licences was that of the Brown and Bigelow company, whose annual quintuplet calendar was known throughout the continent. By 1936 the company had paid the quintuplets one hundred thousand dollars. They were still under contract as late as 1945.

These figures suggest that the Carnation Milk Company got a remarkable bargain when, for just three thousand dollars, it sewed up all rights in its field to the exclusive use of the quintuplets' names and pictures. The deal was made with the original guardianship on November 26, 1934, before David Croll entered the picture, and later resulted in an acrimonious dispute.

Earlier than that, however, the public was entertained by the Great Corn Syrup Lawsuit. Both the Canada Starch company, maker of Crown Brand Corn Syrup, and the St. Lawrence Starch company, maker of Beehive Corn Syrup, had been running advertisements announcing that theirs was the syrup given the quintuplets in the first week of their existence. On May 16, 1935, the makers of Crown Brand applied for an injunction to compel the makers of Beehive to cease advertising, pending a damage suit for $150,000. The injunction was not granted, and the suit did not come to trial until December, 1936. By then most of the principal actors in the drama, who were understandably preoccupied at the time, were unsure about what had actually happened. There was, however, some interesting testimony regarding moneys paid over by both syrup companies. Immediately the news of the birth was published, Bertram Bell, a resourceful Beehive Corn Syrup salesman from Bracebridge, sped to the Dionne farmhouse to try to find out which brand of syrup had been used, or, as the lawyer for the rival firm suggested, to try to convince all those involved to claim that Beehive had been used. A short time later, the president of the St. Lawrence Starch company, W. T. Gray, turned up in Callander and gave Dafoe one hundred dollars for the quintuplets' trust fund, obviously with the hope that Dafoe would say that Beehive syrup had been used. Later Gray paid out another thousand dollars to the first guardianship in return for an exclusive contract that would allow his company to advertise that the quintuplets had been fed the Beehive brand. Finally, the president of the rival Canada Starch firm went to see Dionne, who, in exchange for a downpayment of five hundred dollars and a two-year contract, agreed to say that Crown Brand was the first syrup used.

On the witness stand, after some considerable soul-searching, the Dionne faction lined up with Crown Brand and the Dafoe faction with Beehive. Yvonne Leroux, vague at first, finally recalled that she had used Beehive; she had at this point left the hospital, had recently concluded a lecture tour of the United States sponsored by NEA Service (for which she was paid three thousand dollars), and was that month conducting a regular radio program in New York dealing with her experiences. Alma Dionne, Oliva's sister, contradicted her testimony, insisting that Leroux had been asleep when the quintuplets received their formula and that she had used Crown Brand.

The exercise was pointless. The judge dismissed the case, saying that any brand would have been acceptable since none of the babies got more than five drops of corn syrup anyway, though "the public has been led to believe that this Beehive syrup was a continuous diet fed to the children."

The power of the quintuplets as an advertising instrument, however, was shown by the starch companies' testimony. In one year following the babies' birth, the St. Lawrence company, makers of Beehive, had more than doubled its sales. The Canada Starch company, moving in belatedly with its Dionne contract, had lost a hundred thousand dollars as a result of the Beehive onslaught.

When David Croll took over the management of the quintuplets' affairs, he turned most of the details over to his deputy minister, Joseph Sedgwick, who was to become one of the country's best-known trial lawyers. Sedgwick set off for New York almost immediately to confer with the NEA picture service, whose one-year contract negotiated in the summer of 1934 was about to expire.

We were babes in the woods, you know. So we made a deal under which we gave NEA the exclusive copyright on all these photographs because the photographs were the key to any deal we were able to make. The NEA people approached the prospective licensees for us. Their cut was that they had the copyright on the pictures, which would appear in the ads. Freddie Ferguson, the president of NEA, would make the preliminary soundings and decide if it was a dignified thing and see that they were all right. Then we would make our own deal. I was picked for the job by sheer accident because I was available and because I knew David – the government was smaller then and not nearly so complicated, and David and I had been friends long before that. So I became, in effect, legal and business manager of the quintuplets.

I went up to Callander in the depth of winter with Fred Ferguson and we met Roy Dafoe. Roy was very lonely – a very lonely man. He was the only man in that village with any formal education. I don't say this pejoratively, but they were all peasants, really. On three or four occasions we took him down to New York. We would have some of our principal licensees, particularly the NEA people, come up to the suite, you know, and chat and have a drink with him. All those trips were paid for by the company. We made a deal with Ferguson that whenever he had some prospects he thought we should see, NEA would pay my way down. Every entrepreneur on Broadway was trying to secure a piece of the action. I remember Walter Winchell, whom I didn't much care for, coming over and repeatedly chatting and having his picture taken with Roy and then taking Roy out on the town. Roy loved that. Roy really had to make a dime, and it was really at David

Croll's insistence that he made a dime here and there. And, of course, he did pretty well in the making of the film for Twentieth Century-Fox. He got ten thousand dollars from that picture for the use of his name.

David and I made that contract, and there's an interesting sidelight about that. All the movie people were after us. We didn't know anything about that kind of deal – what we should go for. So we got in touch with Mary Pickford, who, as you know, came from Toronto. She was living in a suite on the top floor, I think it was, of one of the better hotels. She was a good-looking woman then; she would have been in her forties – strong . . . strong! And I can still see her as she talked about the movie deal. She said, Whoever you deal with – get it in cash! Get the most you can, but don't take any overages or royalties because you won't get it back.

I made the contract with Joe Moscowitz, and David, he was dickering in every direction, trying to get the best price he could. But we made the deal because we kept in mind Mary's advice to get what you can in cash. So that is what we did.

The quintuplets received a guarantee of one hundred thousand dollars cash in advance against 10 per cent of the net proceeds for each of the three motion pictures made by Twentieth Century-Fox. As soon as the contract was signed in November, 1935, a crew of twenty technicians left Hollywood by special train for Callander to film scenes with Jean Hersholt, who would play the Dafoe character, and Dorothy Peterson, cast as the nurse. Charlie Blake, who had sold the original screenplay to Darryl Zanuck for five thousand dollars on the basis of a three-hundred-word letter, came along to write the script with the help of a Hollywood professional, Sonya Levien.

The accident of casting changed the career of Hersholt, then a minor character actor. The role had originally been intended for Will Rogers, perhaps the most beloved public figure in North America and a leading box-office draw. But on August 15 Rogers, travelling on a round-the-world flight with Wiley Post, was killed when the plane crashed at Point Barrow, Alaska, in the fog. The news of his death was almost as stunning as that of John Kennedy's a quarter of a century later. As a result of his role in *The Country Doctor*, Hersholt soared to immediate stardom. Two further films with the Quints established him firmly in the Hollywood pantheon and led, in 1937, to a lucrative contract with CBS, under which he played the same role of country doctor in the radio drama *Dr. Christian*.

What was not known at the time was the extent to which Dafoe was profiting from the quintuplets' fame. The general public believed that he was refusing all commercial offers, and the press reinforced that belief. On September 22, 1935, the *New York Times* reported that "the doctor has said he would like to go to the studio as technical adviser on 'The Country Doctor' . . . but he has declined to accept money for his services, an attitude that has caused Hollywood to view him with something akin to alarm." Actually, Dafoe was to receive thirty thousand dollars for his assistance as "medical adviser" on the three Fox pictures.

The following March Charlie Blake wrote that Dafoe had turned down a million dollars in various commercial offers. Blake also reported that a magazine had offered Dafoe five thousand dollars for his life story and that Dafoe had replied: "No thanks. I don't see where my life would be of interest to anyone else."

But Dafoe was already being interviewed by Frazier "Spike" Hunt, one-time editor of *Cosmopolitan* and the author of several biographies, including one of the former Prince of Wales. Hunt had been assigned to write Dafoe's life story by the *Saturday Evening Post*; later it was published in book form. Whether or not Dafoe received a fee for his part in the project is not known, but it would be remarkable if he had not because he took substantial sums for lectures, endorsements, radio broadcasts, and articles in professional publications. When the quintuplets were born, Dafoe was virtually penniless. But when his will was probated in 1943, it was found that he had amassed $182,466 – almost all of it invested in stocks and bonds. That was almost exactly what each of the Quints was worth at the time.

It is hard to understand how the myth of Dafoe's non-commercialism could have been perpetuated, for his picture appeared continually in magazine and newspaper advertisements endorsing everything from Karo Syrup to Chevrolets. On April 7, 1936, for instance, the *Globe* reported that Dafoe had been the guest of General Motors in Oshawa, where he had lunched with the president, R. S. McLaughlin, and his wife at their home, Parkwood, and taken delivery of his new Chevrolet Master Deluxe Coach, which, it said, he had ordered to replace the model he was driving. The inference was that Dafoe was buying the car. Actually it was part of his fee for an endorsement, but if any connected the story with a half-page General Motors ad published the previous month, showing Dafoe standing beside his Chevrolet, they made no comment.

Dafoe did not exactly hide the fact that he was making money from testimonials, but he did not go out of his way to publicize it or to correct the clear impression of non-commercialism that the press had spread. In December, 1934, following his first trip to New York, the doctor hired a Toronto solicitor, William B. McPherson, to act as his agent for the usual 10 per cent fee. In January he told his brother that he was going to tell McPherson "that the hospital and the babies are under my control; that any arrangement made with me is personal, and not to be given to the guardians as to what I might be paid; I don't mind the guardians knowing there would be a contract with me." Some time that spring he revoked the 10 per cent deal and decided to pay his lawyer on a straight fee basis. Though not all of Dafoe's endorsement fees were made public, his collateral contracts generally seem to have been worth about 10 per cent of the sum paid to the quintuplets.

At some point, Dafoe had a falling out with David Croll. There is a "Dear Chief" letter from the doctor in the Hepburn Papers, dated February, 1937, asking the premier to instruct Croll not to issue any further contracts regarding the quintuplets "until I have had a chance to talk to you on your return." What connection, if any, this had with Croll's resignation as the Quints' guardian on February 25 is anybody's guess. On that date Croll simply declared that the quintuplets had become big business to such an extent that he had to choose between his work as guardian and his work as a cabinet minister. He suggested that he be replaced by Percy D. Wilson, who had recently been appointed official guardian for Ontario. That suggestion, which had originally been made by the Opposition in 1935, was acted upon immediately.

One month later, Leopold Macaulay, a Conservative MPP, urged in the legislature that all receipts and other data regarding the quintuplets' involvement in commercial advertising be tabled. Hepburn, while stating that "this advertising is nauseous to me personally," refused to divulge any details of the contracts on the ground that this would reveal too much information to future advertisers. Two days later, however, under intense Opposition pressure, he gave in.

Then, on April 14, Croll and Arthur Roebuck were fired from their cabinet posts by the premier in a *cause célèbre* still green in the memory of Ontario trade unionists. The issue was the strike at the General Motors plant in Oshawa, which John L. Lewis's Congress of Industrial Organizations was attempting to organize. It was the CIO's first incursion into Canada, and Hepburn, who had moved considerably to the right since his election, swore that foreign agitators and Communists, as he called them, would never be allowed to gain a foothold in the country. Anybody who wasn't with Hepburn was against him. Croll and Roebuck, by their silence, were seen to be disloyal. Out they went, and Croll, in his formal letter of resignation, used a phrase that has never been forgotten: he would, he said, rather walk with the workers than ride with General Motors.

Joseph Sedgwick was swept away with Croll, and a new business manager was appointed for the quintuplets in the person of Keith Munro, the *Star* troubleshooter, who had been one of the first newsmen on the scene at the time of the birth. The appointment was Dafoe's. He liked Munro, a bulky, soft-spoken man who had a pronounced stutter like his own. The new business manager was to be paid six thousand dollars a year.

One of Munro's first jobs was to dig into the files to make himself familiar with the details of the contracts that had been signed by Croll. They weren't there. The former minister of welfare had taken them home to Windsor. Nor would he turn them over to Munro: "I hope you will appreciate the Quintuplet file is a personal one and not the property of the government and so I prefer to retain it, but it is open to you at all times."

Wilson asked Croll to return the files. He wrote to him three times between September and December, 1937, before he received an answer. But Croll did not release the material. Instead, he came to Toronto to talk personally to Wilson. Another year passed. Then, in November, 1938, R. L. Kellock, legal counsel for the guardianship and later chief justice of Ontario, asked for specific series of files and letters. Croll allowed him to come to Windsor and examine two cabinet drawers. When war broke out, David Croll joined the armed forces, but still the files were not made public. Before he left for overseas he burned them all; to this day nobody is sure what exactly was in them.

Munro, meanwhile, was faced with a delicate political problem involving the Carnation company.

Almost everybody who remembers the quintuplets remembers the Carnation milk advertisements, which seemed to be everywhere. The inference was that the babies practically bathed in the milk, which came, as the ads put it, "from contented cows." The company itself had boasted that the Quints had consumed twenty-five hundred tins in the first eighteen months. Munro was appalled at the three-thousand-dollar fee paid by the company for the privilege of using the quintuplets' names and pictures. Now it was insisting that it had the entire milk field – including whole milk and ice cream products – tied up! Moreover, the so-called Carnation babies actually *hated* Carnation milk and refused point-blank to drink it. Faced with this, the new guardianship asked Kellock to sue the company.

This was too much for Harold Kirby, government whip and minister of health. Kirby was convinced that the cancellation of the contract would affect the price of milk in Elgin County, the premier's home riding. He phoned Hepburn, who told Percy Wilson to order Kellock to hold up. Kirby also phoned Wilson with a blunt message: the welfare of the government, he said, outweighed any objections that might be raised about the Carnation contract. If Wilson and the others wouldn't play ball, new officials would be appointed who would. Kirby added that it would be well to get Munro down to Toronto at once for a private meeting.

Wilson, a good Liberal who had run unsuccessfully for office in the 1934 election, did as he was told. In vain Munro protested that "this was a right and proper course, which should not be interfered with." The situation was resolved quietly, with the Carnation company agreeing to a small increase in payments. But, compared to the sums that other firms were paying for the Dionne name, it still had a tremendous bargain.

In the United States, several companies tried to cash in on the words "quintuplets," "quints," or "quins" by using them generically in their advertising. Their argument was that the words all belonged in the dictionary and lay within the public domain. Croll had engaged a distinguished American lawyer, Arthur Garfield Hays, to handle the problem. Hays's advice was to sue in every instance, even though the law on the subject was hazy. "Businessmen hesitate to infringe when threatened with a lawsuit," he pointed out. Half a dozen actions were commenced before the Government of Canada on March 19, 1937, passed An Act for the Protection of the Dionne Quintuplets, securing for the exclusive use of the babies a list of two hundred articles, ranging from wheelbarrows to eyebrow pencils.

The children were still not three years old, but already they had taken on all the appurtenances of a major Canadian industry.

TEN:
Cashing in

Hindsight, that rueful sense of might-have-been, suggests that the Dionne quintuplets could have been returned to their parents at some time between the ages of two and three without any serious threat to their well-being. They were healthy children – normal in every way, as everybody connected with their upbringing was at pains to emphasize. Their natural parents were raising their other six children (Elzire Dionne would later give birth to a seventh) without any major problems apart from the usual childhood diseases. Thanks to the Quints, the family was well-to-do. The new guardians kept referring to the day when all the Dionnes would be united, but somehow that reunion continued to be postponed. It was also announced from time to time that the twice-daily showings would soon cease in order to allow the children to lead a more normal life. But this did not happen.

As early as 1935, Dafoe had predicted to the wives of American physicians in Atlantic City that the quintuplets would be reunited with their family "in three or four years." By 1937 he had moved the date back a decade. "Dr. Dafoe believes it will be many years before they can be free of the strict isolation that is theirs today," Lotta Dempsey wrote in *Chatelaine* magazine. "The quintuplets haven't the stamina yet to face the rough and tumble of daily living. . . . Today they are five splendid physical specimens. But take them away from their special environment . . . leave them open to infection, exposed to disease, and Dr. Dafoe doesn't believe they could stand up against it. . . . How long must they stay at Callander . . . moving no farther from their own beds than a few paces? 'Ten years, perhaps.' "

Dafoe sincerely believed it – or believed that he believed it. That he loved the children is beyond question. On his daily visits to the hospital he romped and played with them, and they returned his affection. For a lonely widower past middle age, they were like a spring tonic. In a sense, Dafoe was like an overprotective parent who hates to see his offspring driven out into the cruel world. But there was more to it than that. There must have been a realization – subconscious in the minds of those who cared for the children, closer to the surface in the minds of those who cared less – that the Quintuplet Industry had achieved a momentum that would be difficult to brake. Blatz was neck-deep in his research; it would not count for much unless he could follow it up over the years. Dafoe was involved in his tri-weekly radio broadcasts. Fred Davis was closeted with the children every morning for a full hour, feeding the insatiable demand for photographs. Future films and more newsreel shorts were contracted for. Commercial requests continued to pour in. And, above all, the burgeoning tourist industry of Northern Ontario depended almost entirely on the continued showings of the five children in their new playground.

There was also the built-in quintuplet bureaucracy. The annual cost of maintaining the babies, which had been a mere eight thousand dollars in the first year of their life, had soared to just under seventy thousand by 1937. Each guardian received twenty-five hundred dollars a year. Keith Munro, the business manager, was paid six thousand. In those years of low taxes, these were substantial sums. In 1977, for a man with two dependants to earn take-home pay equivalent to Munro's would require an annual income of more than forty-five thousand dollars.

The pressure to keep the quintuplets isolated was aided by the popular view that it would be disastrous to return them to their family. Most popular journalists continued to portray Dionne as an ignorant and shiftless farmer. It was widely believed that he could not handle money and that if the quintuplets ever went back to the farmhouse, they would quickly lose their fortune through foolish investments. Even worse was the vision of these royal children suddenly plunged into a home that many believed to be little better than a pigsty. "Cultural deprivation" – a new phrase in the Thirties – would certainly result.

That was Dafoe's own belief. His view was expressed with savage bluntness in a cruel magazine article by one Edith Johnson, published in May of 1938:

As with most primitive people, emotion has triumphed over reason with the Dionnes. Consciously or unconsciously they cannot bear the prospect of their famous children acquiring a culture superior to the six little Dionnes at home. Already they have seen signs of what highly intelligent twig-bending does to children, for the quints are infinitely prettier and more attractive looking than the other children, and that would still be true if the quints were put into the same clothes that the six at home wear. They have acquired a certain graciousness and charm as a result of superior association and training.

Dafoe clipped the article, pasted it in his scrapbook, and wrote in the margin the words "Very good."

The reporters who were sent to Callander by the big-city newspapers were near the top of the pyramid of the journalistic elite. Many had incomes as high as or higher than Keith Munro's. The cream of the *Toronto Star*'s reporting team were paid between $125 and $180 a week. As well as earning a take-home salary equal to or greater than that of a fifty-thousand-dollar-a-year man today, all of them lived high on expense accounts. They travelled far more than the average man in the Thirties; they ate better; they stayed at the finest hotels; they travelled first class on steamships and while on the road were able to bank the bulk of their salaries. Sophisticated and worldly, cynical to the point of insensitivity in the accepted tradition of their calling, they found it next to impossible to place themselves in Dionne's situation.* Besides, he would not let them past his own front gate.

They could not believe that Dionne knew anything about handling or saving money. Yet in spite of his new-found affluence, he seemed to be remarkably frugal. His fees as a guardian, which were shortly increased to three thousand dollars a year, his income from the photo contract with the *News* syndicate, the profit from his souvenir booth (there would soon be two), which sold everything from hot dogs to English woollens, all went into the bank. There was little outward evidence that he was splurging. He did not travel or buy fancy clothes for himself or his wife. He put a new porch on his home, but he did not paint it. He installed electricity but not plumbing. It may be that he felt that to do anything more ostentatious would be a sign that he was high-hatting his neighbours. To affluent strangers, however, it was a sign of shiftlessness, as an article in *Parents* magazine in January, 1937, suggests:

Though the Dionnes are better off financially than they have

*There were one or two exceptions: Lee Hartshorn wrote a remarkably sensitive article for the *Nation* in June of 1935 and Gregory Clark in the *Star* in 1937 wrote a warmly sympathetic piece about the Dionnes.

ever been, you would never guess it from the outward appearance of their house and farm. The house stands unpainted with sagging porch, all curtains down in front. . . . The farm itself gave little sign of care or work, though when old Grandfather Dionne had it, it was a prosperous place. . . .

It is an odd situation. On one side of the road the immaculate, up-to-date Dafoe Hospital . . . across the way the father's souvenir stand and ramshackle house. . . . The father and mother . . . are free to come and see their children whenever they like, but far from being appreciative or even understanding of what is being done for their children they are said to be suspicious and resentful. . . .

This was the general tenor of the reportage emanating from Callander: the Dionnes were getting their share – why were they making such a fuss? The media seemed to resent the fact that Dionne was making a good living. "He continues to profit from his fame," reported *News-Week* in May 1937. "At his own stand he gloomily signs his autograph for twenty-five cents, day after day." The selling of autographs irked people more than anything else. It was considered cheap – demeaning.

Dionne's motives in the long struggle over his children were certainly mixed. He resented the fact that strangers were making money out of the quintuplets. "Here we are, living on next to nothing, while my babies have thousands of dollars and all the luxuries," he said in 1938. "Everyone but me is making money out of my babies." Like Dafoe, Dionne played down his new affluence; his store alone netted about eight thousand dollars during the tourist season. Yet he was ambivalent about money. He would take twenty-five cents for an autograph but turn down fifty dollars from a man who offered to pay that sum just to shake his hand. He was known to refuse lucrative advertising contracts because the deal usually included Dafoe. When the NEA syndicate tried to ingratiate itself with him in the early days by sending him an expensive radio, he turned his back on the agent and slammed the door in his face. The offer of a package of cigarettes got one photographer a picture; the offer of four thousand dollars in cash from another failed.

Dionne once declared that he got into business to make enough money so that people would listen to him. The statement has the ring of truth. Money talked. When Dionne was able to hire a lawyer and pay somebody to type his letters, his campaign to reunite his family began to be noticed. But the idea that he was a thoroughgoing mercenary determined to squeeze the last dollar out of his fame persisted, as a single anecdote demonstrates.

When Fox made *The Country Doctor*, the Dionnes refused to go to the hospital to watch the children at work because they objected to being photographed for publicity purposes without being paid. The company then offered to pay a fee of seven hundred dollars if the parents would give it permission to cast two Hollywood players as Oliva and Elzire Dionne. When this was refused, the studio simply changed the names and fictionalized the story. To play the father it engaged John Qualen, a character actor skilled in portraying half-wits and funny Scandinavian immigrants. His performance made a comic figure out of Dionne, who was humiliated by it. When the company returned to make a second picture, ironically titled *Reunion*, it was not able to make contact with Dionne. Qualen, meanwhile, hearing of Dionne's distress, wrote him a letter of apology and regret, explaining that he had simply followed the lines in the script and instructions of the director. He sent along a portrait of himself and asked in return for an autographed photograph of Dionne, enclosing a dollar bill to cover postage and costs. Dionne, mollified, immediately wrote back to the actor expressing his appreciation and enclosing the requested picture. Shortly afterward, *Movie World News* carried a wisecracking paragraph reporting that what a troop of actors could not do for *Reunion* a dollar bill had done.

Dionne's one luxury was his automobile. He loved cars; even in the worst days of the Depression he had owned one. Now he was able to afford a new one every two years. This, too, was turned against him. Implicit in the reports about each new auto was the suggestion that the quintuplets' father was a money-mad spendthrift. Dafoe contributed to the myth that Dionne changed cars every six months. "Dionne salts away a neat income from his concessions," the doctor told a reporter. "In the spring he bought a new La Salle car. He had a Packard last year."

If Dionne was profiting from his children's popularity, so were his neighbours in Callander and North Bay. "You can cash in on the fact that they are in your district," Jack Hambleton, the director of the Ontario publicity bureau told the North Bay Chamber of Commerce in April, 1935. The following year the *Star Weekly* used the same phrase in reporting that more people had become familiar with Northern Ontario in the preceding twenty-four months than in the fifty previous years of the province's history because of "Canada's champion trade-pullers," the Quints. "Everybody cashes in on the babies," the paper reported. All of the province's tourist advertising referred to "Quintland." Pamphlets on the subject were printed in the tens of thousands:

By car, by bus, by train . . . All roads lead to Callander since the arrival of the Quints! Highway 11 runs straight north from Toronto; Highway 17 brings you from Ottawa, Canada's capital; and from the west, you will come through Sault Ste. Marie and Sudbury over 294 miles of good road. The Canadian National Railway passes right through the town of Callander, and the Canadian Pacific through North Bay, the "Gateway to the North," only three miles distant. Each road traverses beautiful country, touches important Canadian cities and towns. And around this most famous nursery in the world lies one of Ontario's loveliest playgrounds, with many comfortable places to stay, both rustic and luxurious . . . with wonderful fishing, good bathing and boating. The whole family will be happy in Quintland this summer!

The Quints saved North Bay from financial disaster. The city, staggering under an annual relief bill of a quarter of a million dollars, ran out of funds in June of 1936 and was unable to persuade the provincial government to bail it out. In order to meet relief payments, it was forced to dip into its reserve fund for uncollected taxes, an action that caused Roy Thomson to resign as alderman. The future Lord Thomson of Fleet protested against the city fathers assuming any further responsibility for relief payments.

But North Bay had that summer turned the corner, with the help of the quintuplets. The 1936 tourist season turned out to be the most profitable in the community's history. The city's banks cleared almost two million dollars in U.S. currency; Canadians left another half million in the town. Men on relief began to find jobs on the new road the government was pushing through from Callander to Corbeil. Accommodation was at a premium. The mayor, James Bullbrook, gave credit where credit was due. The tourists would flock to Quintland for at least a generation, he said.

By 1937, the relief rolls in North Bay had reached a record low for the Depression years. There had been by then a mild business upswing across the country, but nothing like that enjoyed by Northern Ontario. The overall increase in the Canadian tourist trade in 1936 was a modest 8 per cent; in North Bay it was 75 per cent. Suddenly empty streets became busy again, automobiles were parked bumper to bumper along the curbs, the city's six hotels were jammed, and half the private residences in town doubled as tourist homes.

If North Bay received a financial injection from Quintland, the village of Callander was transformed. In 1935 it was virtually bankrupt; its relief office was closed and forty families were deprived of the means of sustenance. Within two years there was no need for a relief office; every able-bodied man was working. Three-quarters of the residents were taking in overnight guests. The village had become, in the words of the *Nugget*, "a little Broadway complete with bright lights, throngs of people and traffic whizzing by." The Callander Hotel added another floor and doubled its accommodation. A second hotel, the Red Line Inn, described as "palatial," rose across the street. Another restaurant opened up; it was so busy that customers sometimes had to wait an hour for service. Léon Dionne installed five pumps in his service station, named them after the Quints, and in two years increased his annual gallonage from two thousand to thirty-eight thousand. The old railway station, a wooden coach with a tin smokestack through the roof, was hauled away to be replaced by a new brick building with a fireplace and a panelled waiting room. And suddenly the village found that it was on the main bus routes to the big cities.

The post office had difficulty coping with the avalanche of mail. Each day between two and three thousand items bore the now-coveted postmark. People wanted it stamped on their hats, autograph albums, and arms. The daily pick-up of cards from Oliva Dionne's booth alone amounted to eight hundred. A good deal of the mail carried American stamps; the recipients were forced to pay at the other end.

After January 1, 1938, a selection of sixteen ready-made greeting messages from Callander was available at the Canadian National telegraph station. They could be ordered by number at a cost of forty cents apiece. All were datelined "Dafoe Nursery, Callander, Ontario," and there was one for every type of tourist:

Greetings from Canada. Just visiting the Quints and it was well worth the trip to see the famous babies. They were simply wonderful.

Interesting trip through Ontario. Arrived today at the Dafoe Hospital and saw the Dionne Quintuplets. They are intensely interesting and well worth seeing.

Just saw the world's five most famous babies and believe me they are grand.

Property values in Callander shot up. A parcel of land that had changed hands in 1933 for two hundred dollars was quoted in 1938 at five thousand. The town that once had difficulty accommodating seventy-five visitors now found room for fifteen hundred. Tourists were urged to make their reservations months ahead. The tourist camps and lodges – almost two hundred of them – were strung out along the highway to North Bay for four miles; they employed nineteen hundred people each season.

All over the continent, automobile bumper cards bore the legend WE HAVE SEEN THE DIONNE QUINTUPLETS. In the eyes of the tourist trade, Quintland's great value lay in the fact that it was known as a "family attraction" – as opposed to the hunting and fishing holidays that appealed only to men and boys. It was known that if women went along, progress was more leisurely and spending more liberal.

A visit to Quintland involved a round trip of at least five hundred miles from the nearest border point. In many cases, foreign tourists travelled double that distance from their home towns. Even with fast driving such a trip kept them in the province for three days; a more leisurely trip occupied five days. Many thousands spent their entire vacation in the nearby resort country. It was reckoned that at six cents a gallon each driver contributed a minimum of a dollar and a half to the provincial treasury in gasoline tax alone.

The total value of the American tourist traffic in Ontario in 1938 was estimated at between $100 million and $125 million. The federal government's travel bureau figured that the quintuplets were responsible for at least a fifth of that figure. This made them one of Canada's most important businesses. Capitalized at 4 per cent, the going rate in 1938, they were a $500-million asset to the province of Ontario.

Two miles and a half from Callander, on the old Dionne and Legros farms, once studded with shattered rock and stunted trees, lay the cluster of hospital buildings and souvenir shops that *News-Week* called "Canada's Coney Island," dominated at the far end by the ungainly bulk of the midwives' pavilion. The building, on the Alexandre Legros property, was actually owned by a North Bay merchant, Philip Adams.

The two midwives, who fronted for Adams, worked in the pavilion, Mme Labelle in the kitchen making hot dogs and Mme Legros out front, running the store with the help of her young daughter Margaret, who never forgot the excitement of the spectacle going on outside.

I remember that like it was yesterday. We never quit talking about it. There were so many people there on Labour Day, I remember, that all the parking lots were full and the cars were stretched along the road all the way to Callander, and people actually walked all the way from Callander to see the Quints. And nobody ever complained. Everybody was so thrilled. They often fainted in the sun, but even then they didn't complain. Often, you know, people went around again to see them a second time.

One thing interested me very much and that was to see the rich people. They were the only ones who would get on the road and travel, especially from the United States. They arrived in limousines with the dark chauffeurs and dark maids. My gosh, the women, eh? In those days they wore such extravagant clothes. And, of course, you'd never go out without a hat. And the wonderful diamonds! I couldn't get over that, being so poor ourselves – we never realized what was going on in the outside world. We were poor people in the country. And then all the doctors and all the nurses from all over the world, it seemed, came to talk to my mother.

And the questions! We had so many. We went to bed at night answering questions and we woke up in the morning answering questions in our sleep. The people, they asked how cold it was in the winter. And, you know, many of them arrived with snowshoes and skis and fur coats. And they wanted to know about the birth. My mother, Mrs. Legros, ran the store and talked to the people. She loved people. She wasn't like the Dionnes, who hid when the public came along. She always had time for the public.

In the fall when the visitors were gone we saw the Quints as often as we could. We never got tired of seeing them. My gosh, they were cute. They had such character.

If Quintland was a northern Coney Island, it was a very Canadian one. There seemed to be, as one writer noted, "a deliberate effort to avoid the most rudimentary principles of salesmanship and merchandising." The Canadian lack of ostentation – which some might call the Canadian lack of showmanship – was never more clearly in evidence. There were no nightclubs, no motion pictures, no neon signs, no sideshows, no huge billboards heralding the nearness of the spectacle, no taverns, no carnival rides, no conducted tours in fancy vehicles: just three or four souvenir shops, two washrooms, a parking lot, the nursery compound, and, for a time, a single Indian in a tepee whose picture could be snapped for a quarter.

This underplaying of the continent's greatest human interest spectacle may have been one reason why the visitors were so cheerful. They seemed perfectly prepared to line up, often for an hour or longer, in the intense heat that radiated from the rocks and then enter a dark corridor, which in midsummer was so stifling that every season people were carried out unconscious. Another reason for the uncomplaining attitude was that the show was free; the government did not even charge for parking. The guardianship was genuine in its desire not to seem to be exploiting its charges. But the most important reason for the visitors' good humour lay in the children themselves. It was not possible to be out of sorts in their presence. Everyone agreed that the sight of them playing in their compound made the trip worthwhile.

For supervisors such as Dorothy Millichamp, Blatz's deputy, working inside the compound, conscious that every eye was on the babies and that the babies themselves were aware of it, the spectacle was less of a thrill and more of an ordeal. The teachers and the nurses suffered from a kind of stage fright: what if something terrible should happen in front of all those people?

Every day you coped with thousands of visitors. The children knew the visitors were there and we knew the visitors were there. It was a very great strain. The children became very aware. They'd get up on the jungle gym and they'd pose. They knew perfectly well what they were doing. I can remember you'd feel that you were calm and collected, and then at the end of an hour and a half you'd be just dripping with perspiration. It was a real, stressful situation. And, of course, the children got wicked, too. They'd take their hats off and throw them over the garden, and then you'd try to get them and their hats back together again. And the visitors could be demanding. Once, I remember, the line got stalled because one woman wouldn't move until she had seen that Marie could walk. Marie was playing in the sandbox at the time. It held the whole show up.

For four summer months the show went on, twice a day. The government, which had removed the quintuplets from their parents because they didn't want the children placed on exhibition, was now itself in a form of show business with those same children. It was in the best of taste – controlled, supervised, well-organized, relatively undemanding. But it was show business all the same. And it drew the customers. Dionne had been criticized for making a profit out of the accident of the quintuplets' birth, but his was a pittance compared to the revenue accruing to the taxpayers of Ontario.

Up the rising knoll that led to Quintland the cars rolled in a steady stream, year after year: Terraplanes and Hupmobiles; Auburns and Singers; Chevrolets with "knee action"; McLaughlin-Buick straight eights with Torque Tube Drive; cars with running boards, cars with rumble seats, cars with the new skirted fenders, cars with "streamlining" (a word suddenly used to describe everything from ashtrays to kiddie-cars); Airflow Chryslers and Airstream De Sotos; green Pierce Arrows, long as a city block, it seemed; gleaming white Cords – the car of the future that had no future; Baby Austins, tiny as toys; Willys-Knights and Lincoln-Zephyrs, snazzy as all get-out; deluxe Frontenacs with Free-Wheeling; Essex Pacemakers with Duco finish; Dodges with Floating Power; Oldsmobiles with Turret Tops; Pontiacs with Syncro-Mesh transmission; baby blue Hudsons with Tru-line Steering and Double Carburetion; Graham Superchargers and black Packard eights with knife-sharp grills and uniformed chauffeurs; the occasional monstrous Dusenberg; sleek La Salles, Whippet coaches, and Durant coupés; new cars and old cars, cars held together with pieces of wire, cars polished to a fine gloss – an unending portable automobile show rolling on to Quintland.

The parade of cars brought celebrities from all over the world to the steps of the Dafoe Hospital. W. K. Kellogg, the inventor of corn flakes, travelled six hundred miles from Battle Creek, Michigan, just to see the babies whom he called the Eighth Wonder of the World. Alexander Woollcott, the *New Yorker*'s theatre critic and an international figure because of his weekly *Town Crier* radio program, arrived in a chauffeur-driven limousine. Prince Chichibu, the younger brother of the Emperor of Japan, on his way to the coronation of King George VI, insisted on breaking his journey at Quintland. Bette Davis, the Warner Brothers' star, turned up wearing yellow horn-rimmed glasses and announced that she'd never play in a movie with the Quints because they would steal the picture. Amelia Earhart and her husband, the publisher George Palmer Putnam, missed the regular showing because of engine trouble at Orillia but were allowed to see the quintuplets anyway; she was itching to return to Oakland, California, to resume her round-the-world flight. The date was April 23, 1937; five weeks later she vanished forever.

The cars poured in at the rate of one a minute from all over the continent. People insisted on telling the policeman on duty how many miles they'd travelled. Some came from as far away as Cuba and the Canal Zone. The first Alaskan tour arrived in March, 1937 – the Polar Bear hockey team. The following year, five Hawaiian school teachers turned up wearing leis and dressed in beach pyjamas. A visit to Quintland conferred a kind of instant status. "We will be the envy of everyone in Iowa when we go back and tell them that we actually saw and heard the quintuplets," said Mr. and Mrs. Albert Hart; they had driven a thousand miles to see the babies on their third birthday.

Strangers, rubbing shoulders with each other in the queue, became life-long friends. In the summer of 1937, Annette Gingolf and Sydney Marcus met at Callander and on November 7 were married. The same year Evelyn Tussing and Norval Kenouse of Findlay, Ohio, came to Callander expressly to be married in "Quint City." A Cleveland woman changed her mind about motherhood after seeing the Quints. "I can't tell you how different my life has become," she wrote to Dafoe, "how much more full and happy it is and promises to remain forever."

Many a new arrival was astonished to find any vestige of civilization in the area. Thirty members of a women's club who came up from Baltimore sounded slightly disappointed because they had expected "a trip through the wild and woolly waste." But the real disappointment came when, because of illness (usually a cold) or because of the weather, the Quints were not shown at all. Then there were protests from those who had driven north for days with one single purpose. Some stuck it out until the showings resumed. Mr. and Mrs. W. C. Laird, who had shipped their car from Honolulu to San Francisco and then driven all the way across the continent to Quintland, were among the stubborn ones. "We came into this part of the country expressly to see those babies and we're not going to leave until we do see them," said the Lairds. Nor did they. Few, even the most phlegmatic, remained unmoved by the sight of the children. Many women emerged from the observation gallery their cheeks wet with tears. Occasionally, one or two neurotics would fall on their knees in the dust and shriek and pray aloud.

A later generation, surfeited with a steady diet of TV glamour, might well ask: What was all the fuss about? Why did these five girls cause such a commotion? Why did millions leave their homes, in the depths of the century's worst depression, to drive hundreds of miles into the back country of Ontario just to watch a group of children playing together?

It is not easy to recapture in words the public's infatuation with the Dionne quintuplets. They were international stars of the first magnitude – greater than Garbo or Barrymore or Harlow. Nobody, with the possible exception of Roosevelt, enjoyed a higher visibility. No week went by without the newspapers carrying a picture layout of the five babies. A quintuplets scrapbook – and tens of thousands kept quintuplets scrapbooks in the Thirties – became an anthology of photographic clichés. Every season, feast day, and national holiday was marked by photographs of the famous five, dressed in witches costumes for Hallowe'en, ogling turkeys at Thanksgiving, lighting candles at Christmas (with Dafoe as Santa

Claus), emerging from giant valentines on February 14, patting bunnies at Easter, ushering in winter with toboggans, skis, snowshoes, and skates, spring with new bonnets, summer with identical bathing suits. When, in 1937, all five had their tonsils removed, it was front-page news everywhere.

THE SENTIMENTAL OLD REPROBATE!

It was impossible to escape the Dionnes. You could not pick up any major magazine without encountering either in the editorial section or in the display advertising at least one photograph or painting of the Quints. In the theatres, they romped through the Pathé newsreels or turned up in special one- and two-reel short subjects. Radio programs thrived on quintuplet jokes. Movies (such as the Marx brothers' *A Night at the Opera*) made reference to "those five kids in Canada." Even a Broadway play had a plot turning on the isolation of the babies in the Canadian north woods.

As public favourites they had several advantages over the other big names of the period. They were beautiful babies – so cute, so chubby, so cuddly that one longed to pick them up and hug them. In this area, only Shirley Temple could compete with the Quints. But there was only one Shirley Temple; there were five Dionnes, absolutely identical to the untutored eye. *That* was the real marvel. Until 1934, the word "quintuplet" was all but unknown. For the rest of the decade it was synonymous with the Dionnes.

Finally, there was the near certainty of being able to see them in the flesh. One might visit Hollywood and never catch a glimpse of a movie star. But you could drive to Callander knowing that twice a day the quintuplets would be on display. The bulk of the North American population, living north of the Mason-Dixon line and east of the Mississippi, could easily manage the trip within the confines of a two-week summer vacation – a vacation which, as an added bonus, took the visitors into the much-touted scenic wilderness that Hollywood labelled "the north woods." The Quints were fashionable. In the mid-Thirties, a visit to the Dafoe Hospital became The Thing to Do.

This helps to explain why the decision to display the quintuplets could not have been reversed. The public on both sides of the border would never have stood for it. Indeed, it is probable that if the babies had not been displayed at the outset, thousands would have arrived anyway and demanded that they be shown. Several members of the hospital staff later remarked that the people would have smashed down the doors if necessary to catch a glimpse of "their" babies. For the possessiveness that Dorothy Millichamp noted was very real. As in so many cases of hero-worship or celebrity-worship, the public cared very little about the privacy or the personal welfare of popular deities. As Lindbergh and Garbo had discovered, it demanded that they be visible and available. It was as if the quintuplets had been born to satisfy a deep personal need, and the commercialization of the babies, through testimonials, allowed the public to indulge that need without any stirring of conscience. If the babies were being displayed in advertisements for profit, it followed that they could be displayed in the flesh for the enjoyment of all.

The quintuplets could not see the people lining up four abreast an hour and a half or more before each showing. But they must have heard "a sort of dull, rhapsodic hum [that] fills the air from early morning until nightfall." They were taken from the nursery porch and conducted to the play area along a pathway that was hidden from the road by a high white screen. As they grew older, they realized that they were on display. Years later, Annette recalled the day when Marie, at the age of five, held up a toy monkey, and Emilie, who was always making comical remarks, said to her: "You'd better drop that monkey or they'll think there are *six* of us." They also sensed that they were special. As one of their nurses, Cécile Michaud, discovered, they knew that they were the Quints.

They could hear the sounds of children and crying babies in the audience. They couldn't see them, but they began to realize as they got older that these people had come to see the Quints. They'd say that in French: that people were coming to see the Quints. They knew that they were the Quints. But they weren't excited about it. I don't think they realized how important "Quints" meant.

163

They were little mimics, beautiful actors. They just loved to pose for pictures. There were no problems with that at all. They were full of joy and laughter all the time. At the shows, they co-operated very well. We'd keep them on their tricycles so they'd make the rounds so everybody could see them. But when the father and mother would be there, they'd disturb them, and they'd get all in a cluster. And the people viewing them, not too many would see them. So we'd have a little bit of a problem there. They didn't talk to us, the parents. Mr. Dionne, he wouldn't mouth us or anything, but she would. She was quite hostile. And, of course, in her French way of speaking she would get quite excited. We just ignored that; it was the only way to deal with it. I remember one day I was sitting in the double swing; she was sitting on the other side. She was threatening me, I can't remember what for. But the people in the audience were asking the guards: Was Mrs. Dionne going to strike the nurse? She did attempt to, but I stayed back on the swing. I can't remember what she accused me of; I think the children kept running to me and asking me something when they were playing. I'd say: Go and see your mother; go ask your mother. I think she accused me of trying to take the children's affections from her. She accused all the nurses of doing that. I just didn't answer. It was hard. I always felt sympathy for them because, in the first place, they lacked education. I guess it was hard for them to understand what all this was about, really. There was no sense trying to explain because they wouldn't listen anyway; they had their minds made up.

They had, indeed; and they had just begun to fight.

ELEVEN:
The French-Canadian connection

During the first four years of the quintuplets' lives, there was one aspect of Oliva Dionne's character with which nobody had reckoned – not the press, not the public, not the people charged with supervising the health and education of his unique children. That quality was pride. By 1938, Dionne was an embittered man, suspicious of the world, trusting in no one. But he was far from beaten; his pride, wounded though it was, would not allow him to suffer defeat. Reuniting his family had become an obsession with him that went further than mere parental love. Something had been taken from him. Until it was returned, he could not hold up his head. In Corbeil, the father was always the master of his own family; alone among his neighbours Oliva Dionne was not the master of his.

His wife's obsession was just as fierce, but her motives were less complicated. Elzire Dionne loved all her children. She wanted them with her, to cuddle, to feed, and to train, not as royal celebrities, but as future mothers or nuns. This was at the root of all her difficulties in the big hospital across the street. The nurses, she felt, were stealing the affections of her own children, alienating them from their real mother. She could not bear it. Occasionally, the Dionnes would go into North Bay to take in a Saturday-night movie, but sometimes her nerves became so affected that she would break into tears on the way and ask to be taken home. Although Dafoe and the guardians made a point of stating publicly that she could visit her children whenever she wished, the meetings did not always work out in practice. The mornings, when the doctor romped with the children and Fred Davis demanded his hour for picture taking, were especially difficult. Mealtime, nap time, Blatz time all ate up a good deal of the remainder of the day.

The Dionnes became rather like upper-class Victorian parents, dropping into the nursery just before tea to relieve Nanny for half an hour. The difference was that for them the routine was not a voluntary one. After Mollie O'Shaughnessy arrived in December, 1936, she was able, with the help of Jacqueline Noël, another new nurse, to ease the situation.

I felt terrible for the Dionnes. They weren't allowed to come and see the children when I first went there. They weren't granted too many privileges. It was just that the doctor loved the children so much. He felt they were his. I don't think he meant to be mean to Mr. Dionne. It was just the way he was. But after Miss Noël and I got working on it, we got the doctor to see the point: that the mother should get in whenever she wanted. Well, there were certain times when she could and when she couldn't. She couldn't have free rein to come morning, noon, and night or stay for meals. But after I was there for some time, they could come more freely. We more or less talked to the doctor: Well, after all, they are their children; and, How would you like it to have your children taken from you and given to someone else?

When Mrs. Dionne used to come over, she was very good in this respect, that when she would leave them she wouldn't tarry too long and make a big to-do about it. She would gracefully slide out and say, I'll see you later on. I thought that was very nice of her. I know one nurse laughed at her because she had come over and one of the children was crying for her, and she'd gone out and then come back when she heard the child crying. She said, So-and-so is crying; and the nurse said, No, no one is crying. That would be very hard. My heart bled for her. I remember once, Cécile was very ill. She had an ear infection. We'd had quite a time – I'd been up for two nights, and I was bushed. Cécile really became quite ill. At twelve o'clock the doctor came. He doused his lights, you know, when he came by the family house so they wouldn't see him going there at night. He didn't want them coming over. Of course, Mrs. Dionne, being a true mother, she was all eyes and ears. He'd no sooner left than she was over, and that night she stayed all night. She was very nice. She said to me, She's a very sick little girl; if anything happens, don't you worry too much. She was a real diamond in the rough.

For Oliva Dionne, 1938 marked a pivotal point in his long struggle to bring the family under one roof. That struggle had been going on for four years without any glimmer of success; it would continue for another four. But the tide was turning, and several factors were responsible: a slight but observable falling off of interest in the quintuplets, which would be accelerated by the coming war; a rise of nationalistic feeling among the French Canadians; and a subtle change in attitude among some sections of the press and the intellectual elite.

On August 29, 1937, an editorial had appeared in the *New York Times* expressing concern about the future of the quintuplets in the goldfish bowl of public curiosity. This produced several letters to the editor urging that the children ought to be returned to their parents to live "a normal life."

The same question was debated two months later in the lobby of the Royal York Hotel in Toronto during a remarkable symposium in which two hundred leading authorities met at the invitation of Dr. Blatz and discussed the quintuplets. The argument split on national lines. The *Times* managed to gather some opinions in advance of the meeting. The American experts generally insisted that the babies would be better off with their parents or parent surrogates. The Canadians disagreed. One Canadian educator expressed the prevailing Toronto opinion when he said: "You Americans are the most sentimental people in the world. You are still thinking in terms of pioneer days when a mother had to keep her baby clinging to her breast while she shot at an odd Indian. All I can say is that I wish I had had a child that is as happy as the quintuplets under the experts. I know of no children who have had such good physical and social surroundings."

The Americans took an opposite view. Helen Watson of the Child Education Foundation remarked it was not possible to give a proper education to "children brought up under that system of solitary confinement, make it as pleasant as you like. These poor quintuplets have not had as much experience of reality as my dog. . . . They need to trot around the kitchen in an ordinary home, to see other children and life going on around them."

For the first time, the controversy was out in the open, and at a high level.

Meanwhile, a strongly nationalistic government was entrenched in the province of Quebec. Maurice Duplessis's Union Nationale party had swept into power in August of 1936, winning seventy-seven of the ninety seats in the Quebec assembly. The Depression had been especially hard on French Canadians, whose feelings of isolation from the rest of Canada were intensified by the obvious truth that economic control in their province was vested in Anglo-Saxon firms that continued to make high profits but cut wages back to destitution levels. One of the many blatant examples will suffice: a textile company, controlled outside the province, made profits of 24 per cent on its invested capital but paid its male employees an average weekly wage of only $13.43. Its women employees averaged a weekly $9.73. Some two hundred of its workers were paid less than eight dollars a week – literally starvation wages. As one historian has remarked, "Given the great strength of Canadian regional pride, it is remarkable that the depression did not produce a powerful secessionist movement."

Duplessis's rise strengthened the aspirations of French Canadians everywhere. He was seen as the champion of religious and language rights. Gregory Clark, talking to the people of Corbeil, was assured that "Duplessis would get the Quints away from Hepburn. You wait and see."

Racial friction had always been especially high in Northern Ontario, where the French-speaking population was larger and more visible than in the industrial south. To the Anglophones, the Dionne quintuplets were, in the phrase of Rev. C. E. Silcox, the secretary of the Social Council of Canada, "the symbol of a great fear" – that the French Canadians were deliberately trying to outbreed their English-speaking neighbours, even though doing so might lower the standard of living for all. The *Globe*, in its very first editorial hailing the birth of the Quints on May 30, 1934, had remarked in passing that "these latest arrivals will arouse afresh apprehensions regarding French ascendency in Northern Ontario."

To the French, however, control of the quintuplets by Anglophones represented another kind of danger: a subtle attempt to wean French-Canadian children away from the roots of their culture, from their language, their religion, and their traditional form of education. And the symbol of that danger was not so much Allan Roy Dafoe as it was Dr. William Blatz.

Dionne clearly sensed this, and when his moment came he moved with a sureness that belied his public image as a slow-witted farmer. Early in February, 1938, Blatz fired Claire Tremblay, the quintuplets' teacher. Shortly after that Dafoe, or more likely Brown, fired Jacqueline Noël, one of the nurses. The reason given, in each instance, was insubordination. Both women were French Canadians; both were strict Catholics; both were squarely in the Dionne camp. Although they had been given some weeks of instruction at St. George's school before assuming their duties at the hospital, neither could or would follow the Blatz system. Worse, in Dafoe's eyes, they were carrying tales to the Dionnes. Both women were teetering on the edge of nervous breakdowns.

Dionne acted with dispatch. The slightly pathetic and bewildered peasant with the Chaplin moustache and the Stan Laurel haircut was no more. The touch of affluence and bitter experience had transformed him. On February 26 he wrote to Aimé Arvisais, the secretary of l'Association Canadienne-Française d'Education d'Ontario in Ottawa, asking for his help.

The association, founded in 1910, had chapters in most parishes in Northern Ontario. Its membership was open to all French-Canadian adults of Roman Catholic religion living in the province. Its aims were to fight for the rights of French-speaking Canadian Catholics, especially the right to be instructed in their own language by teachers of their own religion in the separate schools of the province. The vice-president of the association was Edmond Cloutier, managing director of *Le Droit*, the only French-language daily in Ontario, whose editorial principles coincided with those of the ACFEO. Together they represented a considerable political force.

Dionne wired Cloutier, threatening to go to the newspapers unless Cloutier came at once to North Bay. Cloutier came.

Dionne had already outlined his specific grievances:

a. Dr. Dafoe had not for my wife and myself the consideration which we would expect from him.
b. My daughters are brought up "à l'Américaine." They train them to act in films but not as Catholic and French children should be brought up.
c. The new teacher speaks very poor French and I object that my girls be Anglicized.
d. Miss Tremblay and Miss Noël are in sympathy with us and are loved by the quintuplets. . . . We want to keep them.
e. I am opposed to any dismissal of members of the staff without my being consulted. . . .

These grievances were discussed at length at a private meeting between the guardians – Valin, Dafoe, and Dionne – and Cloutier and Judge J.A.S. Plouffe, the district president of the association. The arguments went on long into the night, but in the end a consensus on several points was reached.

Blatz was out. Judge Plouffe declared that education should not be left in the hands of a man whose faith and language were not the same as the parents' (Blatz was a lapsed Catholic). Nobody, it turned out, had been able to figure out Blatz's exact status or who, if anybody, had granted him authority over instruction in the nursery. He had simply moved in one day with Dafoe's tacit approval, and the guardianship had accepted him, even hiring teachers and nurses on his recommendation. In future, the meeting agreed, the education of the children would be left to the director of bilingual education of the Ontario Department of Education.

The guardians also agreed that the family should be reunited under one roof, although the details and timing were not specified. The biggest argument came over the dismissal of Tremblay and Noël. Dafoe let the government know that he was prepared to resign if either woman was reinstated. As the attorney general, Gordon Conant, said: "I don't think the government or the people would stand for any arrangement that would oust Dr. Dafoe."

The dismissals brought the Hepburn government under heavy pressure. Protests poured in from several French-Canadian groups in northern Ontario. French Canadians had voted Liberal since the 1890s, but here was an issue that could turn them against the party, as they had turned against the Liberal government in Quebec. The Catholic Young Men's Association of Sturgeon Falls and the Saint Jean Baptiste Society of Sudbury could not be ignored. Hepburn was sensitive about the North; his closest cronies and financial supporters were entrepreneurs such as J. P. Bickell and George McCullagh, whose fortunes came out of the mining country. The Ontario Women's Liberal Association had already taken up the Dionnes' grievances with the premier. Suddenly, the quintuplets had become a political hot potato. Hepburn tossed it into the lap of the Official Guardian, Percy Wilson.

Wilson was a former Ottawa lawyer and a one-time sportsman who had played hockey, football, and baseball as a student at McGill. A handsome man with a neat military moustache, slightly bald at forty, he was universally liked and respected. "Kindly," "soft-spoken," "inflexible" were adjectives used to describe him. A former president of the Ottawa Liberal Association, he had failed to gain a seat at the time of Hepburn's landslide victory, being beaten by his close friend Arthur Ellis in what was called "the cleanest, friendliest campaign in the province." One cannot help admiring Wilson; in the struggle that was to come – a struggle that was often mean-spirited and petty – he never forgot himself, never lost his temper, never took sides, and never lost sight of his real job, which was the welfare of five little girls.

Wilson left in mid-March for North Bay to conduct a careful personal investigation into the Noël-Tremblay charges. Both women had made written statements. Dafoe, they said, had told them that the parents should not kiss the children: "It's not hygienic." Dafoe had refused to allow members of the family to eat with the quintuplets: "You have enough of them once a year. . . . They carry germs." Blatz had ordered them to speak English to the Quints in order that they might appear in more movies. Dafoe had urged Noël to teach the children to sing English songs, also for the movie. Dafoe had not wanted the children brought up convent style; he would not let them buy a Sacred Heart for the babies. Further, they objected to the Quints being photographed naked in their bath. Tremblay claimed Blatz had told her, "You know we want these children to learn English and you have not co-operated. You will leave today."

From other members of the staff, especially from the neutral Mollie O'Shaughnessy, Wilson heard the other side of the story. O'Shaughnessy was also a Roman Catholic, but her Catholicism was much broader than that of the other two women. Both were teaching the quintuplets to avoid all men, she said. Both had set out to turn the children against Dafoe, telling them repeatedly in French: "Doctor is dirty. He isn't nice. If you go near him, Little Jesus will cry." Noël had urged O'Shaughnessy to keep a book to use against the doctor "because he is in league with the Devil to get the children." They also taught the quintuplets to be conscious of their own nudity, a fact that Nora Rousselle, Tremblay's replacement, confirmed. When one of the little girls came out of the bathroom partly dressed, the others hustled her back, saying that she was bad and that Little Jesus would cry.

O'Shaughnessy was convinced that the isolation at the hospital had affected both women to the point where they had lost their mental balance. They rarely went out on their afternoons and evenings off. Their only social contact was with the Dionne parents. Tremblay had developed fits of temper and a feeling that she was being watched and followed and so was afraid to venture outside the compound. Noël spent days crying and once told O'Shaughnessy, "I saw the devil in the nursery. He had the face of Dr. Dafoe."

It was clear that, whatever the truth of the accusations, both women were by nature and upbringing totally out of sympathy with the Blatz program and that their presence had contributed to an atmosphere of incredible tension in the nursery. Wilson in his report wrote that Dafoe would have been derelict in his duty if he had not fired them. As for Dionne, Wilson pointed out that he had refused to attend any meetings of the guardianship and therefore could hardly complain that he was not consulted.

Conant, the attorney general, took the political situation seriously enough to make a personal visit to Callander, expecting to see Dionne. But Dionne avoided him, probably because he couldn't reach his newest lawyer, Henri Saint-Jacques, in Ottawa, for advice. Saint-Jacques, a director of the ACFEO, was a skilled and stubborn advocate for his client and would remain so over the next four years. But when Saint-Jacques demanded a judicial inquiry into the affairs of the guardianship, Dafoe fought back:

"Now that they [the Quints] have $600,000 there is a strong interest being shown in them. . . . It looks to me as if outside interests are trying to get control."

There was no inquiry. But Conant did suggest that in the future "in all the affairs affecting the Quintuplets, the father should be consulted. . . ." This represented a considerable change in the official attitude toward Oliva Dionne.

As a result, the guardianship agreed to leave educational decisions in the hands of the provincial department, to educate the other children at the expense of the quintuplets' trust fund, to raise Dionne's allowance by five hundred dollars a year, to appoint an architect to draw plans for a new home for the entire family, and to give Dionne the right to reject or confirm appointments in the nursing and teaching staff. Dafoe would continue to have supreme authority in the matter of the children's health.

Dionne had won a considerable victory, but for him it was not enough. He wanted Dafoe completely out of the picture – out as guardian, out as medical adviser, out of public favour. At the moment this was impossible. The popular press (save for the *New York News*, which had that spring published scoop after scoop from Lillian Barker, its pipeline into the Dionne household) was still heavily on Dafoe's side. And after his public statement about "outside interests," the doctor's mailbag bulged with letters from admirers.

From Mount Dennis, Ontario: "What a heap of trouble those Contemptible Dionnes have given their wonderful friend and Doctor. . . ."

From New York City: "Such ungrateful people! . . . Filthy lucre has obscured the sense of Duty, Justice and Right. . . . "

From Cleveland: "We, the people, are with you! If it were not for you, Dionne would be glad to get potato parings. What's wrong with that damned frog?"

Dafoe's popularity was undiminished. In Chicago in the fall of 1938, where he went to defend himself against Ivan Spear's million-dollar damage suit, he was, as usual, treated like visiting royalty. He rode to his hotel in the official limousine of the Medical Officer of Health – the same Herman Bundeson who had awakened him more than four years before in the grey hours of a May morning. Bundeson turned up the siren, and they shot through red lights to Dafoe's hotel where the Governor's Suite, with a drawing room "like a lesser lounge on the Queen Mary," had been reserved for him. Sixty-two lawyers were on hand to represent Dafoe and his co-defendants. (Dionne's name had been removed from the writ.) Rudy Vallee sat at the counsels' table and lunched with Dafoe at his club. The judge threw the case out after hearing the evidence, and the jurymen, who were not required to leave the box, crowded around the little doctor, asking for his autograph, along with Spear's own lawyers. But the world was occupied with bigger news, for that was the day that Neville Chamberlain was returning from Munich to announce "peace in our time" following the Czechoslovakian crisis.

Because of the continuing flow of photographs showing Dafoe with the quintuplets, the public impression was that he virtually lived at the hospital that had been named for him. That was not true. Some days, in fact, he did not bother to turn up but simply phoned in. He had long since abandoned his practice; too many visitors wanted to consult him just so that they could say they had met him. Although he was medical officer of health for the district, he does not seem to have performed many duties in that capacity. The Red Cross unit at Callander reported that he refused to do vaccinations unless he was paid for it and that their representative got "less cooperation from Dr. Dafoe than from any other physician."

Although his name appeared on articles, medical papers, and a daily newspaper column, Dafoe wrote none of these himself. Every major speech he gave to the various medical associations that clamoured for his presence was written by his younger brother. William Dafoe also answered much of his brother's correspondence and handled his speaking engagements before he acquired a secretary.

In October 1938, Hearst's King Features Syndicate announced that a new medical column written by Allan Roy Dafoe would appear in some two hundred newspapers across the continent. The job was actually done by his new personal secretary, George Sinclair, who that month replaced Gordon Moffatt, who had left after thirty months. A young man just turned twenty-two, the kid brother of one of the most famous reporters in the country, Sinclair would eventually rise to the presidency of Canada's largest advertising agency. But the experience at Callander was not one he was likely to forget.

I was out of work when Fred Davis called to say he was looking for a ghost-writer for Roy. He hadn't the least intention of doing it himself. So for thirty dollars a week I went up there and drafted the column – five hundred words a day. The basis on which I was hired was that I would read the fan mail and judge what people were interested in and then pull medical books down from his library and turn conventional advice into layman's language. I was to do my best to produce a style that might be a country doctor's style, and the idea was that Dafoe would go over it and rephrase it and perhaps add an anecdote. But he shipped the stuff off almost without reading it.

Dafoe would leave home about ten, go out to the hospital, where he'd spend about half an hour or so, then up to North Bay to sit and chat with Keith Munro and maybe Judge Valin. Then he'd be back for lunch, and then in the afternoon he'd nap to about three-thirty. Then he'd bustle in and spend a few minutes with me and then back to his fireplace and his books. He rarely went out. It was an incredibly constant routine. The loneliest man I ever saw in my life. Terribly lonely. A charmless man, really. He had no friends whatsoever and no connections in the village. The one person with whom he might now and then have a conversation was the local Catholic priest. He had an old bitch of a Scottish housekeeper there who guarded him. He hated her; she hated him. They made no bones about that, but they liked living together because he wanted nothing to do with any social contact whatever. I think he'd gone to Callander so he could be the only educated man in town and in a position to snub anybody. He detested the French Canadians. Despised them. Every reference he made to them was in a disparaging tone.

He never addressed me by my Christian name. He neglected formal address. Never Mr. Sinclair, or George, or Hey-you. It was a very formal relationship.

He revelled in publicity. He liked every excuse he could find to go to New York or Chicago as long as someone else would pay. He would usually find someone asking him to make a speech and get his expenses and fee and off he'd go.

He was a remarkably indecisive man. I had to look after his mail. I'd do the mail in the morning and the column in the afternoon. I'd draft answers for routine things, but some of the letters asking him to be on the board of governors of a hospital or a university or something would be fairly important. I'd save them. He'd come in, stand there with his pipe, and throw down the letters without comment. I'd say, What should we do about this? He'd say, Oh, I don't know; see what you think. So I'd put it aside and bring it up again next morning. But over and over again he evaded decisions. Sometimes I'd show him the letter three or four times, and then I'd answer it.

He had a desire to upstage people. There was the time when Jimmy Stewart came to town and he wanted to come in and see the doctor. That was arranged. But when Stewart was due to arrive, Dafoe quite specifically said to me, Now, when he comes, show him in there – pointing to the little barren room where his patients used to wait – and then tell me. So I did this. And Jimmy Stewart and his wife sat there waiting in the straight-backed chairs. I wandered back to let Dafoe know they were there. He said, You go and sit down, that's fine. I went back into my office and he let maybe another minute go by, and then he bustled out saying, Come back in here, come back in here. And he took them into his sitting room.

You know, this was one of the most affecting times of my life because of the mail. It comes back to me now, very strongly, the shock and pressure of some of that tragic fan mail. The Germans had moved in, first into Austria and then Czechoslovakia, and the Jewish people wrote to Dafoe – he was the only name they knew in North America. I remember vividly one letter written on elegant stationery in a beautiful hand – obviously a girl wrote it – and in perfect English, saying she was the daughter of a very successful doctor in Vienna. We must leave Austria, she wrote, because we are Jewish; my father thinks there is no hope, but I have read about you, Dr. Dafoe, and I write to ask whether you could use an assistant. And then she went on to describe the honours her father had, the degrees from the universities, enclosing what was a self-respecting but, you know, a dreadful plea. It seems there is nothing else for us, she wrote, but, even though my parents believe there is no hope, I must write to you.

God knows – she probably ended up as cinders.

TWELVE:
Under one roof

Nineteen thirty-eight – that pivotal year – came and went. Czecho-slovakia tottered; Anthony Eden quit; the Soviet Union contin-ued its macabre series of show trials; Orson Welles scared the wits out of a continent; Douglas Corrigan flew solo across the Atlantic and claimed he had gone the wrong way. And still the quintuplets did not move from their nursery. The talk of a new home, which had been announced early in May, remained just talk.

Dafoe still clung to the idea that there should be two separate buildings, a nursery for the children and a home for the family nearby, both to be erected on a new site. Because of their lack of resistance to infection, he insisted, the quintuplets would still re-quire some segregation. No doubt Dafoe was also aware that once the family came together under one roof, his own usefulness would diminish.

For once he and Dionne were in agreement. The location for the new home, they believed, should be a site overlooking Trout Lake, less than three miles from the old. There were excellent rea-sons to support this move. The water supply on the existing prop-erty was dangerous. Drainage from nearby swamps was seeping into the wells. The tourist washrooms, overtaxed, were polluting what soil there was to pollute. Every spring hordes of mosquitoes and blackflies rose out of the marshes. The site itself was not large; moreover, it was being ringed with booths and shops – "an ever-growing midway, to which I, for one, object," wrote Dafoe.

The department of public works agreed that the Trout Lake site was far superior. It provided plenty of fresh water, freedom from insects, and beaches on which the children could play without be-ing disturbed. "Remember, these children . . . can never run about and find such places for themselves," Dafoe argued. "They can never come down to the beach for an afternoon's bathing as others can. . . . The only privacy they can ever have is what they buy. This makes the choosing of a proper site all the more important, for where we put them now they will undoubtedly live until they are grown. . . ."

But Dafoe had about as much chance of moving the Quints from Quintland as the British prime minister would have had in moving the King out of Buckingham Palace. Once the announcement was made, a storm blew up among the commercial interests of Callander and North Bay.

In May, 1938, when the subject of a new home was first mooted, the Liberal Administrative Committee for Nipissing passed a resolution that it be built near the Dafoe Hospital. In July, when the Trout Lake site was announced, a chorus of protests rose. Callander foresaw its business cut off by the removal of its chief attraction. The reeve of North Himsworth called it "a bolt from the blue" and immediately led a deputation of businessmen to see the attorney general and protest any transfer. North Bay businessmen filed a similar protest. The mayor of Parry Sound informed the premier that "any change in location would greatly lessen their [the Quints'] value as attraction for tourists." The Parry Sound Board of Trade and the Callander Liberal Association joined in the chorus. Philip Adams, who owned the midwives' pavilion, wrote to everybody.

Hepburn left well enough alone. The Trout Lake project was postponed until the following spring on the ground that the price of the land was far too high. The question of an alternative site was never again raised.

For the babies continued to be big business. In the summer of 1939 a quarter of a million people drove up to Callander to see them. Although NEA claimed that interest in their photographs was waning – some newspapers were only offering half as much for them – it was still prepared to pay fifty thousand dollars for a two-year contract extension. Dafoe appeared on the Eddie Cantor radio program that fall for a fee of one thousand dollars and expenses. "Handies" had replaced Knock-Knock jokes as the current fad, and there was one about the Quints. You held up your right hand with the five spread fingers pointing upwards. You pointed your left hand down toward it and wiggled those fingers. "What's this?" you asked. "Give up? It's the five Dionne quintuplets under the shower." Then you turned your right thumb down and added: "One of them just bent over to pick up the soap."

Everyone, it seemed, wanted a look at the Quints. The new king was coming to Canada on a coast-to-coast tour designed to cement Commonwealth relations in a year of crisis; it was said that the Queen had specifically asked to see the quintuplets. Everyone assumed that the royal couple would visit Callander because Dafoe said the children could on no account be moved. Earlier, the Toronto city council had debated the idea of inviting the five to live in Casa Loma, the monstrous and improbable stone castle in downtown Toronto built by a pre-war millionaire. The board of control turned the project down by a narrow vote. "They'd be worth more to Toronto than fifty industries," said one controller wistfully.

Two world's fairs were being planned in the United States, one in San Francisco and one in New York. Both wanted the quintuplets. The Golden Gate International Exposition went so far as to pay Arthur Slaght a retainer of one thousand dollars to try to persuade the guardianship to move the children. As the fair's chairman, Atholl McBean, put it, "It seems to me, he enjoys a strong political position." Slaght certainly did. He had not only been one of Hepburn's chief lieutenants in the 1934 victory but he was also Allan Roy Dafoe's legal counsel and a federal MP for Parry Sound to boot. The conflict of interest didn't worry Slaght: he did his best, but his best was not good enough. A howl of protest rose up over the idea of the Americans cashing in on a Canadian tourist attraction. McBean's comment had a sour-grapes note to it. "If the lives of these little girls are going to continue to be guarded by such a grasping lot," he said, "they certainly have my sincere sympathy."

Behind the high wire fence of the hospital, the five little girls, now reaching school age, continued to live a cocoon-like existence that resembled scarcely any other on earth. Even their games were unique. How many other children in those days could pretend to grind a movie camera and direct imaginary films with the expertise of these five? For the quintuplets had made three feature pictures and scores of short subjects.

The differences between them, which had begun to be noticeable in their early months, became accentuated as a result of their isolation. Small variations, attributable to the order of their birth and physical condition, became more emphatic. Yvonne, the firstborn, was entrenched in her position as the acknowledged "mother" of the group, the one who looked after the others and was most respected by the others. Marie, the smallest and last born, and also the weakest physically, was looked up to least. There was, in fact, a social gap between the two mirror twins, Emilie and Marie, and the three "older" sisters, Yvonne, Annette, and Cecile. Sometimes the three oldest would ostracize the other two, insisting on playing apart from them, as older girls will often ostracize their younger sisters and friends.

Both Yvonne and Annette, the two earliest born, tended to boss the other girls around, but while Yvonne's bossiness was maternal (she oozed charm, rarely quarrelled, laughed and chattered a lot), Annette's was more aggressive. Annette invited quarrels when she knew she could win and was single-minded in her pursuit of her own goals. Nurse Leroux had predicted that Yvonne was "destined to be a housewife" while Annette "might well become a businesswoman." The remarks, in hindsight, are more ironic than prophetic.

Cécile, the middle Quint, was a thoughtful child who went her own way and often played alone. Marie and Emilie had a pixie temperament. Emilie, the most pious of the five, was also the most mischievous. Marie, who sometimes had difficulty keeping up with her sisters, loved to dance, to clown about, and to entertain the others, perhaps as a way of seeking their attention. She continued, also, to be the most affectionate, perhaps for the same reason.

While the Americans continued to woo the quintuplets, Dionne and his lawyer, Henri Saint-Jacques, were keeping up the pressure on Dafoe and the other guardians. Saint-Jacques's first target was the heavy expenditure made for the care of the Quints, much of which was clearly unjustified. He protested Dafoe's long distance bills; most, he said, were for the doctor's private business. He protested George Sinclair's salary; that, he said, went for the doctor's personal publicity. And he protested the one hundred and fifty dollars a month paid to William Flannery, secretary-treasurer to the guardianship, who was also the partner of Kenneth Valin, the nephew of Judge Valin; Saint-Jacques hinted here at nepotism.

Although Dafoe's position both as guardian and as head of the hospital seemed unassailable, Dionne and Saint-Jacques realized that there were two flaws in the carapace of rectitude that had been built up around him, both of his own making. The first was his inability to speak French; the second was his vulnerability in the matter of commercial contracts. Saint-Jacques resolved to concentrate his first attack on the latter front. The doctor had continued to allow the press to depict him as a man unconcerned with money and untainted by commercialism. As late as November 1938, Merrill Denison in *Harper's* referred to "the abhorrence felt by the little doctor for almost anything commercial." Now his enemies were determined to use his public image as a lever to remove him as guardian.

If Dafoe was aware of this gathering cloud of opposition, he did not show it: quite the opposite. On March 30, 1939, he wrote to

Percy Wilson, "I am thinking what's the harm in telling those French where they get off at. It might be a good time right now. Poppa is causing a lot of friction at the hospital, steadily using our teacher as a catspaw. . . ." Then he went off to New York to be initiated into the Circus Saints and Sinners Club at a luncheon in his honour. It was a serious mistake. Dafoe's very malleability, his casual acceptance of any kind of invitation, his "Sure, why not?" attitude that had once captivated New York were about to bring him down.

A few weeks later Saint-Jacques sent the attorney general a copy of a clipping from the *New York Sun*.

DR. DAFOE MADE "DOCTOR OF LITTERS"
Circus Saints and Sinners Initiate
Physician

Dr. Allan Roy Dafoe, famous physician of the Ontario quintuplets, was initiated this afternoon into the Circus Saints and Sinners Club. At a gala luncheon at the Hotel Astor, clad in a pink and white mortarboard and bathrobe, Dr. Dafoe was invested solemnly with the degree of Doctor of Litters. In return, he distributed among the 700 guests stones from the Dionne farm which he announced were "cherished by the superstitious as portents of fertility."

Driven into the room in a horse and buggy labelled "RURAL FREE DELIVERY", he was faced with a setting based on the circus while a dummy stork suspended from a wire fluttered to and fro bearing a picketing sign: "DR. DAFOE UNFAIR TO ORGANIZED STORKS. NO MASS PRODUCTION OF BABIES."

"I've had a swell time," said the country doctor when it was over. "Babies are all I know about, but taking care of the quins has become a job for a doctor, general manager and publicity agent. When I first went to Callander, I climbed to the Dionnes over a trail. Now the quins have paid for good roads everywhere in the district."

Dr. Dafoe was the "FALL GUY" of the show. Tex O'Rourke, the humorist, declared that the forgotten people in Callander were Poppa and Momma Dionne. He said: "While they are at home milking the cows, guys like the Fall Guy are taking the bows."

There was a stage show. A lone figure sitting in the stocks turned out to be cast for Poppa Dionne. When asked for the secret of his success he pulled the handle of an adjacent slot machine. Babies began to fall out of it one after the other. They turned out to be five Saints and Sinners disguised as Quins.

"I ask you," Saint-Jacques wrote to Conant, " . . . is it fair that Mr. Dionne should be compelled to keep this clown as guardian of his five children?"

Saint-Jacques advised Dionne to sue Dafoe for libel. The writ was issued on May 23, the day before the quintuplets met the King and Queen of England in Hepburn's private suite in the Queen's Park legislative buildings at Toronto.

Although Dafoe had said he could not risk a journey to Toronto with the babies, he was persuaded to change his mind after the formal invitation arrived. Significantly, it was addressed not to the guardians but to Oliva Dionne.

The quintuplets had found a photograph of the Royal Family in a picture book, which they promptly pinned to the wall of their playroom. Then, led by Yvonne, they stood in line and each in turn curtsied to the picture. Cécile and Emilie, the two chatterboxes, decided to talk to the photograph, asking how the little princesses were and whether they were like the princess in the Snow White fairy tale. Yvonne, taking the part of Their Majesties, answered all the questions. By the time the meeting took place, the five little girls were self-rehearsed.

A streamlined air-conditioned special of the Temiskaming and Northern Ontario Railway was placed at their disposal. Newly painted in crimson and gold, it included a baggage car, a day coach for police and reporters, a business car for the guardians and railway officials, a nursery car in which the Quints could sleep and frolic, and a combination dining and parlour car. Marie insisted that her oldest doll should also meet the Queen. Yvonne took a duck, Annette a bear, Emilie a three-year-old toy monkey, and Cécile a ragged blue dog. The *Star* engaged Dafoe himself to by-line the story of the events. All the other Dionne children were taken to Toronto as well, the boys dressed in new Eton jackets, the girls in white organdy. But the family reunion ended at the door of the Hepburn suite. The parents, doctor, teacher, and nurses were admitted together with the Quints. The other siblings had to wait outside without a glimpse of the sovereign and his consort.

The royal couple was photographed with almost every Canadian public figure *except* the quintuplets. Again, commercial considerations prevented the obvious picture. At the start of the tour, the government had announced that no one would be allowed to make exclusive photographs of Their Majesties; all pictures would be pooled. NEA Service was asked to waive its exclusivity clause for this one occasion but refused. On the contrary, Fred Ferguson, the president, wanted an iron-clad guarantee that the guardians would do everything in their power to prevent others from taking photographs. It was, of course, impossible. Arthur Sasse of International News Service boarded the train as a pool photographer and managed to take several unauthorized pictures, over the protests of Fred Davis. Ferguson, infuriated, put a ban on all further photographs; none were taken of the quintuplets until December of 1939.

The truth was that Ferguson was having second thoughts about his $25,000-a-year contract. That fall the war effectively dried up the European market and began to push domestic photos off the picture pages of the American newspapers. Ferguson tried to squeeze a free year out of Keith Munro, but Munro already had an offer in his pocket from King Features Syndicate. The NEA contract was allowed to lapse without further payment, and Fred Davis went to work for the Hearst group.

Dafoe was having his own troubles. The writ for libel was followed in six weeks by a second court action. Dionne was now demanding that the doctor turn in to the quintuplets' estate all the funds allegedly realized by him on advertising contracts in which the pictures or names of the quintuplets were included. He demanded a full inquiry into these contracts. The notice before the Nipissing District Court sought the production of contracts with forty companies.

Dafoe's lawyer, Arthur Slaght, charged that the suit was "a piece of personal venom" inspired by "subversive interests." He tried to have the case dismissed on the ground that the jurisdiction was not within the scope of the Nipissing court. Judge Plouffe – the same Judge Plouffe who was the local president of the ACFEO – found against him. A week after the action was announced, Dafoe signed a new three-year collateral contract with the Colgate company that paid twenty-five hundred dollars a year. The company said it wasn't interested in signing any kind of contract with the quintuplets unless the doctor was included. At the guardianship meeting, Dionne protested the contract but was overruled by Valin and Dafoe. Munro, as business manager, was enthusiastic. He wrote to Hepburn that the average advertiser wasn't interested in the Quints' endorsement unless Dafoe's went along with it. "They go together like bacon and eggs," Munro wrote. Some advertisers, in fact, wanted *only* Dafoe: "I personally believe that the day Dr. Dafoe severs his connection with the Quints, interest in them will drop fifty percent."

But Slaght, as a good Liberal and a Hepburn crony, was concerned about the public reaction to the suit and the revelations that would follow. There would, he felt, "be a very injurious effect [that] . . . will gradually create a bad taste in the mouth of the public . . . thereby destroying what has been a very proper and natural asset to our country." It was made clear that the government did not want the case to come to court.

Dafoe had other problems that wartime fall. "I have my hands full . . . I'm afraid of my nurses quitting. Judge [Valin] is *non compos mentis* at times," he told Wilson. Valin, who had always supported him against Dionne on the board of guardians, was lapsing more and more into senility. Mollie O'Shaughnessy was also ill and off duty, "still a nervous wreck" in Dafoe's words. The two other nurses, Cécile Michaud and Louise Corriveau, were at daggers drawn with the new French teacher, Gaëtane Vézina, who was solidly in the Dionne camp.

Oliva Dionne, acting on his lawyer's advice, was making efforts to be civil to reporters. "And so," Dafoe told Wilson, "we have to walk easy and be extra nice to the press. Public opinion so far is with us . . . but we can't take chances. . . . They [the Dionnes] torment the nurses every day and try to upset the children. The teacher is dangerous and spends all her spare time with the parents and the Barker woman. . . ."

As a result of Dionne's charges before the board of guardians at a June meeting that the nurses were poisoning the minds of the quintuplets against him, both Michaud and Corriveau decided to keep daily handwritten notes of the events during the summer. These notes reveal an impossible situation at the nursery, with the quintuplets being pushed and pulled in two directions by their mother, teacher, and siblings on the one hand and the two nurses on the other, often in full view of the public.

July 5, 1939: . . . Mrs. Dionne refuses to sit near Miss Michaud and I, remarking to her daughter, Thérèse, she could not sit near us as the honoured people around there were the nurses.

July 10: Mrs. Dionne in observation. Annette sitting in swing with her, and kept calling other children to her and disturbing play. When Quints refused to go to her she scolded them. . . . Yvonne and Cécile came to me crying. . . . Mother came to me, accused me of telling the Quints not to go to her. . . . Mrs. Dionne told Miss Michaud in front of her children and Quints I was a real devil and hard hearted towards the Quints.

August 16: Cécile brought in to be bathed . . . said her mother had said Dr. Dafoe, Misses Corriveau and O'Shaughnessy and Michaud were dirty and not nice, not to listen to them, they were crazy, only to listen to Miss Vézina. . . .

August 22: Mrs. Dionne . . . accused me . . . of turning the children from her and that I was dirty and that she had witnesses from the public, etc. . . . . I got up and walked out of the office and she followed me, yelling insults and threats so loud everybody could hear her. . . .

August 29: Children brought into bathroom for bathroom routine. Emilie and Marie admitted telling dirty stories: Miss Michaud and Miss Corriveau were dirty; we were bathing them and using towels to wipe their posterior with – Dr. Dafoe was dirty; only Miss Vézina and Mrs. Dionne were clean. . . .

September 2: After observation children played nicely with Thérèse and Pauline till 4:00 p.m. Mrs. Dionne came in and broke up their play. Called children to her and they refused, saying *maman* told them stories. Mrs. Dionne very angry, scolded Marie telling her that she was dirty and that she played with her posterior, told Emilie that she was a crazy little girl. Marie, Emilie, Cécile very hurt and refused to go to their mother. Mother very angry, got up and marched into the observation playground and started to cry and told children she was going to their father. Miss Corriveau and I went in and brought Annette and Yvonne in for bath. We told the other children to play with Thérèse. Thérèse pushed them and told them to go away. Children brought in for bath very upset. . . .

At the same time, Dafoe found himself under continual attack from *Le Droit* and sections of the Quebec press: "It would seem that Dr. Dafoe was Lord and Master in his domain. He acts like a dictator in the choice of the nurses. . . ." Dafoe was quick to send the editorial to Hepburn. "Dear Chief," he wrote, "this just adds fuel to my suspicion that we are in for a good, old-fashioned blitzkrieg again."

But Hepburn did not want a blitzkrieg (a new word that year). He wanted a quiet, out-of-court settlement between Dafoe and Dionne that would not damage the image of the quintuplets. The details were hammered out that fall between Slaght and Saint-Jacques. As of December 26, 1939, Allan Roy Dafoe was no longer a member of the board of guardians of the quintuplets. Oliva Dionne had won another round.

In addition to Dafoe's resignation, Saint-Jacques exacted a series of conditions: Mollie O'Shaughnessy would be replaced as head nurse. Construction of a new school, which all the Dionne children could attend, would begin at once. Wilson would replace Dafoe as an active guardian. The doctor would continue as medical adviser in full charge of the hospital and would also continue to hire the nurses but not the teachers. In return, all of Dionne's claims against Dafoe would be dismissed. The doctor would not be forced to produce in open court the details of his collateral contracts with commercial firms.

Dafoe's name was scarcely off the board when the New York World's Fair, having failed in its bid to attract the Quints during the first year of its operation, mounted a high-powered if desperate campaign to secure them for a second season.

In several ways, the story of the New York fair resembles that of the Chicago Century of Progress Exposition five years before. Both fairs were launched with rosy prospects and high ideals. Neither fulfilled the hopes of its sponsors. Both tried to bolster their fading fortunes by exhibiting the Dionne quintuplets. The theme of the New York fair was "Building the World of Tomorrow"; its secondary purpose was to promote the cause of world peace. But before the fair had entered its second season, the World of Tomorrow was crumbling around the heads of European refugees and the cause of world peace was lost.

If the fair was a financial flop it was, that first summer, a publicity man's dream. Its symbol – a connected spike and ball pretentiously named Trilon and Perisphere – became as well known as the M-G-M lion. The most popular commercial pavilion, the General Motors Futurama, purported to show how all traffic problems would be solved by superhighways by the year 1960. Gypsy Rose Lee, Frank Buck's Jungleland, and Billy Rose's Aquacade were big attractions, but they failed to lure the fifty million people the fair's promoters had confidently forecast. When the exhibition closed its gates in November, 1939, only half that number had paid their admissions. Worse, several European nations were forced to withdraw, including the Soviet Union, whose vast pavilion had been a smash hit of the first season, drawing sixteen million visitors. The fair's board was confident that the quintuplets would replace the Soviet exhibit. The fair would reproduce the entire hospital complex, playground and all, as well as the original farmhouse in faithful detail, and with some added refinements including soundproofing, air-conditioning, X-ray glass instead of wire mesh, and water maintained at the exact temperature required by Dafoe. The entire household – nurses, cooks, policemen, servants, plus all of the Dionnes – would be taken to New York by special train. And extraordinary precautions would be taken to forestall the threat of kidnapping.

On January 11, Mayor Fiorello La Guardia announced officially that the quintuplets would come. More important, perhaps, Walter Winchell also announced it. But in Canada there was an instant reaction. The *New York Times* had just posted a resident correspondent in Ottawa who sent back a bewildered first report. The public was far less interested in the war effort, he wrote, than in whether or not the five girls would go to the fair.

Some of the commercial interests were alarmed at the prospect. The Colgate-Palmolive-Peet Company said flatly that if the quintuplets went to New York its contract would be valueless. But the biggest loss would be to the Canadian tourist industry. The press took up the cry against the move. "No greater mistake could be made," cried the *Toronto Star*. "Ridiculous and outrageous," said the *Ottawa Citizen*. The *Sudbury Star* proclaimed that the stigma would take years to live down. The *Montreal Star* likened the proposed exhibit to that of "some man with a rubber skin or a woman with two faces." Dafoe added his own opinion. "We do not consider them freaks," he said.

These comments were echoes of similar ones voiced five years earlier at the time of the Spear contract. The situation, however, was different. The quintuplets were all healthy and perfectly able to travel. All the fair had offered to do was to duplicate or even improve on the exact conditions under which they were being exhibited in Ontario. One might well ask (but no one did ask): If the Quints were to be seen as freaks in New York, what were they in Callander?

On January 13, 1940, the fair's vice-president, J.C. Holmes, a former member of the U.S. diplomatic corps, arrived in Toronto convinced that he could persuade the guardianship to release the Quints. "I won't give up until I have a definite yes or no," Holmes declared. On January 15 he got his No; the Red Cross, which was to benefit from the scheme, spurned the hundred-thousand-dollar guarantee. Holmes declared himself flabbergasted and left, announcing he still remained hopeful. But it was clear that the quintuplets were going to stay put.

The Americans were not at war, and most Canadians did not yet feel any strong sense of being embroiled in a worldwide conflict. Dafoe had not even bothered to tell his charges that a war was taking place in Europe. "Why should we tell them?" he asked. "The war doesn't seem to us to have any bearing on the immediate problem of bringing up these five little girls." Then in the spring, the panzers began to roll and people suddenly stopped singing that most foolish of war ballads, *We're Going to Hang Out Our Washing on the Siegfried Line*. That summer the war's impact was felt strongly in Northern Ontario when the attendance figures at the Dafoe Hospital dropped sharply. The major loss came from the United States; the number of tourists crossing the border into Canada that year was reduced by 40 per cent.

The tourist slump was immediately seen as a Nazi plot. All nine provinces, through their tourist bureaus, combined in an effort to stop what was called Tourist Sabotage by the Germans. A series of radio programs extolling the advantages of visiting Canada was planned, and the quintuplets were called in to man the front lines. They appeared for ten minutes on *Ontario Night*, sponsored by the two transcontinental railways and broadcast over a network of forty-seven stations. They sang French songs and one English hit, *Oh, Johnny*, which they could not finish because of their limited knowledge of the language. "Come up and see us some time," said Cécile to her American listeners. Meanwhile, Keith Munro urged that the children be put out in the observation playground even on rainy days in order to avoid further tourist disappointment. The *Nugget* applauded the idea. "While theoretically it is not beneficial to the Quints it is believed such showings would simplify many tourist difficulties. . . ." Suddenly, in the face of an economic slump, all the public worries about the common cold and the children's low resistance to disease vanished.

Dionne and his supporters continued to harass – there is no other word for it – the guardianship and the nursing staff. Arvisais, the secretary of the ACFEO, sent an angry wire to Wilson complaining about the choice of songs on the tourist broadcast and "the quality of French used by the nurses attending the quintuplets." Cécile's phrase of invitation was pronounced shocking; it was, after all, the siren call of that painted goddess of sin, Mae West. Dionne even threatened legal action.

Dionne's tactics were purposely obstructive. He would object on every possible occasion and veto every suggestion put forward by Munro who, as an English-speaking appointee of Dafoe's, was considered an enemy. No issue was too small to draw a complaint from him or his lawyer. The Case of the Missing Hair provides a good example of the continual nit-picking that plagued Percy Wilson during these difficult years.

On September 3, 1940, Saint-Jacques wrote directly to Conant, the attorney general, to protest that "stealthily, behind the mother's and the Guardians' backs, the nurses Miss Dubeau and Miss Chaput, have cut short the hairs of our Quintuplets. *These hairs have disappeared*. They must be found and returned to the parents. . . . Whoever has committed this trespass must be punished. We insist that the hairs be returned to the owners without delay. I have advised the father that he has an action, in fact, several actions, against the author of this piece of vandalism."

Dionne's purpose was to weaken Dafoe's position as head of the hospital by forcing the dismissal or the resignation of all his nursing appointees and having them replaced by French-speaking nurses of his own choice. For language was now the lever to be used to pry the doctor away from control of the quintuplets. If the children were to speak French and French only, how then could Dafoe converse with them? Of what further use would he be as their medical adviser?

Dionne himself had not the slightest prejudice against English. On the contrary, he spoke it himself in preference to French and with only a mild accent, in spite of the patois that the newspapers sometimes put into his mouth. He had switched schools as a boy to learn it. English as much as French was the language of the Dionne household; the other children spoke it fluently. Now, however, he insisted that the quintuplets become completely proficient in French before learning any English at all. In this he had the enthusiastic support of French-Canadian nationalists in Ontario.

The Dionne camp was never satisfied with the French spoken by Dafoe's nursing appointees. *Le Droit,* in an editorial at the end of 1940, charged that in spite of their French names they "speak a jargon which . . . is certainly not conducive to the learning of perfect speech." It repeated the argument that Saint-Jacques had been hammering home: the nurses were stealing the children's affections from their mother. In the face of this persistent campaign, Wilson capitulated. Corriveau had already resigned. Now Leona Dubeau was replaced by Gertrude Provencher. Shortly afterwards Dubeau, suffering from tuberculosis and a generally run-down condition, was hospitalized. "I feel certain," she wrote to Munro, "that conditions at the nursery contributed to my illness."

On Sunday, May 11, 1941, the language issue came to a head. The quintuplets had been engaged to appear on a CBS Mother's Day broadcast to invite Americans to "come up and see us this summer" and to sing *There'll Always Be an England,* a particularly appropriate selection with Rommel's panzers streaking towards the Suez canal. The Saturday afternoon rehearsal went well. Chaput, one of the nurses, drilled the children in the few English words they would need to say. But one hour before the broadcast, all five struck, and there was nothing that the producer, Rai Purdy, could do about it.

I remember that I was quite new at CFRB at the time because Dick McDougall had been sent to Callander to be the regular announcer on the show that the good doctor was featured on for Lysol, and that's how I got my first job in radio as a cub announcer at twenty-five dollars a week. So I was very surprised to be sent up to do this job in

Callander for CBS, which, of course, to me was an enormous thrill because I'd never been on a network before. You see, I'd only just started. I can't remember all the details of it now, but I do remember that there was some squabble there, and just before we were to go on the air – of course, it was all live in those days – that somebody said, Nobody's going to speak English; they absolutely refuse to speak English. So, rightly or wrongly, I felt that maybe if we got something moving we might just sorta get them on the air; and so I got down on my hands and knees, and I got all five of them on my back, and I crawled around the floor like a pony and then – WHAP! – we were on the air.

The instigator of the revolt was Yvonne, whom Blatz had singled out as the mother-figure among the Quints. "Don't speak in English," she told her sisters. "It's not nice."

Nor would the children agree to sing *There'll Always Be an England*. "You can't get them to sing that song. They've been told not to sing it and that's that," an anonymous hospital official was later quoted as saying. The broadcast went on, and the quintuplets spoke only in French. The resultant controversy shared front-page space with the arrival in Scotland of Hitler's right-hand Nazi, Rudolf Hess, on his abortive "peace mission."

The repercussions were violent. In Toronto, the Orange-leaning *Telegram* headlined the story "BAN ON QUINTS' ENGLISH THREATENS POLITICAL BLOW-UP." Another unnamed official was quoted: "It's dynamite. There's bound to be a showdown one of these days between Quebec and the remainder of Canada. In Ontario right now, the situation as to French Canadians is not any too good. Anything the government might do in this issue will not help the situation."

North Bay, as usual, was concerned about the tourist industry. "From a mercenary standpoint alone the whole affair is likely to have an adverse effect," the *Nugget* wrote. "All parties concerned should get together to make sure that the Quintuplet picture is such that it will draw a maximum of visitors from the United States. . . ."

Two weeks later, the Ontario government tourist bureau persuaded the American newscaster and author Lowell Thomas to preside at the Quints' birthday broadcast. Thomas diplomatically decided to rehearse the quintuplets in two short sentences only – and both in French. He would ask them to help out in the current Victory Loan Campaign, and they would reply: "Oui, oui, Monsieur Thomas." Then they would send a message in French to Dafoe, who was seriously ill in a Toronto hospital. It may well have been this last suggestion that caused the embarrassment; at any rate, when Thomas asked his question the quintuplets refused to say a word, let alone convey a message to the doctor. There was no doubt about who was manipulating the children. Dionne, however, maintained his bland approach. "Had the other guardians consulted me in this connection instead of always doing things behind my back, my wife and myself would have soon convinced our children to speak English and all that adverse publicity would have been avoided," he told the provincial secretary.

Dafoe's condition was serious. In April he had been operated on for cancer of the lower intestine; a colostomy was performed. He did not return to Callander until early June and was still too sick to resume his duties. When another doctor was appointed to fill in for him, Dionne immediately protested the choice.

In the meantime, Dafoe had received a hard rap on the knuckles from Judge Plouffe, who, after examining the accounts for the previous several years, revealed that the annual cost of administering the hospital and the fund came to a third of the total amount earned each year by the Quints. The expenses, he said flatly, were not justified. He went on to write that he had been under the impression that Dafoe's sole income consisted of his monthly payment of $210 for looking after the children. Now, he discovered, the doctor had a considerable income from collateral contracts. He did not accuse the guardianship of misrepresenting the facts, but he was annoyed by what he called their "mutism" on the subject. He cut Dafoe's annual compensation by a thousand dollars and warned that further cuts would probably follow.

Revenues were continuing to decline as the war crisis deepened. Quintuplet dolls were no longer selling. Munro's New York agent, F. Darius Benham, had already reported that "the children have died out as an advertising medium. The public figures they have passed the danger point." They would be much more valuable, especially in radio commercials, he added, if they would only speak English. "I've discussed this . . . with . . . twenty advertising agencies and each one said 'Get these kids speaking English, they'll have tremendous advertising value.' " The word from Hollywood was the same. Fox had been considering a fourth picture, but the idea died when it was learned the Quints would only speak in French.

Photographic royalties from King Features Syndicate were dropping to a trickle. It was possible to sell pictures of the quintuplets only on their birthday and at Christmas. Even this was becoming difficult because of Mrs. Dionne's adamant refusal to let anybody but herself fix the children's hair. For years the public had been charmed by the photographs of the five girls with beautiful dark brown curls. Few realized that the quintuplets' hair was actually straight and that it had to be freshly waved every morning of their lives. Clark Kinnaird of King Features protested that the new straight hair style was unattractive and disorderly and made the children look older than they were. He pleaded for a professional hairdresser. But Mrs. Dionne remained unmoved. Through Saint-Jacques she indicated that any curling of the children's hair would be an "ordeal." Munro was convinced that this was still another tactic to harass the nurse on duty.

This harassment did not cease when finally the quintuplets' education was placed in the care of an order of nuns from North Bay. To Dionne, North Bay was anathema. He wanted to make his own choice – an order from Nicolet, Quebec. When he refused to give the new Sisters free rein over details of the children's schooling, the Sisters withdrew.

To Wilson there was only one solution. There must be a firm plan for the reunion of the family that had been talked about since the spring of 1938 but never acted upon.

Wilson's recommendation reflected the general change in attitude among the public and the press toward the Dionne family. Friendly articles had appeared in several mass magazines, notably the *Ladies' Home Journal* and *True Story*. The Barker syndicated articles had also had an osmotic effect. Equally important was the Roman Catholic lay press, which took up the Dionne cause. Two articles by Francis Talbot, published in *America* in the fall of 1941, produced dozens of letters advocating the return of the quintuplets to their parents. They were widely reprinted. *America* editorialized that "Mr. and Mrs. Dionne seem to be normal, respectable and responsible parents, not the degraded, moronic and greedy type that most Americans believe them to be."

The idea began to spread that the children were unwilling prisoners in a plush jail. An article in *Le Droit* reported that they had jumped the playground fence "where they were held as little prisoners and had tried to run away." The paper declared they were living in "an enervating and suffocating atmosphere."

In September, the government accepted Wilson's recommendation. A new fifty-thousand-dollar, seven-bedroom brick home for all the Dionnes would be started the following spring. There was no mention of Trout Lake. The house would be built as close to the nursery as possible. The original hospital would be turned into a school for the entire family. The teachers would be the nuns from Nicolet – the Sisters of the Assumption, who had always been Dionne's choice. The government also let it be known to the guardianship that the father of the quintuplets was to have his own way as far as the care of his children was concerned.

Immediately this announcement was made, Oliva Dionne ceased his campaign of opposition. He had, in fact, achieved almost everything that he had set out to achieve. There remained only one final victory, and that was not long in coming.

Dafoe would have to go. For more than five years Dionne had been working toward the moment when he could force the doctor's resignation. Now that moment had arrived. Actually, Dafoe's control over the hospital in the autumn of 1941 was token only. Sick, tired, and disheartened, estranged from the quintuplets who now refused to speak to him, his visits became fewer and fewer. The children spent both Christmas and New Year's Day with their family. On February 1, 1942, all five went along with their father and mother to break ground for the new home. Dafoe was not present. Five days later, Dionne served notice to the guardians that he wished to have sole supervision over the nursing staff and the health of the quintuplets. "The Guardians agreed unanimously that under the instructions of the Government, Mr. Dionne was to have control of his children, that he was quite within his rights in asking this." At the guardianship meeting, with Dafoe absent, Dionne demanded the doctor's resignation, effective that day. Wilson refused to support such a move; he would, he said, try to persuade the doctor to resign.

The announcement was made by Mitchell Hepburn on Valentine's Day. "It is no secret," the premier said, "that things have not been harmonious there for some time and his position as physician to the Quintuplets has been made almost impossible by reason of the fact that the children are not allowed to speak English."

Dafoe made his final professional call at the hospital the following day to bid the quintuplets goodbye. The details of that last confrontation are meagre, but it must have been inexpressibly sad for the doctor. The world had thought of him as their real father, and doubtless he himself had felt a similar bond. At Christmastime the quintuplets had firmly believed that he was at the North Pole, helping Santa Claus. When a painting by a leading artist had arrived at the nursery, Cécile was convinced that the doctor himself had painted it; the doctor, she thought, could do anything. But when Dafoe stretched out his hand to say farewell, the five girls held back and did not take it. The man behind this stunning rebuke was Oliva Dionne. Now, if not before, Dafoe was made to realize who the real father was. The bonds of blood proved stronger than any other.

"I have never made a barrel of money," Dafoe said in an interview that week. That was scarcely true. As for Dionne, he said nothing. Hepburn asked him for a public statement, but several days passed before Dionne replied. He said that he had been in bed with flu but would have liked to say that the press had grossly exaggerated the differences between the doctor and himself. That was not true, either. Flu or not, Dionne had the strength to ensure that the metal plaque bearing the doctor's name was removed from the stone gates in front of the hospital.

Miraculously, all the problems that had irked Dionne in the days when Dafoe was in charge melted away. The quintuplets began immediately to learn English. And, on their eighth birthday, the hair-curling ritual that the Dionnes had objected to as an ordeal was restored. Clara Ogilvie, a fashionable New York hairdresser whose clients included some of the biggest names in show business, came all the way to Callander to supervise the new style. And the summer showings, which Dionne, through his lawyer, had once damned as "Barnumesque" and injurious to the children's health, were also continued. But the crowds dwindled.

The following October, the quintuplets paid their second visit to Toronto to appear at a Victory Loan rally in Maple Leaf Gardens. Out onto the stage they rolled, pedalling white tricycles, dressed in red velveteen with white slippers and socks. It was noticed that they all had new permanent waves. For the first time it was their father who introduced them to the crowd. At his word of command all five tumbled off their tricycles and grouped themselves around the microphone. They spoke to the crowd in English and then sang *There'll Always Be an England*. For Oliva Dionne it must have been a magic moment. His total mastery of his family had at last been demonstrated to fifteen thousand applauding spectators and hundreds of thousands of radio listeners.

Had he ever thought beyond this moment? Had he ever considered the future of the reunited family, with its two disparate arms? The quintuplets were his. To Dionne, savouring the applause, that was enough; it was what he had worked, battled – even schemed – for. But was this really the end of the struggle? Did Dionne foresee the hollowness of the victory, the eventual price of the triumph? It is hardly possible. For to Oliva Dionne, the recapture of his children had become an end in itself.

Allan Roy Dafoe was not present that night. The news stories did not comment on his absence. He had not seen the quintuplets since that painful leave-taking at the hospital; nor would he ever see them again. On June 2, 1943, he died suddenly of pneumonia. The news, which might have made larger headlines, was overshadowed that day by another tragedy. Leslie Howard, the film star, had vanished in a plane over the Bay of Biscay.

Wartime shortages slowed the construction of the new home, but finally, on November 17, 1943, more than nine years after the original separation, the Dionne family was reunited under one roof, and the press was able to report that the quintuplet melodrama had, at last, a happy ending.

"It's lovely to have mamma and daddy always near," Yvonne, the leader, was quoted as saying. "I am so happy. It is just like the picture books, our new home is so nice."

But like so many other chapters in the Dionne quintuplet story, the reality behind the public image was quite different. Twenty years later, Yvonne and her three surviving sisters savagely revised that quoted statement.

"It was," they wrote, "the saddest home we have ever known."

THIRTEEN:
Aftermath

If the story of the Dionne quintuplets proves anything it proves that people believe in fairy tales and that the media believe them too, even when they know better; or perhaps it is more accurate to say that the media invent fairy tales for the public to wallow in. The story of the quintuplets' birth was a fairy tale. The Good Fairy was Dafoe; the Wicked Fairy was Oliva Dionne. Dafoe had feet of clay – who hasn't? – but, having invented a Legend, the newspapers stuck to it. During Dafoe's lifetime no reporter had the temerity to suggest that in his later years the doctor was little more than a figurehead and that his personal dollar profit from the miracle of Callander was as great as that of any one of the five babies. Perhaps a later generation of journalists would have treated Dafoe with greater realism, but that was not the Thirties' style.

The media's handling of Dionne is more complicated. By the time the quintuplets were returned to their family the Bad Fairy had somehow been transformed into a Hero on Horseback, freeing his children from the clutches of Authority. Newspapers love an underdog who wins out against insurmountable odds, and that is how Dionne came to be portrayed.

The newspapers of the Thirties and early Forties tended to treat the stories they reported as melodramas. The soap opera, after all, was the real theatre of the masses, and the typical soap opera dealt with ordinary people facing up to and surviving against almost hopeless odds. The titles themselves often suggested the content: *Brave Tomorrow, Against the Storm, Bright Horizon, Valiant Lady*.

To a remarkable degree the soap operas evoked a cosy bygone era of tree-shaded small towns, where folks were folks – the kind of small town and the kind of small-town people depicted in the hugely successful Andy Hardy movies. *Big Sister* was set in "Glen

Falls," *Aunt Mary* at "Willow Run Farm," *The Great Gildersleeve* in "Summerville," *Ma Perkins* in "Rushville Centre," *Seth Parker* at "Jonesport, Maine," *Young Dr. Malone* at "Three Oaks." The very names of the villages have a wistful sound to them, suggestive of pleasant streams, little waterfalls, sunny skies, spreading foliage. The soap-opera people did not live in apartments or tenements; they lived in detached homes – "the small house halfway up in the next block," to quote the opening of *Vic and Sade*.

The melodrama tended to centre around a professional or business figure who unselfishly helped his neighbours. David Harum was a small-town banker; Just Plain Bill was a small-town barber; Dr. Hackett, of *County Seat*, was a small-town druggist; John, of *John's Other Wife*, was a small-town storekeeper; and, of course, Dr. Christian was a small-town doctor, directly based on the public image of Allan Roy Dafoe.

By contrast, the crime and detective shows took place in big cities. "Death stalks the city," cried the announcer on one episode of *The Green Hornet. Big Town, Gangbusters,* and *Front Page Farrell* were all set in congested, crime-ridden city streets, which the public tended to identify with Chicago. (New York, by contrast, was all glamour and high drama, typified by such programs as *Grand Central Station, First Nighter,* and *Grand Hotel.*)

Though the majority of the population had long since shifted out of the rural areas, the radio listeners lived vicariously. Like the pastoral setting, the happy ending was mandatory; there were so few in real life. Hollywood changed almost every classic it bought so that the final reel would be upbeat. Life must mirror art. Thus, in the story of the quintuplets, there was a series of "happy endings." First, the Good Fairy saved their lives when almost everybody had given up hope. Then, when the Bad Fairy tried to spirit them away to Wicked Chicago, they were saved again, in the nick of time. Further attempts by evil forces were made upon them, but again Good triumphed over Evil. At that point, the world believed that the quintuplets really would live happily ever after. The newspapers assured their readers that no other children anywhere were receiving better care. The newsreels and the still photographs showed them romping cheerfully with their kindly protector. "Happy Little Quins!" as the Palmolive ads exclaimed.

That soap opera ended; a new one began. Subtly, over the years, it came to be believed that the quintuplets were living in a prison – a gilded prison, certainly, but a prison no less. A totally new script was created in which a poor but struggling farmer was seen to be battling to reunite his family. Did they not have, as the soap opera said, the Right to Happiness? By November, 1943, when the Quints were finally returned to their parents, the public was convinced, again, that the new melodrama had the conventional happy ending. "I am so happy," little Yvonne had been quoted as saying; and in the decade that followed, the public was periodically led to believe that the labyrinthine tale was over, neatly packaged in that final scene with the little girls tripping across the road to their big new luxury home.

"All in all," the *Star Weekly* reported in 1948, "the quintuplets seem to be happy and contented, particularly when they are left alone. They appear to be devoted to their parents and according to Sister Superior, value nothing more highly than the friendly, fatherly counsel they receive from papa."

Lillian Barker, in her second book about the quintuplets, *The Dionne Legend*,* published in 1951, re-emphasized the joy the quintuplets felt at being reunited with their parents:

> . . . no displaced persons . . . ever tried more conscientiously to adapt themselves to their new family. . . . They just wanted to be happy themselves and to make everybody else happy, above all, their parents. . . . [They] had no condescending or patronizing ways. They were just five sisters who had prayed to live at home. Their prayers had been answered, *et voilà*, what more could they ask? That seemed to summarize the quintuplets' attitude.

The quintuplets continued to make headlines from time to time. In 1943, they visited Superior, Wisconsin, to launch five Liberty ships named after them. Fifteen thousand people attended. They all visited the Marian Congress at Ottawa in 1947. The same year, the former nursery was turned into a school (named Villa Notre Dame) where the quintuplets and nine other girls, hand-picked from various Northern Ontario and Quebec communities, studied together under the Sisters of the Assumption. In 1950, they visited New York as guests at the hundred-dollar-a-plate Alfred E. Smith Memorial Dinner. It was noticed at the time, but not commented upon, that Emilie disappeared for part of the program, apparently with a headache. The girls' drawing power seemed undiminished. When they returned from New York through Montreal, a thousand people jammed the station to greet them and an additional four thousand milled about the entrance. In 1952, they made an-

---

*Miss Barker's book was withdrawn from distribution in Canada because of "certain inaccuracies." Its publication aroused a storm of protest because the book was strongly antagonistic to Dr. Dafoe.

other public appearance at the St. Paul winter carnival. But apart from these well-publicized outings, the five children were rarely seen, even in North Bay and Callander. They remained hidden behind the high wire fence that now surrounded the Big House (as it came to be called), a circumstance that Audrey, Danny Dionne's new girl friend and later his wife, would never forget.

I'm from New Brunswick and, of course, I'd heard of the Dionne Quints. I'd seen them in the Colgate ads and in the movies. But when I read about them it was just like reading about the Sleeping Beauty. It wasn't real, you know? So when I met Danny and got his name, Daniel Dionne, it didn't mean anything to me, either. Then I mentioned him to somebody I was working with, and he filled me in: Don't you realize who he is? And then he told me about it.

You know, this was another part of the world to me. But I realized what it was all about fast enough when he brought me to Callander to meet the family one Saturday; and I saw the big fence, and, you know, you couldn't get through the gate, even though you were one of the family. I remember Danny got out of the car at Callander and went to the garage and phoned the parents to unlock the gate because we were coming in; and I thought, What the heck is going on? You know – coming from a small village in New Brunswick, I thought he was putting me on. But we walked in and his Dad gave him a kick in the rear, you know, and his brother hid behind a chair. . . . But I remember his mother best of all. She had a real French-Canadian motherly look about her – a beautiful-looking woman! . . .

At that time the whole family had to be protected. You know at one time they had two big bears around the house for protection: live bears – tied up. And the police! You couldn't go out, either, because there were too many people around – strangers. There was the threat of kidnapping. . . . Even in 1952, after I was married, you couldn't let your kids play in the yard because people were still coming around wanting to talk to you or yelling at you for information, thinking that any one of us was the Quints because we were all dark-haired.

The Quints were shy. When people would come around, they'd find an excuse to go up to their room. They were very, very shy. Their father was strict, up to a point, but then he had to be. I remember one time they couldn't understand why they couldn't go out, just the five of them together. Because when you went out with them, two would have to walk together and one would walk with another member of the family. But it was only to protect them that he did that. . . .

On their eighteenth birthday, in May, 1952, Dionne announced that his daughters would leave home for the first time to attend school at the convent of the Sisters of the Assumption at Nicolet, Quebec. The following year, in August, Marie announced her intention of becoming a nun; she was enrolled at the Convent of the Holy Sacrament in Quebec City, where it was reported she would be treated "just like any other girl." Yvonne also separated from the others to study at the Congregation of Notre Dame in Montreal. Her three sisters continued their schooling at Nicolet.

In late July, 1954, Emilie made headlines. She had been found wandering about Montreal, lost and disoriented, and had been taken to the police station and finally to the Archbishop's palace. The stories that emerged were garbled; some suggested that Emilie had been in jail. The truth did not come out for many years: Dionne had kept secret the fact that Emilie, too, had decided to take the veil and had enrolled as a postulant at a convent in Ste Agathe, the Laurentian ski resort north of Montreal. Meanwhile Marie had become ill and homesick and had been sent for a rest to a convent at Richelieu. She called for Emilie, her closest sister. Emilie immediately took the bus from Ste Agathe to Richelieu but became confused and got off at the Montreal stop in error. She had never been on a bus alone in her life; nor had she ever wandered alone in a big city. Montreal bewildered and frightened her. Finally, a police car picked her up and an official at the Archbishop's palace was able to direct her to the proper bus line. Had she not been a quintuplet, the story would not have made news. Though she asked the police to preserve her anonymity, one of them leaked the tale to the press.

Within two weeks she made headlines again, and for the last time. Alone, in her bed at the convent, she suffocated to death during an epileptic seizure. The world was shocked. No hint of her condition had ever crept into the newspapers. The affliction had not become apparent until she was twelve – three years after she moved into the family home. The Dionnes, feeling that it was shameful, had kept it a dark secret. Emilie herself always had a forewarning of her attacks, and her sisters knew exactly how to treat her when she suffered from one. Mrs. Dionne had let Mollie O'Shaughnessy into the secret at the time of the New York visit, and the former nurse, now Mollie McMillan, had agreed to accompany the group. She attended Emilie when the girl realized, during the Al Smith dinner, that she was about to suffer another seizure. But even Dr. J. E. I. Joyal, Dr. Dafoe's replacement, was ignorant of Emilie's affliction, although he revealed, in a remarkable statement after her death, that there was "much hearsay" about such attacks.

The Sisters at Ste Agathe had been warned by Mrs. Dionne that

Emilie was subject to convulsions and should never be left alone, but they apparently did not take the warning seriously enough. The day before her death she had suffered a seizure in the convent hospital, where she fell and bruised her ankle. No physician was called to treat her. She experienced three further attacks and asked not to be left alone, but the nun who was supposed to remain in her bedroom departed briefly for Mass. On her return, she found Emilie dead.

For Emilie's four identical sisters, the tragedy was almost unbearable. It had not occurred to any of them that one might predecease the others. The funeral that followed was a nightmare for all, a repeat performance of that spectacle of an earlier decade – cars bumper to bumper along the highway from Callander to Corbeil and the police patrolling the grounds in an attempt to preserve some kind of order.

The four survivors all moved to Montreal. Marie, whose health was failing and who felt the loss of her sister more keenly than any, could not return to the convent. She and Annette enrolled in the Collège Marguerite-Bourgeoys, one to study music, the other literature. Yvonne and Cécile entered the Hôpital Notre-Dame de l'Espérance as student nurses. In September, 1955, Marie made another attempt to adjust to convent life, but it was short-lived. Late in November she was reported in hospital in "very precarious condition."

That December, the quintuplets burst once again into the news. Eight-column headlines in the *Toronto Star* announced:

PAPA DIONNE DECLARES QUINTS
IGNORED FAMILY AT CHRISTMAS

Dionne himself called a press conference, a remarkable action for a man who had once shunned the media. But then, the Oliva Dionne of 1955 was not the Oliva Dionne of 1935. He had long ago come to realize the power of publicity, and it may be that he now felt that publicity would help to hold his family together as it had once helped to reunite it.

"We were not surprised when the Quints did not come home at Christmas," he told the newspapers. "We have realized for months that they have been drifting away from us. . . . The Quints lately have been treating their brothers and sisters with contempt."

He added that the four girls had not even bothered to send a Christmas card. In addition to the father, two of the boys were interviewed. "They act as if they are queens or something," said Victor. "We are like dirt to them," said Danny, an attitude of which his wife, Audrey, was well aware.

Danny's attitude was that he was bitter about being separated from them. He used to say that they were like two families. They were one and the Quints were one, and if he wanted to see his sisters, he'd have to ask permission. I remember lots of times when he would talk about the past; he'd say, How would you like to live the way we did? If I wanted to see my sisters, I'd have to go first and look at them through a fence. He probably never even touched their hands until they were home together in the Big House.

Dionne, echoing an old phrase of Dafoe's, blamed "outside intruders" for the separation: "We suspected that outsiders were trying to influence the Quints some time ago, and we were sure of it by the way they acted toward us after they left home, and then more so when they reached their 21st birthday and came into some money."

By "outsiders" Dionne meant Germain Allard, who had met Annette during his fourth year in college and was now her steady escort. There was also another man on the horizon, of whom Dionne was not yet aware: Philippe Langlois, a CBC technician, was taking Cécile out on a regular basis. Both girls kept these romantic involvements a secret from their father for some months. These were the first and indeed the only boyfriends either girl had ever known. Both were married within two years; some years later both marriages broke up.

They're my age, you know. When I was eighteen I was married to their brother Danny, and so we were all very close. When they needed someone to talk to, they'd come to me. They couldn't figure out the kind of life I had. They would wish they could have been more like that. And they would question me about love: How does it feel to be in love? How does it feel to have a man care for you? How do you know he cares for you yourself and not because you're a Quint? To me, they were lost. They were my age but they hadn't started to live yet. When you're seventeen or eighteen, you don't realize much. Like any teenagers, they were boy crazy, but they didn't have a chance. They didn't have the chance to go out with boys like I did. It was different for them. If there were parties, boys were chosen to be their escorts. I doubt at the time if a boy had asked them out if Mr. Dionne would have let them go, unless he knew the family of the boy very well. I think sometimes he was a little overprotective, but then he had to be.

I remember one time when I was pregnant with my first baby, and I was out in the fields with Annette, picking berries, and she got to wondering if she would ever be as happy as I was. And she started asking me questions: How do you know you're in love? How does it feel to be

married? How can you tell when a man really loves you? And I said,
You can't really answer that question; nobody can. And she said,
Well, how do you know when the right one comes along? How do you
know he's the right one? And I said, Well, you just know; things just
happen. That was before she met Germain. . . .

All that Christmas week of 1955, the schism in the family made
headlines. The quintuplets did their best to paper over the breach.
They explained to reporters that their Christmas cards had been
held up in the mail; that, traditionally, presents were not exchanged among French-Canadian families until New Year's Eve;
that they could not come home because Yvonne could not be released from her duties as a nurse-in-training, and all four liked to
do things as a group. Finally, Yvonne, Cécile, and Annette made
the pilgrimage to Callander for the New Year. Marie was too ill to
travel. Annette brought along her boyfriend, Germain Allard, a
cheerful, extroverted young man whose sister had gone to school
with the Quints at Corbeil. Allard never forgot the arctic atmosphere he encountered in the Big House or the attitude of Oliva
Dionne, which was more than faintly reminiscent of Mr. Barrett
of Wimpole Street.

There was a feeling of tension as soon as we came in. A cold wel-
come: just phrases like, Hello, how was the trip? Remarks about the
weather. That kind of thing. Annette finally decided after a few mo-
ments to introduce me to her father and to the other members of the
family. They were all very, very cold. We could feel the tension. No-
body wanted to go straight to the point – the fuss about the Christ-
mas cards. That had been the topic, apparently, in the family all
during the previous few days, but they didn't want to bring it up.

I got the impression that Mrs. Dionne was more human, more sym-
pathetic. But she didn't want to say anything because the boss was the
father. She is of the old, old mentality – that the woman is to be the
slave of the husband. In other words, she has to say the same things
that he does. But she seemed to be more honest, and I had the feeling
the girls would go more easily to the mother than to the father.

Annette and I had bedrooms on the second floor with a connecting
bathroom. The next morning Mr. Dionne, who was complaining of
many things, finally told me: I know all about you and my daughter;
last night you were walking from one bedroom to the other. Meaning
that I had slept with her! In his own house! I was so mad, I don't re-
member exactly what I said, but I told him, in effect, Do you believe I
would be crazy enough to sleep with your daughter in your house
when I had hundreds of chances to do it in Montreal? My reputation

was affected and my pride was affected . . . . Young Oliva, he was sleeping upstairs and could hear the tone of our conversation. He came down angry, and he wanted to settle things outside. I tell you, my friend, if I had had a car of my own, I would have driven back to Montreal, right then and there. . . .

But the cracks in the family's façade were covered over. By the end of the week Dionne had issued a statement that it was all a misunderstanding. The entire family (sans Allard) smiled cheerfully together for the photographers.

Another year went by. In April, 1956, Marie decided to open a flower shop in Montreal, named the Salon Emilie after her dead sister. It was a financial disaster. Marie gave away as many flowers as she sold and suffered a forty-two-thousand-dollar loss. Depressed by the failure of her first business venture, she suffered a nervous breakdown in the spring of 1957. She was given shock treatments for her condition and radium treatments for the tumour in her right leg, which had bothered her all her life. Annette married Germain Allard early in October of that year. Cécile followed with a ten-thousand-dollar wedding at Corbeil to Philippe Langlois. A year later Marie was married secretly to Florian Houle, fourteen years her senior. She did not inform her sisters until the night before the marriage; they stayed away in order to preserve her privacy. Nor did she make any attempt to tell her parents. The three girls settled down to raise families. Yvonne, who had been studying art and sculpture, put them aside and announced, in 1961, that she intended to become a nun.

By this time, those who still remembered the Dionne quintuplets had come to a vague realization that all was not right between the four survivors and their parents. But the depth of the gap of understanding was not made public until the four girls put their names to a series of articles that began appearing in *McCall's* magazine in September, 1963. Written by James Brough and later published in book form under the title *We Were Five*, the articles tore away the curtain of secrecy behind which the family had hidden itself since the day of reunion.

We Were Five is a bitter and sometimes brutal book. It confirms almost everything that Alfred Adler predicted in his much-maligned article in *Cosmopolitan* magazine. By separating the quintuplets from their family – physically, psychologically, and financially – and by treating the five sisters as royal celebrities, artificially reared, constantly on display, and identically attired, the Ontario government and its appointees had created a schism within the family that could never be healed.

The book was written after a series of thirty interviews that Brough conducted with Cécile and Annette and their husbands and with Marie. Most of the material came from Annette, who, as a child, had been tabbed as the most aggressive of the quintuplets. Annette's husband, Germain Allard, was by then acting as the spokesman for the four; it was he who handled the financial arrangements with Brough and *McCall's*. Yvonne did not take part, although her name appears in the multiple by-line. Florian Houle, Marie's husband, attended the first two interviews and then refused any further participation. His marriage to Marie was already on shaky ground.

After the articles appeared, Houle wrote to Oliva Dionne: " . . . when I realized the feeling of hate and grudge that your daughters gave to their comments, I told my wife that I disapproved . . . and . . . refused all other interviews or invitations with the author." Houle said that he had tried to have the articles toned down after the author submitted a rough draft for approval, urging his wife and her sisters to "withdraw statements which were most impolite and harsh to you." But when Marie phoned Annette, the two agreed that the suggested changes were not justified.

"I realize," Houle wrote to Dionne, "that you were looking for an explanation for the conduct of your daughters. I realize also that it is hard for a father to admit that his own daughters talk this way about their father. Alas! It is the pure and simple truth."

The quintuplets not only stood by the book, which paid them an estimated hundred thousand dollars from royalties and serial rights, but Annette also went to New York after its publication to take part in some thirty television, radio, and newspaper interviews to help push its sale. She has since referred to it as "a sensitive and accurate account of our life story," and to this day she and her sisters put off prospective interviewers by referring them to *We Were Five* as the final word. The book is harsh in its assessment of the Dionne parents, but the truth is that the quintuplets' own feelings – especially toward their father – were even harsher at the time it was written. Brough did his best to soften the blow.

The four sisters started off by making it clear that, contrary to what was believed in 1942 and 1943, they had loved their years at the Dafoe Hospital. This was, they said, the happiest period of their lives; after the move to the Big House, they often dreamed of their nursery days and longed to go back. To them, the new environment was far more prison-like than the old and the discipline far harsher. In one sense, *We Were Five* is the story of a clash between two systems of child upbringing – the modern system of Dr. Blatz and the age-old system of Roman Catholic Corbeil.

It was rarely possible for the quintuplets to leave the grounds of their new home and never by themselves. Those trips that were made, they wrote, were always an ordeal because of the presence of motorcycle police escorts with blaring sirens, which attracted crowds and "gratified some deep-seated desire of Dad's for recognition." Nor were they allowed to make friends outside the immediate family: all their letters, incoming and outgoing, were opened and read by their father.

Through the eyes of these identical children, Oliva Dionne appears as a distant and unloving man, impossible to grow close to, embittered by the events of a decade, suspicious of strangers and acquaintances, and hungry to assert his total control over his daughters, whom he rarely if ever praised. The entire family held him in awe, and all the children accepted his commands without question. "Nobody argued with Dad; to disobey was unthinkable. Yet in almost indefinable fashion, he was afraid of Mom, as if there lingered in his heart a sense of guilt or obligation for fathering five daughters in a single birth. . . ."

"Guilt" was a word that turned up several times in the book. Elzire and Oliva Dionne behaved "as though they were partners in some unspoken misdeed in bringing us into the world. . . . We were drenched with a sense of having sinned from the hour of our birth . . . we were riddled with guilt."

To the quintuplets, both parents seemed to be searching constantly for physical proof that their restored daughters loved them. They must demonstrate that love continually. Good-night kisses were mandatory; if the five girls forgot, Oliva Dionne pulled them back to the living room to maintain the ritual. Yet he himself remained at a distance, insisting that when they spoke to him in French they use the formal *vous* rather than the intimate *tu*.

The family leaned over backward in its attempt to make sure that the five sisters would receive no special treatment. (They were dismayed on the first day to find themselves separated from each other in individual bedrooms.) But they *were* different from the rest of the family. They had been brought up in French; their siblings spoke fluent English and laughed at their attempts to converse in the strange language. They were treated not as separate individuals but as a single entity. They were obliged to dress alike but could not choose their own clothes; their mother purchased identical oversize dresses for them in the splashy flower prints she enjoyed but the girls hated. "We felt as though we were in uniform," they wrote. They were not allowed to do their homework in their rooms, as the others were, but had to study in the living room under their father's watchful eye. They grew fat on the milk their mother forced on them but were not allowed coffee until they were twenty; their brothers and sisters drank it at fourteen. Make-up was also forbidden.

Oliva Dionne enjoyed showing them off. "When neighbours were asked in for the evening, we were invariably part of the show, to be ushered in for inspection." Even after they were asleep, they wrote, strangers were sometimes taken through their rooms.

Their parents insisted that they lend a hand at chores. The five girls, who for the first nine years of their lives had never had to lift a finger to perform a single service, found it irksome and felt it unfair. In their book they insisted that they were treated as slaves and made to work far longer hours than other members of the family: they scrubbed their bathrooms, milked cows, fed chickens, sheared sheep, helped in the haymaking.

Money was also a divisive factor. Indeed, the financial imbalance between the Quints and the rest of the family was almost certainly the chief reason for the split that was to come. The quintuplets wrote that they were constantly reminded of their wealth, yet all they received was a tiny allowance. When they went to the movies *en famille*, they were expected to pay. At Christmas, it was assumed that they would each buy an individual present for every member of the family; the others were allowed to club together. Whenever a COD parcel came to the door, it was the Quints who paid for it – or so they claimed.

They themselves had no idea how much money was held in trust for them. In fact, they wrote that they believed all through their childhood and teens that it was their father's money they were spending. This, too, brought a sense of guilt. "It was impossible to spend a nickel without wondering if he could afford it." Dionne even refused to allow them to have a bicycle apiece. Two would be enough for five, he said; anything else was unnecessarily extravagant.

In their early teens they suffered from a series of communicable childhood diseases to which they had little natural immunity because of their isolation in the Dafoe nursery. Emilie's epilepsy first showed itself when she reached puberty. Her seizures were brought on by emotional domestic scenes and by her menstrual periods. Dionne warned his family never to discuss Emilie's affliction.

Love and sex were regarded as equally shameful. Pregnancy was unmentionable; when Mrs. Dionne grew heavy with another child, nobody made any comment. The facts of life remained a mystery. Boyfriends were taboo. It did not occur to any of the five that they might someday marry and have children of their own; the tacit assumption was that marriage was not for them.

At school in Nicolet, their existence remained confined. They believed that the nuns, too, leaned over backwards to avoid preferential treatment and thus made things harder for them. Although it was made clear to them that they were the richest children in the school, their allowances of two dollars a month made them paupers compared to their classmates. Unlike the other students, they were not allowed to leave the school grounds for any reason; Dionne had given strict orders against it. When the others went out, the five girls were sent to their rooms to write letters. But, they wrote, they had nobody to write to except their parents.

Inevitably, the breach came. After Emilie's death, when the four survivors left Corbeil to lead lives of their own in Montreal, Oliva Dionne was "offended and outraged." The much-publicized reunion following the Christmas headlines of 1955 only emphasized in the sisters' minds their father's possessiveness: "He could not bear to let us go. He had fought tooth and nail to prevent it. He wanted to keep us for himself alone."

In Montreal, the four girls "raised without a shred of independence or mental muscle, introverts through and through," found that they did not know how to handle money, how to enter a store, how to approach a salesclerk, or how to choose their own clothes. Clinging together, they discovered that they were immediately identified. Crowds gathered. They fled. Shopping expeditions consisted of sudden furtive dashes into stores to purchase the first item they could lay hands on – generally something black and a size too large.

Meanwhile their father had started to turn up unannounced, and there is a strange account of two of them hiding under their own bed while he hammered vainly on the door of their apartment. The four girls insisted in their book that their father had actually hired private detectives to spy on them and on their boyfriends. They knew this, they wrote, because the fees for the job were charged to the quintuplets' trust fund. When Dionne finally met Germain Allard, he told him: "You are only interested in Annette because of her fame as one of my daughters and because of her money."

Money, the sisters wrote, changed their father's nature. "There was so much more money than love in our existence. It took a long time to realize the effect it had on all of us. . . ." At twenty-one, they were due to come into a fortune that exceeded eight hundred thousand dollars. But they were pressured by their father, they said, to sign a trust agreement that would give them only the interest on the principal until they reached the age of thirty-one.

Two-thirds of the principal was to be divided among them in instalments at the ages of thirty-one, thirty-nine, and forty-five. The remaining third was to be shared by their children or, if there were none, by the other members of the Dionne family. If one died unmarried, her estate would go to her parents and then, in equal shares to each brother and sister. The Big House and the land on which it stood would remain in their parents' hands for their lifetime. Years before, Dionne had lost his children because the government of Ontario believed he did not know how to handle money and would become an easy prey to the unscrupulous. The terms of the trust fund made it clear that he now felt the same way about his own offspring. Subsequent events suggest that he was right.

"We have no wish to hurt anyone," the sisters wrote in the final chapter of *We Were Five*. To the other members (such as Audrey Dionne) of what was and still is a closely knit family – who saw the story from a totally different point of view – this is hard to believe.

That book really hurt them, hurt them deeply. You're looking at two old people that haven't really lived, not through their own fault but because of something that happened to them. All they want is quiet, now. I cannot honestly believe that the Quints themselves would say anything like that against their parents, because I know the rest of the family. I still say there is someone behind pushing them to do this, and I think it was Annette's husband. He had a lot of influence on those girls – an awful lot. And he was always the spokesman for the Quints. It just doesn't make sense why they should be so heartless when the rest of the family is all so human. They are all beautiful people. I mean, you just don't do that to your parents.

Of course, they were hurt in their early childhood, and they are taking it out on somebody else now, which isn't really fair. Of course they had chores. At the time I met them, each and every one had chores, like all the other boys and other Dionne girls. They had to help with the housework. Mrs. Dionne never really had a maid. I don't think she could have stood anybody in her work kitchen. The only help I remember were some women who came to the Big House to do the cleaning once a year – cleaning walls and things like that. Mrs. Dionne, she did everything herself, and the Quints did their share of the work and the other girls and boys, too. And they had to learn to knit and to sew; that's something I can't do, but their mother taught them to do it. You know she made all the baby clothes for our babies, made all the christening sets, all the clothes you'd need for your kids. That's not being a bad parent.

There was always a lot of action around that house. The Dionnes were a big family – always lots of children around. I can't remember, except for the time at school, when any of the Dionne kids were away from home. Every one of them always came home at the holidays. Christmas was beautiful. Christmas – that was really family life, something like I had never seen before. It was a beautiful time of the year, and I always looked forward to Christmas with them. When we were married and living in Toronto with little babies – we had five in the first ten years – we wouldn't have dreamed of spending Christmas away from the Big House. At Christmas time, you know, you hear about French-Canadian meat pies? I remember making about thirty or forty of them and a great big Christmas cake and all the fruit and the big turkey! She used to make all her own wine, her own soup – everything you ate, she made it.

And in the summertime – we used to play baseball and take long walks and pick berries, and there were always sing-alongs and home movies. And at night we would get together and pray in front of the big statue. It was a good life. It brings back some pleasant memories for me. . . .

For the quintuplets, raised during the most formative years of their lives with a totally different philosophy, there were few pleasant memories. The breach was complete. For twelve years, from 1958 until 1970, Yvonne and Annette did not see their parents. Cécile had tried to achieve some rapprochement during a visit to Corbeil in 1969, but her friends said she returned home deeply hurt because of the continuing coldness of her father.

Tragedy struck the Langlois home in 1962 when one of Cécile's twin boys died at the age of six months from cancer of the kidney. Two years later the marriage broke up. Although Cécile, like her sisters, was a devout Catholic, she sought more than a legal separation; she sued for divorce and retained custody of her four other children, all boys.

Marie's marriage broke up the same year. "It would have been impossible for any man to live with her," Germain Allard, her brother-in-law, has since remarked. Of the five interwoven tales, her story is the most tragic. The feeling of having been raised in a goldfish bowl never left her; she could not rid herself of the obsession that people were staring at her wherever she went. Yet Florian Houle dated her for two months before he learned who she was. Houle, an employee of the provincial sales tax department, knew Marie only as "Denise Mousseaux," a pathetically thin girl with thick glasses, a little lame in one leg, who dressed cheaply in black and carried a one-dollar plastic purse. One night when a waitress urged him to fatten her up (she weighed just ninety-one pounds), Marie remarked that she had weighed barely a pound at birth, and it began to dawn on Houle that she was not what she pretended to be. When at last he met her sisters, the masquerade was over.

Their marriage lasted six years. Marie's temperament was as changeable as the weather. She flared up easily and was subject to fits of depression interspersed with bouts of gaiety. She had no understanding of money – spent it liberally, often gave it away, and left large sums lying around the house. Once she lavished gifts upon a neighbour and then, after a quarrel, tried to sue her in court for their return. She was not a good housekeeper; her husband did most of the cooking. Her bitterness towards her non-identical siblings was so strong that she refused emphatically to allow her elder sister Rose to be godmother to one of the Houle children.

After her separation she deteriorated physically and mentally. Deeply depressed, psychologically erratic, she began to drink heavily – so heavily that Annette and her husband, with whom she stayed for a time, were forced to lock their liquor cabinet. Often she talked of suicide. In February, 1970, after Marie had moved into an apartment of her own in Montreal, Annette became alarmed because her sister's daily phone calls had suddenly ceased. There was no answer at her apartment; the newspapers for three days were piled in front of her door. Germain Allard gained entrance through a window and discovered what he had suspected: Marie had been dead for several days, apparently of a blood clot in the brain. (The body was in such a state of decomposition that the coroner could not be certain.) At the funeral, Yvonne and Annette saw their parents for the first time in twelve years.

The Allards had bought a home in St Bruno, a suburb of Montreal, half Francophone, half Anglophone. Annette was astonished at her husband's easy geniality and openness. "How can you be like that?" she used to ask him. "You seem so natural. You talk to everybody you meet. You always say what you feel." Slowly, she learned from him to overcome some of her shyness – the kind of hopeless, lost feeling that made her want to hide away when anybody recognized her on the street. In 1967 she wrote that she was "gradually learning to smile and to let the curious stare and to accept their gesture as a normal human response. . . ." Her husband felt she was beginning to blossom as a result of his example.

Then, in the early seventies, the three surviving sisters who had been separated geographically found themselves together again in St Bruno. Cécile returned from Quebec City after her divorce and bought a house near Annette. Yvonne, who had never showed any interest in marriage and who had thrice tried unsuccessfully to become a nun, moved out of her Montreal apartment, lived for a time with the Allards, and then bought a house nearby. The sisters phoned each other constantly, talked incessantly of the past, and drew in among themselves – or so it seemed to Germain Allard.

It was a bad move because by being closer to each other in St Bruno they formed the same closed circle they had formed when they were younger in Corbeil. . . . I would say they interfered in our house. If Annette and I decided to do something about the children in the morning, I would come home from the office in the evening to find Annette had changed her mind because she had been influenced by Yvonne or maybe Cécile. It was mostly Yvonne who influenced the girls. Socially, Annette was adventurous. But Yvonne was smarter, and Yvonne had the influence.

So Annette's attention was going more and more to her sisters and less and less to the family. It was natural because they were Quints. And Yvonne was very persistent. She wanted to get all of Annette's affections for herself; that is a very important point. . . .

Finally I got fed up. I told Annette, Your sister goes out of our home or I go out myself. I wasn't able to stand it any more. We had a fair talk and I told her, Look, I know what you are; I know it wasn't easy for you in the past, psychologically; but the only way to save our marriage is to sell the house and move out of this circle of you and your sisters and try to start all over again.

In other words, she was being asked to choose between me and her sisters. But she wasn't able to make that decision. So it was better for me to go. . . .

Yvonne, Annette, and Cécile still live in the Montreal suburb of St Bruno. Their lives are anything but glamorous. It is not necessary for them to "buy their privacy," as the world once believed, for few people recognize them today. Even if it were necessary, they could scarcely afford the luxury. The final instalment of the trust fund will be paid when they reach the age of forty-five, on May 28, 1979, but the principal has dwindled; Annette and Cécile drew heavily upon it during the period of their marriages. Philippe Langlois, who died in 1975, was a particularly lavish spender; Cécile's share of the fund has been reduced to fifty thousand dollars. She received ten thousand dollars from Emilie's estate and more than twice that sum from her share of the royalties and serial rights from *We Were Five*, but that money is long gone. Because she cannot support her children on the monthly interest from the

211

trust fund, she has been forced to go to work. Few of the customers in a local supermarket realize that the clerk who rings up their order is one of the famous Dionne quintuplets.

Annette is only slightly better off. She will receive ninety thousand dollars from the fund in 1979. Meanwhile she tries to support her four children on the monthly interest – about three hundred and forty-five dollars – and a small additional sum sent by her husband for support. In the spring of 1977, she was trying, vainly, to find a job to supplement her income. She cannot afford even a second-hand car or an evening out.

Nurse Leroux had once predicted that Annette would become a businesswoman in adult life and that Yvonne would make an ideal mother. But Yvonne, who never married, is now better off financially. The interest from her share of the trust fund (the capital amounts to about one hundred and eight thousand dollars) allows her to live comfortably. Leroux's predictions, like so many others made about the future of the quintuplets, have not been realized. Yvonne has little or no social life. She has no interest in male company and, apart from her sisters, sees few people. In effect, she is a recluse. She does volunteer work in the St Bruno municipal library but, in the words of an acquaintance, "goes directly from her house to the library and back to her house again, seeing no one."

Marie's two children live with their father, Florian Houle. Her share of the trust fund, which is now theirs, had dropped below seventy thousand dollars, but Houle has managed to build it up past one hundred thousand. He is the only member of the quintuplets' circle who continues to enjoy a cordial relationship with Oliva and Elzire Dionne. Houle makes a point of taking his children on regular visits to see their grandparents in Corbeil. But in spite of his own efforts to effect a reconciliation, Yvonne, Annette, and Cécile have scarcely any communication with their father and mother. In 1975, when the Dionne parents celebrated their fiftieth wedding anniversary, they received a card – nothing more.

The Dionnes no longer live in the Big House, which has become a nursing home. Their home is a small grey brick bungalow, a few hundred yards away. Nothing remains now of the souvenir shops and the concessions that once marked the spot where the quintuplets were born. But the log nursery can still be seen; it is now a private home.

The original farmhouse is also gone. Danny Dionne and his wife Audrey lived in it for several years but finally turned it over to a local entrepreneur named Stan Guignard, a man of parts whose hand, one suspects, the late Ivan Spear would have been proud to shake. A former Canadian heavyweight boxing champion (118 fights) and a wrestler who toured Europe under the name of Northern Bear, Guignard has been a policeman (he once put his own mayor in jail), a real estate salesman, a used-car dealer, and, above all, a promoter.

After Guignard took over the house, he moved it to a better location in a field next to the Pinewood Motor Hotel on the outskirts of North Bay, where it stands today, carefully labelled for all to see. And here, for an admission price of seventy-five cents (twenty-five cents for students, ten cents for children) visitors can wander through the very rooms where the Dionnes lived before the quintuplets were born and browse among some hundred original artifacts and scores of pictures and paintings that call to mind an era now long gone.

Here is the double bed in which Elzire suffered the painful labour of May 28, 1934, and the kitchen table on which the babies were first bathed in oil and fed. Here is the 550-pound range on which the water was boiled to sterilize their diapers and the wooden machine in which the diapers were washed. Here are the very incubators that were rushed to Callander almost half a century ago and the same eyedroppers with which Marie Clouthier and Yvonne Leroux administered the first droplets of nourishment. Here are the Brecht feeders, which Fred Davis rustled up in North Bay, and the later bottles, complete with the original nipples, with one of which Louise de Kiriline was working when fire almost destroyed the farmhouse.

Here are the quintuplets' bibs, and their knitted woollen soakers, and their baby dresses – five of each, all hanging in rows. Here are dolls, including the inevitable Shirley Temple doll, and a set of five miniature golf clubs, never used, and the silverware that General Trujillo sent from the Dominican Republic. Here are all the special clothes the quintuplets wore on big occasions: their confirmation dresses, the gowns they wore to meet the King and Queen, and the frocks in which they christened the Liberty ships – five of everything, with photographs to match. Everything has been saved, from the five original oil paintings that Andreas Loomis did for the Palmolive soap ads to the five original perambulators, which stand out on the porch each summer, just as they once stood on the porch of the Dafoe Hospital in the Thirties.

Each year more souvenirs arrive from people who still remember the Dionne years. There is, for instance, a large glass cabinet crammed with memorabilia donated by a woman from the States who, like thousands of others, made a hobby of collecting items about the Dionnes when the Quint craze was at its height. Dafoe is represented, too. His entire medical library has been borrowed from the Town of Callander. And here are all of his car licence plates, some marked D-70, going back to the days before the birth, when he appeared to be the quintessential country doctor, forcing his old Chev down the rutted roads of East Ferris township, never caring about his fee.

In one corner are stacked all the visitors' books from the Thirties, containing the signatures of all the people who drove up to Callander and who made their way to the observation gallery to watch the Quints at play in the days when movies were a quarter and a glass of beer was a nickel and admission to the Dionne playground was free. The new visitors like to leaf through these books, looking over the old names of people who came from places that do not seem quite so far away today as they did then.

You know, there was one fella came up here and he spent hour after hour going through those books just looking for one name, his mother's. And finally, after two hours, darned if he didn't find it. She'd actually come up here forty years before. People care. You know, last year I put all this stuff into a trailer and I took it out to the West Coast to the Pacific National Exhibition at Vancouver, and in just ten days we had fifteen thousand people go through that trailer. Line-ups all day long, every day. I remember one couple came over from Victoria, and they had tears in their eyes; they told me that they had "adopted" Marie when she was little. You know what they said? They said, You've brought the quintuplets back to us!

We have people come as far as three thousand miles just to see this museum. Last year we had twenty-three thousand pass through this old farmhouse – twenty-three thousand people who wanted to be reminded about the Quints. One group made a special trip all the way from Chicago just to look at a place where the quintuplets were born. It gets better every year; every year more and more people come – just to see what it was like and to remember that time.

You see, they haven't forgotten. They can't forget. Don't try to tell me that people have forgotten the Dionne Quints.

Notes

page	line	Chapter One
16	35	*Time,* Jan. 11, 1937.
17	14	*Literary Digest,* Dec. 14, 1935.
17	18	*New York Times,* April 11, 1937.
17	22	*Globe,* March 27, 1936.
17	27	*Nugget,* Aug. 14, 1939.
17	40	*Toronto Daily Star,* June 13, 1935.
17	42	*Ibid.,* July 8, 1936.
18	2	*Ibid.,* Feb. 12, 1938.
18	8	*Telegram,* Jan. 18, 1937.
18	11	Dafoe Scrapbooks, "Quintuplets Do Their Own Script," *Motion Picture Herald,* Dec. 21, 1935.
18	12	*Toronto Daily Star,* Feb. 10, 1937.
19	6	*Time,* Aug. 29, 1938.
19	9	*Nugget,* May 25, 1938.

page	line	Chapter Two
20	10	Hoar, p. 19.
20	13	Horn, p. 10.
20	23	*Nugget,* June 8, 1934.
20	24	*Ibid.,* Oct. 31, 1934.
21	14	William Dafoe Papers, A. R. Dafoe to W. Dafoe, Jan. 14, 1934.
21	17	Minutes, Township of North Himsworth, Nov. 15, 1934.
21	21	Scott, F. R., and Cassidy, H. M., in Horn, ed., p. 120.
21	24	Horn, p. 12.
21	37	*Nugget,* Jan. 24, 1936.
23	30	*Toronto Star Weekly,* June 23, 1934.
29	7	William Dafoe Papers, Address to the Conference on Research on the Dionne Quintuplets, Oct. 30, 1937.
29	21	Hunt, pp. 78-79.
29	23	*Ibid.,* p. 88.
30	38	*Ibid.,* p. 154.
31	34	Dafoe Scrapbooks, *Sunday Post,* Boston, *circa* Feb. 1935.
32	37	Hersholt.

page	line	Chapter Three
36	34	Legros and Labelle, pp. 8 and 9.
37	35	William Dafoe Papers, Carnegie Hall address, Dec. 10, 1934.
37	39	*Ibid.*
38	5	*Ibid.*
38	13	Legros and Labelle, p. 15.
39	7	Hunt, p. 22.
39	11	Barker, *The Dionne Legend,* p. 41.
40	10	Hunt, p. 209.
40	17	Interview, Louise de Kiriline Lawrence.
49	21	Interview, Mort Fellman.
53	15	Interview, Marie MacNaughton.

page	line	Chapter Four
56	12	*Scientific Monthly,* July, 1930.
57	21	Carskadon.
57	23	*New York Times,* July 19, 1933.
57	36	Carskadon.
60	6	Dafoe Scrapbooks, *Press,* Cleveland, June 2, 1934.
60	9	Barker, *The Dionne Legend,* p. 57; Hunt, p. 260.
60	32	*Toronto Daily Star,* June 6, 1934.
61	4	Dafoe Scrapbooks, *American,* Chicago, June 6, 1934.
61	14	*Globe,* Sept. 28, 1938, and *Nugget,* same date.
61	26	*Ibid.*
61	34	*Ibid.*
61	38	*New York Times,* May 31, 1934.
61	43	*Toronto Daily Star,* June 1, 1934.
62	7	Hunt, p. 244.
62	26	Dafoe, A. R., "The Survival of the Dionne Quintuplets."
62	45	William Dafoe Papers, Address by A. R. Dafoe to the New York Academy of Medicine, Dec. 13, 1934.
63	31	Hunt, p. 225.
64	27	*Ibid.,* p. 229.
67	10	*Toronto Daily Star,* June 5, 1934.

page line **Chapter Five**

68   4   *Toronto Daily Star,* Aug. 31, 1934.

69   40 Interview, Luis Kutner.

70   8   William Dafoe Papers, Elizabeth S. Hawkes, Springfield, Mass., to A. R. Dafoe, June 12, 1934.

70   16 *Ibid.,* Anon., Grand Rapids, Mich., to A. R. Dafoe, Aug. 11, 1934.

70   22 *Ibid.,* W. Dafoe to A. G. Nicholls, Nov. 5, 1935.

71   21 Dafoe Scrapbooks, *Press,* Cleveland, *circa* June 1, 1934.

71   26 Barker, *The Dionne Legend,* p. 70.

71   36 *Toronto Daily Star,* Sept. 27, 1938.

72   19 *Nugget,* July 4, 1934.

72   32 Neatby, H. Blair, in Hoar, ed., p. 92.

73   10 McKenty, p. 49.

74   36 *Toronto Daily Star,* July 27, 1934.

75   10 *Ibid.,* July 28, 1934.

75   24 *Nugget,* July 25, 1934.

75   29 Barker, *The Dionne Legend,* p. 87.

76   34 William Dafoe Papers, Address by A. R. Dafoe, Dec. 13, 1934.

76   45 McLeod.

77   8   *Nugget,* Oct. 2, 1935.

77   18 Leroux Diary, June 14, 1934.

78   24 William Dafoe Papers, Claire Aubin to A. R. Dafoe, Aug. 18, 1934.

78   38 Dafoe, A. R., "Further History of the Care and Feeding of the Dionne Quintuplets."

79   4   *Ibid.*

79   8   William Dafoe Papers, Mrs. D. Greensman to A. R. Dafoe, n.d.

79   19 *Toronto Daily Star,* Aug. 16, 1934.

79   30 *Telegram,* June 25, 1934.

Chapter Six

81   28 *Toronto Daily Star,* Dec. 4, 1934.

82   6   William Dafoe Papers, A. R. Dafoe to W. Dafoe, Feb. 1, 1935.

84   7   *Herald-Tribune,* New York, Dec. 10, 1934.

84   41 *World-Telegram,* New York, Dec. 10, 1934.

86   18 *New York Times,* Dec. 10, 1934.

86   23 *Journal,* New York, Dec. 15, 1934.

86   30 *Toronto Daily Star,* Dec. 10, 1934.

87   10 Winchell, "Quintuplets? Shucks!"

87   24 *Journal,* New York, Dec. 15, 1934.

88   27 *Toronto Daily Star,* Dec. 11, 1934.

89   10 *Ibid.*

89   21 Winchell, *Winchell Exclusive,* p. 101.

90   12 *Toronto Daily Star,* Dec. 12, 1934.

91   12 *Mirror,* New York, Dec. 14, 1934.

91   32 Dafoe Scrapbooks, envelope postmarked "Long Island."

91   40 *Toronto Daily Star,* Jan. 8, 1935.

93   8   Dafoe Scrapbooks, *Sunday Post,* Boston, *circa* Feb. 1935.

93   20 *Ibid., Times Journal, circa* May, 1936.

93   29 Interview, George Sinclair.

94   14 Vallee.

94   38 William Dafoe Papers, Clark Kinnaird to W. Dafoe, July 26, 1955.

Chapter Seven

95   21 *Toronto Daily Star,* Dec. 22, 1934.

96   12 *Ibid.,* Jan. 21, 1935.

96   17 *Ibid.*

96   19 Leroux Diary, Jan. 21, 1935.

97   31 *Nugget,* Feb. 18, 1935.

97   44 *Toronto Daily Star,* Feb. 9, 1935.

98   30 *Ibid.,* Feb. 5, 1935.

98   43 *Ibid.,* Feb. 6, 1935.

99   22 *Ibid.,* Feb. 7, 1935.

99   29 Interview, Luis Kutner.

99   40 *Toronto Daily Star,* Feb. 7, 1935.

99   43 *INid.,* Feb. 8, 1935.

101 8   *Ibid.,* Feb. 9, 1935.

101 44 *Ibid.,* Feb. 15, 1935.

102 2   *Variety,* Feb. 12, 1935.

102 8   *Toronto Daily Star,* Feb. 12, 1935.

102 12 *Ibid.,* Feb. 15, 1935.

102 25 *Ibid*

102 42 *Ibid.,* Feb. 9, 1935, and *Globe,* Feb. 9, 1935.

103 31 Globe, Feb. 23, 1935.

103 43 Ibid.

104 27 Hepburn Papers, Gen. Correspondence, Paul Martin to Premier Hepburn, March 8, 1935, encl. Martin to David Croll, same date.

104 34 Globe, March 12, 1935.

104 39 Toronto Daily Star, March 12, 1935.

105 12 Nugget, March 15, 1935.

105 21 Globe, March 13, 1935.

105 34 Leroux Diary, March, 1935 [undated].

106 15 Ibid., March 23, 1935.

106 34 Toronto Daily Star, March 16, 1935.

107   2 Sun, New York, March 25, 1935.

107   8 Hepburn Papers, Gen. Correspondence, Feb. 10, 1935.

107 11 Ibid., Feb. 9, 1935.

107 13 Ibid., March 12, 1935.

107 15 George Sinclair Papers, A. Case, San Francisco, to Dionne [copy to A. R. Dafoe], May 18, 1935.

107 17 Ibid., Anon. to A. R. Dafoe, July 12, 1935.

Chapter Eight

108   7 Nugget, May 29, 1935.

108 12 Globe, May 14, 1935.

108 18 Toronto Daily Star, May 29, 1935.

109 16 Ibid. and Nugget, same date.

109 20 Toronto Daily Star, June 19, 1935.

109 25 Globe, Sept. 9, 1935.

109 38 Newman, pp. 105-15.

111 16 Ibid.

111 26 Blatz, pp. 191-92.

111 34 McMillan MS.

112 36 Ibid.

112 39 Dafoe, A. R., "The Survival of the Dionne Quintuplets."

113   1 Toronto Daily Star, May 11, 1936.

113 32 Braithwaite, p. 69.

113 41 Grescoe.

114   3 Canadian, Feb. 3, 1968.

114 28 Globe, April 23, 1935.

114 40 Nugget, April 27, 1935.

115   6 Ibid.

115 22 Globe, May 25, 1935.

115 28 Leroux Diary, June 1, 1935.

119   1 Blatz memorial pamphlet, p. 1.

119 17 Maclean's, April 15, 1932.

119 34 Fletcher and Millichamp, p. 33.

119 36 Blatz, p. 102.

119 44 Ibid., pp. 132-33.

120   9 McMillan MS.

120 19 Blatz, pp. 95-102.

120 42 Bowlby, p. 13.

122 14 Blatz, p. 158.

122 30 Ibid., p. 35.

122 36 Ibid., p. 33.

123 32 Ibid., p. 195.

124 11 Ibid., p. 202.

126 33 Globe, July 21, 1936.

126 38 Ibid., Feb. 29, 1936.

Chapter Nine

129 43 Last Post, "The Company," Feb. 1970, in Horn, ed., pp. 122-23.

130   6 Scott, F. R., and Cassidy, H. M., "Labour conditions in the men's clothing industry, Toronto, 1935," in Horn, ed., p. 120.

130 36 Sann, p. 101.

131 11 MacLennan, Hugh, "What It Was Like to Be in Your Twenties in the Thirties," in Hoar, ed., p. 151.

131 26 Dempsey.

132 29 Official Guardian's files, Dionne Quintuplet Papers, W. M. Flannery to Percy Wilson, Oct. 24, 1936, encl. statement of Gordon V. Thompson, Ltd.

132 32 Ibid., Keith Munro to Wilson, May 15, 1939.

132 34 Ibid., Munro to Wilson, Nov. 6, 1937.

141   2 Ibid., royalty statement to 1937.

141   3 Ibid., McCormick contract, Feb. 21, 1936; David Croll to E. G. Brown, June 16, 1936.

page line   page line

141   5   *Ibid.*, C. J. McCabe to Croll, Jan. 15, 1936, encl. statement.

141   8   *Ibid.*, Fred Ferguson to Munro, Nov. 24, 1937.

141   12   *Ibid.*, Munro to Wilson, Nov. 6, 1939; Wilson to Oliva Dionne, June 12, 1945.

141   16   *Ibid.*, R. L. Kellock to Wilson, July 30, 1937; Kellock to Carnation Company, Oct. 13, 1937.

143   3   *Toronto Daily Star, Globe and Mail, Nugget*, Jan. 13-30, 1937.

145   14   Blake.

145   26   *New York Times*, Aug. 6, 1943.

146   3   William Dafoe Papers, A. R. Dafoe, copy of contract, handwritten, Dec. 19, 1934.

146   8   *Ibid.*, A. R. Dafoe to W. Dafoe, Jan. 28, 1935.

146   10   *Ibid.*, A. R. Dafoe, handwritten note, undated.

146   18   Hepburn Papers, Gen. Correspondence, Private: A. R. Dafoe to Hepburn, Feb. 4, 1937.

146   31   *Globe and Mail*, March 23, 1937.

147   18   Official Guardian's files, Dionne Quintuplet Papers, Croll to Munro, July 7, 1937.

147   21   *Ibid.*, Wilson to Croll, Sept. 17, Dec. 1, Dec. 10, 1937.

147   22   *Ibid.*, telegram, Croll to Wilson, Dec. 11, 1937.

147   25   *Ibid.*, Kellock to Croll, Nov. 3, 1938; Kellock to Wilson, Nov. 3, 1938; Wilson to Kellock, Nov. 8, 1938.

147   29   Interview, Sen. David Croll.

147   43   Official Guardian's files, Dionne Quintuplet Papers, Kellock to Carnation Company, Oct. 13, 1937.

148   5   *Ibid.*, Personal and Confidential Papers, Wilson: Written report of conversation with Hepburn, Dec. 20, 1937.

148   10   *Ibid.*

148   14   *Ibid.*

148   26   *Ibid.*, Arthur Garfield Hays, memorandum, Jan. 13, 1938.

Chapter Ten

149   17   *Globe*, June 13, 1935.

149   27   Dempsey.

150   21   District Court, District of Nipissing, Judge J. A. S. Plouffe's order re Guardianship Accounts, March 19, 1942.

151   7   Dafoe Scrapbooks, "Have-the Dionnes Won or Lost?" by Edith Johnson, May, 1938 [unidentified].

152   12   Littledale.

152   19   *News-Week*, May 29, 1937.

152   26   Dafoe Scrapbooks, John F. Coggswell in *Sunday Post*, Boston, April, 1938.

152   28   Furnas.

152   31   *Toronto Daily Star*, March 4, 1937.

152   37   Furnas.

152   39   Dafoe Scrapbooks, John F. Coggswell in *Sunday Post*, Boston, April, 1938.

153   22   *Toronto Daily Star*, March 4, 1937.

153   31   George Sinclair Papers, typed MS. by Paul Nafe, *Christian Science Monitor*.

153   36   *Nugget*, April 25, 1935.

153   40   *Toronto Star Weekly*, Aug. 1, 1936.

154   23   *Nugget*, July 8, 1936.

154   32   *Ibid.*, Sept. 2, 1936.

154   38   *Ibid.*, Feb. 1, 1937.

155   7   *Ibid.*, July 15, 1938.

155   14   Kelley.

155   141   Denison.

156   5   *Ibid.*

156   32   *News-Week*, Sept. 12, 1936.

157   30   Denison.

159   44   *Toronto Daily Star*, May 29, 1937.

160   9   George Sinclair Papers.

160   13   *Nugget*, June 6, 1938.

160   22   *Ibid.*, Aug. 8, 1938.

163   23   Denison.

163   30   Allard and Rasky.

Chapter Eleven

167   24   *New York Times*, Oct. 17, 1937.

167   31   *Ibid.*

168   4   Quinn, p. 266.

168   6   Hoar, p. 20.

168   11   *Toronto Daily Star*, May 21, 1938.

168   17   *New York Times*, Aug. 29, 1935.

169   3   ACFEO Files.

169   16   *Ibid.*, telegram, Dionne to Cloutier, March

6, 1938; Dionne to Cloutier, March 9, 1938.

169 28   *Ibid.*, Dionne to Arvisais, March 1, 1938.

169 43   *Ibid.*, Report of guardianship meeting, Cloutier to Wilson, March 12, 1938.

170 7   Official Guardian's files, Private, Gordon Conant to Wilson, March 17, 1938.

170 19   *Ibid.*, Mme Emma Poupore to Wilson, encl. "Looking into the Future with Mrs. Dionne."

170 26   Dafoe Scrapbooks, John F. Coggswell in *Sunday Post*, Boston, *circa* May, 1938.

170 30   *Telegram*, Oct. 23, 1936.

171 5   Official Guardian's files, Dionne Quintuplet Papers, Confidential, "Dionne Quintuplet Guardianship Investigation."

171 28   *Ibid.*

171 36   *Ibid.*

171 41   *Ibid.* Munro to Wilson, April 18, 1938.

172 3   *Nugget*, April 22, 1938.

172 6   Official Guardian's files, Dionne Quintuplet Papers, "Dionne Quintuplet Guardianship Investigation," Conant to Wilson, April 28, 1938.

172 27   George Sinclair Papers, Eric R. Beuck to A. R. Dafoe, April 22, 1938.

172 29   *Ibid.*, R. Waulters to A. R. Dafoe, April 22, 1938.

172 32   *Ibid.*, "An Admirer" to A. R. Dafoe, April 25, 1938.

172 41   *Toronto Daily Star*, Sept. 22, 1938.

173 4   *Ibid.*, Sept. 30, 1938.

173 19   Public Archives of Ontario, Public Health Nursing Series, Report of a Visit to Red Cross Unit, Callander, Nov. 27, 1935.

173 26   William Dafoe Papers, handwritten note: "Written for Roy."

Chapter Twelve

176 24   Official Guardian's files, Dionne Quintuplet Papers, Dr. Dafoe's submission to guardianship re Trout Lake site. n.d.

176 28   *Ibid.*, Deputy Minister of Public Works to Wilson, encl. report from J. M. Philip, Superintendent of Construction, May 12, 1938.

177 5   *Ibid.*, Dafoe submission.

177 13   *Ibid.*, W. Aubry to G. D. Conant, Sept. 7, 1938.

177 18   *Globe and Mail*, Sept. 17, 1938.

177 19   *Ibid.*, Sept. 20, 1938.

177 21   Official Guardian's files, Dionne Quintuplet Papers, telegram, W. M. Ketcheson to Hepburn, Sept. 14, 1938.

177 24   *Ibid.*, John Perks to Hepburn, Sept. 15, 1938; Secretary, Callander Liberal Association to Hepburn, Sept. 14, 1938; Philip Adams to Wilson, Sept. 15, 1938, encl. Adams to Hepburn, Sept. 15, 1938.

177 27   *Ibid.*, Memorandum, Conant to Wilson, Sept. 15, 1938; *Toronto Daily Star*, Sept. 23, 1938.

177 34   Official Guardian's files, Dionne Quintuplet Papers, Ferguson to Wilson, n.d.; Munro to Wilson, Jan. 7, 1938.

177 36   William Dafoe Papers, telegram, Sam Weiubord, William Morris Agency, to A. R. Dafoe, Nov. 23, 1938.

178 4   *Toronto Daily Star*, Jan. 3, 1939.

178 10   *Globe and Mail*, April 16, 1937.

178 17   ACFEO Files, McBean to Jack Hughson, Dec. 21, 1938.

178 21   *Ibid.*, Slaght to McBean, Dec. 12, 1938.

178 26   *Ibid.*, McBean to Hughson, Nov. 1, 1938.

179 29   Official Guardian's files, Dionne Quintuplet Papers, Saint-Jacques to Wilson, Oct. 3, 1938.

180 4   *Ibid.*, Dafoe to Wilson, March 30, 1939.

181 3   Hepburn Papers, Gen. Correspondence, Private, Saint-Jacques to Conant, May 16, 1939, encl. *New York Sun* clipping, April 12, 1939.

181 20   McMillan MS.

182 6   Official Guardian's files, Dionne Quintuplet Papers, Ferguson to Munro, March 30, 1939; Ferguson to Guardianship, May 24, 1939.

182 14   *Ibid.*, Munro to Wilson, Oct. 24, 1939.

182 22   *Nugget*, July 3, 1939.

182 24   *Ibid.*, July 7, 1939.

182 28   *Ibid.*, July 19, 1939.

182 32   Official Guardian's files, Dionne Quintuplet Papers, Wilson to Conant, July 10, 1939.

182 40   Hepburn Papers, Gen. Correspondence, Private, Munro to Hepburn, Sept. 16, 1939.

183 2   *Ibid.*, Slaght to Conant, Sept. 4, 1939.

183 6   Official Guardian's files, Personal and Confidential Papers, Dafoe to Wilson, Aug. 13, 1939.

Bibliography

Unpublished Sources

Archival

Anon.	"The Dionne Quintuplets," scrapbook mounted and bound by New York Public Library, New York, 1934-36.
Association Canadienne-Française d'Education d'Ontario	Files, Archives de l'Université d'Ottawa
Hepburn, Mitchell	Papers, Public Archives of Ontario
Wilson, P. D.	Official Guardian's Files, Public Archives of Ontario

Private

Dafoe, A. R.	Scrapbooks
Dafoe, William	Papers
Davis, Yvonne Leroux	Diary
McMillan, Mollie O'Shaughnessy	Manuscript
Sinclair, George	Papers
Walker, Norma Ford	Scrapbooks

Newspapers

Globe	Toronto, 1934-38
Globe and Mail	Toronto, 1938-45
New York Times	New York, 1934-45
Nugget	North Bay, 1934-55
Telegram	Toronto, 1934-55
Toronto Daily Star	Toronto, 1934-55

All New York papers for December, 1934

All Chicago papers for February, 1935

Published Sources

Anon.	*The Dionne Quintuplets Growing Up* (Newspaper Enterprises of America), New York, 1935.
	William Emet Blatz, Institute of Child Study, Toronto, 1965.

Adler, Dr. Alfred	"Separate the QUINS," *Cosmopolitan,* March, 1936.
Allard, Annette, and Rasky, Frank	"I'm a Housewife Now," *Canadian* magazine, May 27, 1967.
Barker, Lillian	"The Most Unusual Mother I've Ever Known," *Extension Magazine,* January, 1955.
	The Dionne Legend, New York, 1951.
	The Quints Have a Family, Toronto, 1941.
Blake, Charles E.	"How They Got the Quints in Pictures," *Photoplay,* March, 1936.
Blatz, William E.	*The Five Sisters, A Study of Child Psychology,* Toronto, 1938.
Blatz, William E., Chant, N., *et al.*	*Collected Studies on the Dionne Quintuplets,* Toronto, 1937.
Bliven, Bruce	"A Century of Treadmill," *New Republic,* November 15, 1933.
Bowlby, John	"Child Care and the Growth of Love," *World Health Organization,* 1951; Pelican ed., Harmondsworth, England, 1953.
Braithwaite, Max	*Sick Kids,* Toronto, 1974.
Brough, James	*We Were Five,* New York, 1965.
Burton, Walter	"Photographing the Dionne Quints," *Popular Science Monthly,* February, 1937.
Buxton, Frank, and Owen, Bill	*The Big Broadcast,* New York, 1972.
Carskadon, T. R.	"Sally Rand Dances to the Rescue," *American Mercury,* July, 1935.
Corbin, William	"Babes in the Woods," *American* magazine, September, 1934.
Corriveau, M. Louise	*Quints to Queens,* New York, 1976.
Dafoe, Allan Roy	*Dr. Dafoe's Guidebook for Mothers,* Toronto, 1936.
	"What the Quints Have Taught Me," *Rotarian,* April, 1942.
	"The Survival of the Dionne Quintuplets," *American Journal of Obstetrics and Gynecology,* 1940.
	"Further History of the Care and Feeding of the Dionne Quintuplets" (read before the Ontario Medical Association, October 23, 1935), *Canadian Medical Association Journal,* 1936.
	Speech, New York Academy of Medicine, December 13, 1934.
	Address, Conference on Research on the Dionne Quintuplets, Toronto, October 30, 1937.
Dedmon, Emmett	*Fabulous Chicago,* New York, 1953.
De Kiriline, Louise	*The Quintuplets' First Year,* Toronto, 1936.

Dempsey, Lotta   "What Will Become of Them?" *Chatelaine*, June, 1937.

Denison, Merrill   "Infant Industry: The Quintuplets,"
Harper's, November, 1938.

Dionne, Oliva   "Whose Children Are the Quintuplets?"
True Story, February, 1939.

Fangel, Maude Tousey   "A Squint at the Quints," *Woman's Home Companion*,
August, 1935.

Fielding, Raymond   *American Newsreel, 1911 to 1967*,
Stillwater, Okla., 1972.

Fletcher, Margaret, and   *25 Years of Child Study: Goals and Growth of*
Millichamp, Dorothy   *Nursery Education*, Toronto, 1951.

Franklin, Stephen   "How Canada's Best Known Parents Coped with Fame,"
Weekend magazine, March 27, 1965.

Furnas, J.C.   "Mr. & Mrs. Dionne," *Ladies' Home Journal*,
February, 1940.

Gauvreau, Emile   *My Last Million Readers*, New York, 1941.

Grescoe, Paul   "Thank Dr. Brown," *Canadian* magazine,
February 3, 1968.

Griffith, Phyllis   "Just One Big Unhappy Family," *Toronto Telegram*,
May 29, 1937.

Hersholt, Jean   "Five Little Stars," *Woman's Home Companion*,
June, 1939.

Hoar, Victor, ed.   *The Great Depression: Essays and Memoirs from
Canada and the United States*,
Toronto, 1969.

Horn, Michiel, ed.   *The Dirty Thirties*, Toronto, 1972.

Hunt, Frazier   *The Little Doc*, New York, 1939.

Kelley, Hubert   "What 5 Babies Did to a Town – and a Man,"
American magazine, March, 1937.

Legros, Mme Alexandre, and   Ministering Angels to the Dionne Quintuplets (pamphlet),
Labelle, Mme Benoit   n.d.

Littledale, Clara Savage   "My Visit to the Quintuplets," *Parents Magazine*,
January, 1937.

Mason, Dr. A.D.   *The Dental Story of the Dionne Quintuplets*
(pamphlet), Toronto, 1941.

McKenty, Neil   *Mitch Hepburn*, Toronto, 1967.

McLeod, Bruce   "My Neighbours the Quints," *Maclean's*,
December 15, 1950.

Munro, Keith   "The Strange Case of the Dionne Quints," *Colliers*,
April 23, 1949.

Newman, Horatio Hackett   *Multiple Human Births*, New York, 1940.

Northway, Mary L.   *W. E. Blatz: His Family and His Farm*, Toronto, 1975.

Peters, William   "The Future of the Four Quintuplets," *Redbook*, May, 1955.

Phillips, Paul   *No Power Greater*, Vancouver, 1967.

Quinn, Hebert F.   *The Union Nationale*, Toronto, 1963.

Sann, Paul   *Fads, Follies and Delusions of the American People*, New York, 1967.

Shultz, Gladys Denny   "The Quints' Future," *Better Homes and Gardens*, January, 1938.

       "Mrs. Shultz Visits the Quints," *Better Homes and Gardens*, February, 1938.

Snyder, Betty M.   "Canadian Mecca," *Readers' Digest* (condensed from *Baltimore Sunday Sun*), November, 1936.

Tunley, Raoul   "I Had a Date with the Quints," *American* magazine, April, 1952.

Vallee, Rudy   "I Stand By," *Pictorial Review*, August, 1936.

Winchell, Walter   "Quintuplets? Shucks!" *Liberty*, April, 1935.

       Winchell Exclusive, New York, 1975.

Woodward, E. L.   "Les Dionnes," *Spectator*, September 13, 1935.

Young, William H., Jr.   "The Serious Funnies: Adventure Comics during the Depression, 1929-1938," *Journal of Popular Culture*, Winter, 1969.

Index

Books by Pierre Berton

The Royal Family
The Mysterious North
Klondike
Just Add Water and Stir
Adventures of a Columnist
Fast, Fast, Fast Relief
The Big Sell
The Comfortable Pew
The Cool, Crazy, Committed World of the Sixties
The Smug Minority
The National Dream
The Last Spike
Drifting Home
Hollywood's Canada
My Country
The Dionne Years
The Wild Frontier
The Invasion of Canada
Flames Across the Border
Why We Act Like Canadians
The Promised Land
Vimy
Starting Out
The Arctic Grail
The Great Depression, 1929-1939
Niagara
My Times

PICTURE BOOKS
The New City (with Henri Rossier)
Remember Yesterday
The Great Railway
The Klondike Quest
Pierre Berton's Picture Book of Niagara Falls
Winter

ANTHOLOGIES
Great Canadians
Pierre and Janet Berton's Canadian Food Guide
Historic Headlines

FOR YOUNGER READERS
The Golden Trail
The Secret World of Og
Adventures in Canadian History (Series)

FICTION
Masquerade (pseudonym Lisa Kroniuk)

Pierre Berton

THE GREAT DEPRESSION
1929-1939

"The most important book written so far by Berton ... *The Great Depression* is the definitive work that will carry our collective memory with us into the next century."

Calgary Herald

"With passion and fury, Pierre Berton has cast a harsh light on one of the darkest corners of Canada's past. The country's image of itself may never be quite the same."

Maclean's

"A vigorous compilation of anecdote and argument, it is also a timely reminder of the war between the wars. Lest we forget."

The Toronto Sun

"Pierre Berton's fascinating and superbly readable account of the Great Depression in Canada prompts the question, why did he wait so long before writing it?"

The Toronto Star

"Berton's chilling *magnum opus* ... [He] has produced something very near perfect. It's clearly written, fast-moving, human down to the dotted i's and so well drafted it reads like a novel."

Times-Colonist (Victoria)

"[*The Great Depression*] is a scalding indictment of the law, big business, the bigots, the police and politicians ... The book is clear, fast-moving and painful – you can almost feel the chilblains of the under-clothed riding rail box cars ..."

Canadian Press

"Were one to read only one account of Canada in the Great Depression, one would not be ill-served by Berton's."

The Hamilton Spectator

Pierre Berton

THE WILD FRONTIER

Pierre Berton explores the richness and variety of Canada's past with stories of adventure and exploration, of courage and endurance: the hardships of British seaman John Jewitt, who became a slave of the Nootka Indians of Vancouver Island; the famous Mounted Policeman, Sam Steele, who wielded absolute authority over a huge part of the country; Mina Hubbard, the widow who trekked across Labrador, and many more.

"The book is a treat. And not just for Canadian history buffs, but for anyone with an evening to spend getting a taste of six intriguing frontier characters you've probably never heard of."

Kitchener-Waterloo Herald

"The book made compulsive reading for me. Berton's vivid, gripping style made it much more than just another history lesson."

The Edmonton Journal

"Good popular history is a rare commodity in this country and Berton is one of the best practitioners of the art."

The Globe and Mail

"He's [Pierre Berton] still the masterly miner who staked a claim on this country's romantic and often bizarre and tragic past and who works that claim with vigour and flamboyance second to none...There's nary a dull moment in the lot."

The Victoria Times

Pierre Berton

MY COUNTRY

Canada's heroes and Canada's history — a heritage as rich and compelling as that of any country.

Pierre Berton brings the past alive with stories of magic and mystery, hardship and romance: the piracy of Bill Johnston, scourge of the St. Lawrence; Sir John Franklin's tragic Arctic expedition; the great Cross-Canada hike of 1921; and many more.

"Pierre Berton has done it once again."

Calgary Albertan

"*My Country* is popular entertainment and information on the grand scale."

Victoria Times

"Berton knows how to whet the appetite of even the most jaded armchair adventurer..."

Calgary Herald